Can Journalism Survive?

For my wife, Jill, and my kids, Dylan and Miranda

Can Journalism Survive?

An Inside Look at American Newsrooms

David M. Ryfe

polity

First published in 2012 by Polity Press

Polity Press
65 Bridge Street
Cambridge CB2 1UR, UK

Polity Press
350 Main Street
Malden, MA 02148, USA

ISBN-13: 978-0-7456-5427-0
ISBN-13: 978-0-7456-5428-7 (pb)

A catalogue record for this book is available from the British Library.

Typeset in 10.5 on 12 pt Plantin
by Servis Filmsetting Ltd, Stockport, Cheshire
Printed and bound in Great Britain by MPG Books Group Limited, Bodmin, Cornwall

The publisher has used its best endeavours to ensure that the URLs for external websites referred to in this book are correct and active at the time of going to press. However, the publisher has no responsibility for the websites and can make no guarantee that a site will remain live or that the content is or will remain appropriate.

Every effort has been made to trace all copyright holders, but if any have been inadvertently overlooked the publisher will be pleased to include any necessary credits in any subsequent reprint or edition.

For further information on Polity, visit our website: www.politybooks.com

Contents

Detailed Contents

List of Figures

Preface

I never set out to study newspapers. After graduate school and a PhD, in the year 2000 I happened to get a first job in a journalism school, not because I wanted to work in a journalism school but because that is where I was hired. Like many journalism schools, the faculty at Middle Tennessee State University was composed mostly of former journalists. Since I had never stepped foot in a newsroom, much less been a journalist, they held me in high suspicion, so much so that the chair of my department suggested I think about interning in a newsroom.

At first, I resisted the idea, seeing it as a distraction from my research and teaching. But then, in 2003, I found myself teaching a media and politics undergraduate course. In preparation, I reread the classics of media sociology, such as Herbert Gans's book *Deciding What's News* and Gaye Tuchman's *Making News*. I also searched for updates to this literature. Much to my surprise, I learned that, by and large, it had not been updated. No significant ethnographic study of newsrooms had been published since 1980. Despite the fact that much had changed in American newsrooms since then, researchers were still referencing texts that were over two decades old.

At this moment, a thought occurred. If I visited a newsroom, I could kill two birds with one stone: allay the concerns of the senior faculty in my department and write an essay that updated a literature that sorely needed updating.

This thought brought me to my first newsroom at the end of 2004. I had no intention of staying very long. Authors of the classic ethnographic studies, people like Leon Sigal, Edward Epstein, and Mark Fishman, actually spent little time in newsrooms. Gaye Tuchman devoted parts of three years to her magisterial study, but on average most ethnographers committed no more than six months to their research. For the purposes of my small essay, I imagined I could get away with three months.

From the beginning, however, I discovered that events were too interesting to leave. I entered that first newsroom alongside a new editor who was intent on shaking things up. Each month became a new chapter in this saga. I couldn't leave until I got to the conclusion. This took two years. In the meantime, journalists discovered the Internet. Not literally, of course. By the mid- to late 1990s, most newspapers had websites. But even in 2004 the web remained an afterthought in newsrooms. At the *Daily Bugle* – the first newspaper I visited – the "web team" consisted of two people (an editor and a programmer). They were shunted to the corner of the room, consigned to "shoveling" content written for the newspaper onto the website. To be sure, editors made note of web traffic numbers. But they had no grand strategy for the web, and, as far as I could tell, reporters considered the new medium as little more than an afterthought.

Then, in 2006, just as I was preparing to wind down my research, interest in the Internet exploded. Partly, this was due to the wide availability of broadband cable, which made the web usable to a larger segment of the audience. And partly it was due to the fact that the spiral of decline in the industry was quickening. Whatever the reason, I could not leave newsrooms just as this new story began to unfold. Through no fault of my own, I had a front row seat at one of the great public dramas of the early twenty-first century. I did not want to give up this privileged position. So I remained in newsrooms for another three years, watching, taking notes, and asking questions. Without meaning to do so, I ended up spending more time in newsrooms (parts of five years) than any ethnographer had ever done.

As the reader will see, the three newsrooms at the heart of this study belong to mid-sized, regional daily newspapers. I have good reasons for choosing such newsrooms. In that they are the primary source of local and regional news for the communities they serve, and employ the vast number of daily journalists working in the United States, these newsrooms represent the backbone of American journalism. For better and worse, the fate of journalism is tied to the fate of these newspapers.

Still, one may wonder about how well these newspapers represent wider trends in the profession and industry. In particular, one may ask about how well they reflect the situation of the elite, metropolitan dailies (e.g., the *New York Times*, the *Wall Street Journal*, the *Washington Post*) that dominate the national picture.

The question of representativeness arises for any ethnography, a method that intentionally sacrifices breadth for depth. In this study, however, I am justified in saying that the dynamics I witnessed at these three regional dailies mirror those at work in the broader profession. In the first instance, the economic trends that confront regional dailies (e.g., declining market penetration, loss of advertising revenue, and so on) afflict all of daily journalism, including elite metro newspapers. The same is true for the challenges to journalism posed by the Internet. These challenges, which arise from the networked structure of online communication, are the same for all reporters, whether they work at large, urban or mid-sized, regional dailies. Moreover, forty years of scholarship has shown that news culture is fairly well organized and dispersed across the profession of journalism. Whether a journalist works at a small-town newspaper, a regional daily, or a metro daily, she has been more or less socialized into the same norms, practices, and principles. The reactions of most journalists, therefore, are likely to be within a small range of variation from those I witnessed in the newsrooms I visited. In short, while no ethnography is entirely representative, mine is representative enough to warrant wide conclusions about the field of journalism.

Before telling this story, let me say a word or two about methods. The bulk of data for this study was collected during fieldwork conducted over five years in three newspapers: the *Daily Bugle*, *The Herald*, and the *Cedar Rapids Gazette*. Fieldwork at the *Daily Bugle* took place from January 2005 to August 2006, at *The Herald* in July 2008, and at the *Gazette* in July 2009. At the *Bugle*, I spent an average of two days per week (and sometimes three) in the newsroom. During this time, I attended budget meetings and other news meetings, observed reporters and editors interacting with one another, conducted formal interviews with every reporter and editor working on the city desk, held many impromptu discussions as events occurred, and followed reporters around on their beats. I also conducted four formal interviews with Calvin Thomas. In addition, from May to July 2006, I worked as a faculty intern for the paper. For two days per week over twelve weeks I reported on and wrote twenty-seven stories for the city desk on topics ranging from government press conferences, to the release of academic studies, to events at the state legislature.

For the content analysis of news content at the *Bugle*, I collected the front and local sections of the newspaper Monday through Friday, from January to February 2005, and again from July 2005 to January 2006. A graduate student and I coded every article that appeared on the first page of these sections according to the following categories: reporter, placement of story (centerpiece, front, or local front page), length of story, story type (daily vs. enterprise), frame (hard vs. soft), and story source (one-time or ongoing event). This process produced a total of 1,369 records on a Microsoft Excel spreadsheet. Figures 2.1 and 2.2 were generated using this software program through simple aggregations of story type and story source trends across stories over time.

At *The Herald* and the *Cedar Rapids Gazette*, I conducted four weeks of fieldwork and visited the newsroom seven days a week during this period. As at the *Bugle*, I attended budget meetings and other news meetings, observed reporters and editors interacting with one another, conducted formal interviews with every reporter and editor working on the city desk, and held many impromptu discussions as events occurred. I also conducted several interviews with the editors, Hank Carlin and Steve Buttry. These interviews took place both before and after my visit. Before visiting their newsrooms I spent several months doing historical research on the newspapers and, from May to June 2008, conducted a content analysis of the front page of their news sites. In addition, I stayed in contact with many reporters and editors for several months after my visit to keep up with events in these newsrooms.

By agreement with the editors, I did not audio-record or videotape any conversation or interview. Instead, I compiled my observations and conversations into ten ringed binders of field notes. These field notes form the core data on which I have drawn in this book, and all observations mentioned come from them. At times, I have had to paraphrase language used by individuals. However, any text placed in quotation marks is a direct quote from one of my sources.

In accordance with an agreement between me, Thomas, and Carlin, and the rules of my university's institutional review board, all names, including those of the newspapers, have been changed in the writing of this book. However, Chuck Peters and Steve Buttry preferred that I use their real names and the name of their newspaper. While I have honored their preference, I have changed all other names of people in the newsroom. Editors and reporters were made aware of these rules when I visited their newsrooms.

Now, to the story!

Acknowledgments

This book took many years to complete and I have accumulated many debts along the way. I want to thank my former department chair, Richard Campbell, for setting me on the path that became this book, and two former deans, Cole Campbell and Jerry Ceppos, for keeping me on this path. I have had conversations with many people about the project. I want to thank a few of them for comments or information that have made their way into the manuscript. They include Alan Deutschman, Bill Winter, Martin Langeveld, Phillip Meyer, Gaye Tuchman, Carol Riordan of the American Press Institute (API), John Murray of the Newspaper Association of America (NAA), Alan Mutter, Earl Wilkinson, Henrik Bødker, Mark Blach-Ørsten, Ed Lenert, and Ward Bushee. Others have done me the service of reading drafts of various chapters and parts of chapters. They include Dominic Boyer, Eric Klinenberg, Mark Deuze, Timothy Majoribanks, Daniel Hallin, Michael Schudson, Rodney Benson, Richard Kaplan, Timothy Cook, Bartholomew Sparrow, Gaye Tuchman, and Vicki Mayer. David Flores and Abbey Smith proved invaluable as graduate assistants at various stages of the project. I also owe a debt to the anonymous reviewers for Polity Press, who provided helpful suggestions for making the manuscript better. A special thank you to my colleague Donica Mensing, who not only read and commented on various parts of the manuscript but helped me flesh out my ideas over several years of lunches. *Journalism: Theory, Practice and Criticism* published two essays from which much of the material in chapter 2 is derived. Here are links to these essays: http://jou.sagepub.com/content/10/5/665.full.pdf+html and http://jou.sagepub.com/content/10/2/197.full.pdf+html. This material has been published in *Journalism*, 10(2), and 10(5). SAGE Publications Ltd. All rights reserved. ©.

Introduction

By some measures – say, employment – the American newspaper industry has been declining only for a short time. But by at least one – percentage of advertising expenditures – its decline began as long ago as the 1920s, and by several others, including market penetration and circulation, it began in the 1970s. In recent years, the rate of decline in nearly every measure has quickened. In the 2000s, newspaper circulation dropped 31 percent from its peak in 1984. As I write in 2011, market penetration of newspapers hovers at roughly 40 percent of households (meaning that the average household now subscribes to less than half a daily newspaper). Something less than 20 percent of people under the age of twenty-five read a daily newspaper. More ominously, advertising revenues have fallen off a cliff. In 2000, the industry garnered about $20 billion in advertising expenditures. By 2009, that number had been halved, to $10 billion, or about the level they were at in 1965. With their revenues dropping, stock shares of major newspaper public companies plunged in 2008 and 2009, falling to pennies per share in some cases. In 2010 stock shares for many of these companies bounced back somewhat, but only because newspapers systematically slashed costs, especially labor costs. According to the website Paper Cuts, from 2007 to 2009 the industry bought out or fired 33,000 journalists. In fact, since 2001, the industry has shed more than 25 percent of its workforce.[1]

Things in the industry got so much worse so quickly, journalists were initially caught off-guard. For years, they had comforted themselves with the thought that, as many have said to me verbatim, "there will always be newspapers." But by 2006 they had been shaken out of this complacence. Why 2006? That year the Knight-Ridder news company unexpectedly died. Knight-Ridder was a combination of two venerable news companies (Knight and Ridder) whose histories stretched back to the beginnings of modern journalism at the turn of the twentieth century. Among journalists, Knight-Ridder was known as one of the "good guys." Its newspapers – thirty-two at the time of its sale, making it the second largest news chain in the country – had a reputation for doing things the right way. They did not cut corners. They resisted the pull of commercialism. They privileged professionalism among their journalists and preached service to their communities. Since their merger in 1974, the Knight-Ridder news chain had won eighty-four Pulitzer prizes, including fourteen for public service. And now, seemingly in the blink of an eye, the company was gone.

Its sale set off a collective panic among journalists. One could almost hear the same thought rising from all corners of the profession: "If it happened to Knight-Ridder . . ." Who will be next? What will happen to us? What will happen to me? WE'VE GOT TO DO SOMETHING! Journalism was like a punctured balloon, one moment upright and stable, the next careening out of control. One moment "everyone knew" that there would always be newspapers, the next journalists were imagining a once unthinkable situation, a world without them. It was as if with Knight-Ridder's demise the blinkers had finally come off for journalists, and they could now see just how vulnerable they and their industry were.

Rachel Smolkin (2006) caught the new mood in an article for *American Journalism Review* published a few months after Knight-Ridder's sale. After reciting facts that had been known but ignored for a very long time ("circulation is falling; newsprint costs are rising; retail, auto, and movie advertising is slumping; classified advertising is available free on craigslist and other online venues"), Smolkin got to the point. The situation has become so dire, she observed, newspapers now have only two options: they can "adapt" or they can "die." Adapt or die. Since then, this phrase has become conventional wisdom across much of journalism. I rarely meet a journalist today who does not believe that journalism *must* either adapt or face the fate of (take your pick) the typewriter, railroad, or telegraph industries.

Have they succeeded? Are they adapting? Will they avoid professional death? Should we care? This last is a fair question. When considering the plight of newspapers, many people say, "Good riddance! Who needs newspapers!" When I hear this sort of reaction – and I hear it a lot – I respond in two ways. First, as Alex Jones (2009) has noted, newspapers (mostly metro dailies) produce upwards of 70 to 80 percent of new information that circulates in most communities. If these daily newspapers cease to exist, we have no good idea of how this information will be replaced. This should give us pause before we dance on newspapers' collective grave. Second, assuming for the moment that the world would be better off without newspapers, it is, nonetheless, still a great story. It isn't every day that an entire industry falls to its knees. We might want to know out of simple curiosity why it is happening.

So the question of whether journalists will adapt or die seems at least interesting and probably important, and it is with this in mind that I began making visits to newsrooms in January 2005. From that time until the summer of 2009 I visited the newsrooms of three metro daily newspapers, and watched as the journalists in these organizations worked feverishly to avoid obsolescence (see the preface for a discussion of this fieldwork). In that time, I talked with dozens of journalists as their news organizations implemented new experiments. I sat in on their meetings. I observed them devise new plans and reorganize their newsrooms. I followed their progress as they worked new beats, learned new tools, and acquired new vocabularies to describe what they were doing. As you might expect, I often heard uncomfortable conversations and intense arguments. On more than one occasion, my interviews lapsed into "bitch" sessions as people vented their frustrations. A few times, I even found myself, strangely enough, offering career advice, and trying to console someone who had finally had enough and quit or, more often, was laid off.

What did I find? The short answer is that journalists have not adapted very well. For the most part, they continue to gather the same sorts of information, from the same sorts of people, and package it in the same news forms they have used for decades. Newspapers have the same look and feel they have had since the 1930s, and newspaper websites still look uncomfortably like newspapers. When journalists have tried to break from tradition, their efforts largely have come to naught. I know of no recent innovations in news that were invented in a metro daily newsroom, and no newsroom, to my knowledge, has adopted the new innovations in a comprehensive way.

I am not the only person to come to this conclusion. In the late 1990s, Pablo Boczkowski conducted one of the first analyses of technology's impact on journalism. In three case studies, which included a visit to the *New York Times* "Technology on the Web" section, Boczkowski (2004) found that, the closer online news came to a conventional newsroom, the less innovation it displayed. When confronted with change, Boczkowski concluded, journalists tended to be "reactive, defensive, and pragmatic" (p. 48). Since then, researchers have duplicated Boczkowski's finding time and again.

Deborah Chung (2007) interviewed twenty-two editors of online news sites nominated for 2002 Online News Association (ONA) awards. Given that they were being recognized by the ONA, you might think that these journalists embraced change more than most, but you'd be wrong. Chung found that these editors were "resistant" to adopting interactive features of online news and had a general "hesitancy" toward innovation (2007, p. 57). Jane Singer (2004) visited with online journalists in four newsrooms at about the same time. She found that even these journalists maintained a sense of "us" versus "them," marking a clear separation between print and online news. Further, far from embracing the digital medium, they "resist[ed] convergence as long as they [could]" (2004, p. 846). Studies in other parts of the world confirm Singer's observation. The idea that online news sites allow for much interactivity, David Domingo (2008) concludes in a study of four Catalan newspapers, is a "myth." In all cases, "the professional culture of traditional journalism prevails" (p. 680). John O'Sullivan and Ari Heinonen (2008) summarize the findings of this literature in the title of one of their essays: "Old values, new media."

Not surprisingly, content analyses of online news sites find much the same thing. In an examination of ten news sites in eleven countries (including the United States), Thorsten Quandt (2008) concludes that the "revolution" in news promised by the Internet "did not happen," at least at traditional news organizations. "Online journalism . . . is basically good old news journalism" (p. 735). David Domingo and his colleagues (2008) performed a similar content analysis of European and American news sites and discovered that "core journalistic culture [has] remained largely unchanged" (p. 339). Ditto for Wilson Lowrey's (2011) analysis of American newspaper websites. "Statis," he writes, "rather than innovation seems the primary tendency for these newspapers" (p. 75). Introducing the findings of several studies included in a special issue of *Gazette*, Richard van der Wurff (2005) writes that "online newspapers [remain] subordinate and subservient to print newspapers" (p. 107).

The upshot seems to be this: even today, journalists rely on the same sources, especially government agencies, as principal sources of news. Their definitions of news and newsworthiness, e.g., immediacy, impact, uniqueness, human interest, and the like – which have been taught in introduction to journalism classes for decades – remain essentially in place. And their role conceptions still revolve around longstanding values like objectivity, facticity, balance, and neutrality. Again, this is not to say that nothing has changed in journalism. News writing today is more informal and conversational than in the past, and more likely to incorporate multimedia elements. But these are changes more of style than of substance. The evidence overwhelmingly indicates that, at least as practiced by metro daily newspapers, online journalism looks very similar to its print counterpart. Consequently, if it (probably) does not die, journalism will likely be greatly diminished in the next decade or two. The evidence for this is already apparent, in the demise of several prominent metro dailies, in slimmer yet costlier newspapers, in newspapers not delivered every day, in the move to online-only news.

The fact that newspapers have not adapted well is relatively easy to demonstrate. Explaining why is more difficult, and will take up most of the chapters that follow. Briefly, however, in my observation the major impediments to change arise from within the culture of journalism. This is a large term – the "culture of journalism." Fortunately, sociologists have been analyzing it since David Manning White's (1964) gatekeeper study. For more than half a century, they have argued over its origins and growth over the twentieth century. They have examined many of its elements, and sorted through how these elements are produced and reproduced in newsrooms. And they have sought to understand how journalists are implicated in this culture. This literature has not addressed everything we might ask of the culture of journalism, but a great deal of good work has been accomplished – enough, I think, to help flesh out a cultural explanation for why journalists have found it so difficult to adapt.

In the rest of this introduction, I want to place the culture of journalism in this broad intellectual context, a discussion that will set the stage for the more specific analyses to follow.

Let me first deal, however, with a preliminary issue, namely the definition of my object of study. Throughout this book you will see me throw the words "journalist" and "journalism" around. When I use them, I mean "journalists who work for metro daily newspapers." Newspaper journalism, especially the journalism practiced at mid-sized and larger metro daily newspapers, is my focus. Partly I use the contraction for reasons of efficiency. Writing (and reading) "journalists who work for metro daily newspapers" over and over would be tedious and cumbersome. But there is also a substantive reason to conflate the two, one that the words' etymologies reveal. According to the Oxford English Dictionary (OED), the origin of the word "news" ("a report or account of recent events or occurrences") is very old, stretching back to the fourteenth century. Usage of "news" to mean "new things" goes back even further, to the mid-900s. In contrast, the first use of the word "journalist" ("one who earns a living by writing a public journal") in the English language occurs in the early 1600s, about the time that pamphleteers first arrived on the scene. And the word "journalism" ("the occupation of a journalist") does not make its debut until the 1830s. It is used initially to refer to the French and English "grub street," and to the American "penny press" – the earliest ancestors of modern commercial news organizations. This is no accident. People coined a new word when they encountered a new organizational form: the commercial newspaper.

I take these etymologies to mean the following. The conflation of the word "journalist" with "people who work for metro daily newspapers" is reasonable because these people were the first to practice "journalism." That being said, it will not do to equate "journalism" with the news, or to imply that all reporters practice their craft within journalism. As I say, today one often hears people claim "there has always been news." The implication is that there must also always be journalism. But the news is not the same thing as journalism. There has always been news, but journalists have not always delivered it, and, in the four hundred years they have delivered it, they have not always done so within journalism. Indeed, the fact that journalists working for commercial news organizations dominate news production is a relatively new phenomenon. If there was a time before journalists produced news within journalism, then, logically, there may also be a time after this is the case. Or, put another way, the news may be inevitable, but journalism isn't.

The Challenge

With these preliminaries out of the way, we might now ask what threatens journalism so much that we are contemplating a future without it. Many observers point to the Internet, or to "new communication technologies," as the culprit.[2] According to Yochai Benkler (2006), for example, the Internet is terribly disruptive to journalism – and all mass media – because it threatens journalism's role as a primary filter of public information. This "is the core characteristic of mass media," Benkler writes: "Content is produced prior to transmission in a relatively small number of centers, and when finished is then transmitted to a mass audience, which consumes it" (2006, p. 209). Online, in contrast, everyone is ostensibly a "user" – a consumer and a producer of information. As users, we "are substantially more engaged participants, both in defining the terms of [our] productive activity and in defining what [we] consume and how [we] consume it" (ibid., p. 138). This is a simple but profound point. The Internet gives individuals much more control over their information environment, and correspondingly dilutes the control of professional journalists.

Part of the challenge to journalism lies just in this fact: that individuals have more choice online. They have more freedom to avoid the filter imposed by professional journalists on the information they receive and, if they choose to do so, to create and distribute their own information. One way journalists sometimes deflect this fact is to say that much of the culture produced by amateurs is, in a word, bad. They are, of course, right. Science fiction writer Theodore Sturgeon even coined a law to this effect: "ninety percent of everything," he famously said, "is crud." Most people, including people producing news, have little talent for it. But another law – the law of large numbers – shows that this does not matter. Today, about a billion people (according to the website Internet World States, over 500 billion of them English speakers) have access to the Internet, and this number will only grow in the future. Suppose that only 1 percent of these people have any talent for cultural production. They write well, or have a nice visual eye, or know a lot about a particular subject. One percent of 1 billion is 10 million people. Each of these individuals possesses as much talent as the average journalist, and together they surpass the number of professionals by a large margin. Even if most of online content is "crud," in absolute terms a large amount – an amount far larger in the aggregate than what is produced by professionals – will be very good. Not only do people have more choice online, then, they also have more choices.

In recent years, researchers have been hard at work analyzing how people exercise their newfound freedom online. They have discovered that people do not choose to interact with others in a random way. Rather, they tend to congregate in "small worlds" (e.g., Barabási, 2002; Ferguson, 2002; Schnettler, 2009). A small world is a network structure characterized by dense clusters of individuals linked together via bridges or connectors. Within these dense clusters, individuals go on with their virtual lives much as they do in their real ones: they interact with people who are familiar, or with whom they share a common interest. Indeed, one way of thinking about the Internet is that it amplifies people's social tendency to interact with others like them, and brings this tendency to scale. This is not to say that people completely insulate themselves from one another online. Much as in real life, they remain linked to other clusters of people through the activities of bridges – individuals who have links to more than one dense cluster. Dense clusters plus these bridges equal small worlds. Scientists have shown that this structure combines durability with efficiency, which may be why it has been duplicated in a great variety of settings – from the human brain, to ant colonies, to electrical grids. At any moment, an individual in a small world can feel the intimacy of dense interactions with familiar others, and yet remain separated from any other individual in a system by as few as six steps (hence, the famous "six degrees of separation" associated with small worlds).

Researchers have learned a few other things about the small worlds we inhabit online. They know, for example, that the distribution of links within small worlds tends to be skewed toward highly active, popular individuals. Why this should be the case is easy to demonstrate. Suppose that there are three individuals, whom we will call "A," "B," and "C." Further suppose that "A" and "B" are linked together, and "A" and "C" are linked together. If a new individual "D" were to enter this network, with whom is she most likely to link? The answer is clearly "A," because "A" gives "D" access to both "B" and "C." Now suppose that "E" enters the scene. Given that "A" provides access to every other individual in the network, "E" is even more likely to link to "A." By this logic, "A" is likely to become ever more popular. This phenomenon, called a "power law," produces a situation in which, the more popular a node is in a network at T_0, the more popular it is likely to be at T_1, the likelier still at T_2, and so on. It produces, in other words, "hubs" – individuals with far more ties than the average person in a network.

Hubs play a special role in small worlds. In fact, their role is so special it makes them utterly unlike anyone else in their clusters of intimates. To demonstrate this point, scientists often turn to the example of height. To find the average height of people in a given population, you simply add the height of all individuals and divide by the number of people. The result gives you a bell curve, with roughly half of the people falling on one side, and half on the other. The average height lies in the middle. Power-law distributions work in a very different way. Because they describe relations between individuals, power laws allow a few people to accrue most of a trait characteristic of a system, leaving everyone else with little of the trait. In the instance of height, a power-law distribution means that most individuals are very short, and a few individuals are very tall.

In the case of online hubs, a power-law distribution creates a situation in which a few highly passionate, highly interested, highly knowledgeable individuals do most of the work of online communication. Hubs are most likely to post content, most likely to engage in collaborations, most likely to link to others and to be linked to. We can be even more precise: about 20 percent of online users (hubs) perform as much as 80 percent of the work. This "80/20 rule," as it is called, is very nearly an iron law of online interaction. If an online community forms around baseball, most of its members will be a little interested in baseball, and a very few members will be highly interested. If an online community forms around a neighborhood, most of its members will be a little interested in the neighborhood and a few people will be highly passionate. And as much as 80 percent of the interaction that takes place in these online communities will be accomplished by the 20 percent who are most interested, most passionate, and most knowledgeable. This can seem unfair. Why should 20 percent of a community's members be responsible for producing the bulk of its activity? In fact, however, this division of labor is key to a small world's success. The willingness of highly active people to do most of a cluster's work makes it possible for everyone else to contribute a little bit. Absent this willingness, online clusters quickly dissipate.

Its structure of nodes, links, hubs, and bridges allows us to see a different aspect of the Internet's challenge to journalism. Imagine for a moment that you are a professional journalist wishing to reach an audience with the news. In a mass-mediated system, you might accomplish this goal in one of two ways. On television, you might broadcast the news to everyone (and therefore to no one in particular), hoping through brute force to catch the attention of a mass audience. Alternatively, in a newspaper, you might compile a large number of news items, with the hope of aggregating an audience by making each item very interesting to a few people. The small-worlds structure of the Internet dramatically alters this situation. Online, individuals have more choice about which information they receive, and more of this information will come from people with whom they have a personal connection or share a common interest (from someone within the clusters they inhabit). As a journalist, you stand outside these clusters of activity. How will you get inside? The answer is obvious. The most efficient way to access a cluster is to appeal to its hubs. They are the only individuals with a great number of links to others in the cluster. Recall that, in a system privileging personal interest and choice, people become hubs because they show more interest or have more passion than the average member of a cluster. If an online group forms around kayaking, for example, its hub will very likely be someone who is very passionate or has a lot of knowledge about this subject. Others link to this passionate person because she represents a "one-stop shop" for all things kayaking.

So, to get inside online clusters, you need to attract the attention of a hub. How will you do so? Well, if hubs tend to be very passionate and/or knowledgeable, then they are likely to respond to you only if you are similarly passionate and knowledgeable. In the small-world, power-law distributed structure of the web, hubs are far more likely to respond to people like themselves – people similarly passionate and knowledgeable about particular subjects. The web, in other words, rewards passion and expertise.

The problem for professional journalism is that, since the 1920s, it has been grounded in ideals of detachment, independence, and objectivity. Journalists in the profession distinguish themselves precisely by their unwillingness to get too involved. Some political journalists even go so far as to refrain from voting, for fear that their subjective choices will interfere with their objective reporting. Online, this simply will not do. It will not do to feign disinterest when trying to reach people who are anything but. It will not do to write for everyone and therefore to no one when individuals prefer to interact with very particular someones: people they know and people they trust. Achieving success online requires journalists to dispense with the very value that has sustained professional journalism for nearly a century, namely, objectivity. This is what journalists are up against. If journalists wish to survive in the densely clustered world of online interaction, they will have to make personal, even intimate, connections with others. They will have to learn to love (read: be passionate about) the issues they cover – and to love the communities of people with whom they interact – *more* than they love their professional identity.

To summarize: online, individuals have more freedom to choose and more options from which to choose, and this has dislodged journalism from its role as a primary filter of public information. Also, when exercising their choice, individuals tend to cluster with like-minded others, much as they do in their daily social interactions. The links within these clusters are skewed toward highly popular individuals – what scientists call "hubs." These hubs are the most active, knowledgeable, and passionate individuals within online clusters. To have a chance of online success, journalists need to exude the same level of knowledge, passion, and interest as the hubs that stand between them and everyone else in a cluster. Success online requires that journalists, far from being disinterested observers, should be interested and active participants – and this requirement challenges a core aspect of journalistic culture.

The Culture of Journalism

As I have framed the issue, the challenge to journalism posed by the Internet is not, at bottom, technological or economic; it is ontological. It goes to the heart of what journalism is, what journalists do, and why they do it. It is a challenge, in other words, to the culture of journalism. And it is here that we will find the root of the profession's inability to change. To see how this is so, it is helpful to learn a few things about this culture: its origins and history, its composition, how it works, and how journalists are enmeshed within it.

Literary scholar Raymond Williams (1976) once called "culture" one of the two or three most complicated words in the English language (p. 87). It derives from the Latin root "cultis," meaning "to make things grow," as in "to cultivate." When I think of the culture of journalism, this is precisely how I see it: the symbols that have grown up within and around journalism to define it as a distinctive social field. No one has ever catalogued – if it were possible – all of the symbols that compose the culture of journalism. Generally, though, they take one of three forms: of principles, like "cover the story but do not become the story"; of shared norms like "objectivity," which any two journalists may define differently but all share as a common reference; or of practices, like the practice of verifying information. The culture of journalism acts as a kind of gravitational force for journalists, pulling them together enough so that they are more similar to one another than they are to members of any other occupation.

The first thing to say about this culture is that it is relatively new. Many of its elements have long histories. When the first news beat was organized is unknown, but James Gordon Bennett created a beat of a kind in Washington, DC, as early as the 1820s. The definition of news as "human interest" dates back at least to the 1830s (e.g., Hughes, 1940; Schudson, 1978). Norms associated with objectivity – detachment, independence, balance, and the like – stretch back to the same period (e.g., Kaplan, 2002; Mindich, 1998; Schiller, 1981). The first news interviews took place in the 1860s (e.g., Schudson, 1995a). However, these elements did not coalesce into a distinctive culture until the late nineteenth and early twentieth centuries.

Before that time, people who produced news saw themselves as engaged primarily in some other activity. In colonial America, for instance, most journalists were first and foremost printers, and referred to themselves as such (e.g., Botein, 1975; Pasley, 2001). During the nineteenth century most newspapers were appendages of the political party system, and most journalists were party hacks (e.g., McGerr, 1986; Schudson, 1998; Smith, 1977). The first commercial newspapers, the "penny press," may have been introduced in the 1830s, but their proprietors were nothing like modern journalists. Many retained direct or indirect connections to the political parties. Those that did not considered themselves businessmen first and journalists a distant second. While they may have sold newspapers out the front door, for example, they often sold dry goods out the back. In keeping with the amorphous nature of journalism, through these years news could come from virtually anywhere and be circulated by just about anyone. It was not uncommon for a mid-nineteenth-century news proprietor to get the news from a traveler just off a train, and to print it as such: "So and so just arrived from Boston and tells us . . ." Through much of the nineteenth century, there were few boundaries between practicing journalism and doing other things.

This began to change in the post-Civil War period. Over a period of decades, several social trends began to converge. Liberal political reformers in the North – many of them newspaper editors – campaigned against the political parties and the partisan press. The professions (law, medicine, the academy, etc.) emerged around the same time. Corporations also grew larger. As a national market developed, these corporations began to see mass media, including large urban newspapers, as vehicles for marketing their products on a national scale. In turn, owners of urban newspapers saw new commercial advantages in satisfying this corporate need. New printing technologies invented in the 1880s gave publishers the ability to reach a mass audience on a daily basis. And then, in the aftermath of the 1896 presidential election, the third-party system dissolved, and newspapers suddenly found themselves freed from public culture to which they had been attached since the 1830s.

This freedom presented newspapers with new opportunities but also a slew of new problems. Commercial newspapers signed contracts with advertisers to print their ads daily. Now that they were no longer tied to the political parties, where were they going to find enough information to wrap around these ads *every day*? Another problem was that this information had to be cheap. Commercial newspapers were, by definition, profit-seeking enterprises. It would do them no good to find costly sources of information when what they needed was *cheap* information. The answer to each of these problems was to position reporters at the only locations in society that produced information reliably and at little cost: government agencies. City hall, the statehouse, the courthouse, the police department, and other government agencies came to form core news "beats" of modern newspapers because they gave newspapers ready access to low-cost information.

In solving these problems, however, these government beats raised another: the problem of credibility. With the political parties weakened, journalists became primary filters of the information that circulated between officials and citizens. But no one elected them to play this role. What gave journalists the right to determine which information the public received and how that information was to be framed? Except for a vague reference in the First Amendment to the freedom of the press, journalism plays no formal role in government. Yet there they found themselves, stationed at government agencies, front and center in the hurly-burly of politics. How could journalists fend off the accusation that they favored politicians over citizens, or one politician over another, or one government department over another?

This is the question sociologist Gaye Tuchman (1972) asked herself when she began visiting newsrooms in the mid-1960s. "The newsmen," she famously discovered, "cope with these pressures by emphasizing 'objectivity,' arguing that dangers can be minimized if newsmen follow strategies of newswork which they identify with 'objective stories'" (p. 664). These strategies include sticking to facts, balancing opposing points of view, attributing significant facts to external sources, and relying on familiar writing formulas, like the inverted pyramid style of writing leads. If these practices did not precisely solve journalists' credibility problem – people have never stopped complaining that journalists are biased – they did allow them to manage it. By adopting "objective" news practices, journalists secured their new role in public life, to say, in effect, "we are rightfully filters of public information because, unlike anyone else, we strive to be objective, independent, detached, and balanced."

Here, then, seem to be the origins of modern journalistic culture. When newspapers were freed from the party system, they faced new problems. Different newspapers adopted different solutions to these problems, and some of the solutions seemed to work better than others. Newspapers copied the success of other newspapers – a process social scientists refer to as "isomorphism." Entrepreneurs took practices that worked in one newsroom and transplanted them to other newsrooms. Professional associations and journalism schools began to teach the "best practices." Once the first steps were taken down the path of professionalization, path dependency took care of the rest. Political scientist Paul Pierson (2000) defines path dependency this way. Once social actors take steps down a particular path, "the relative benefits" of continuing down the path "compared with other possible options increase over time" (p. 252). For example, the choice to place reporters at government agencies set an important precedent. Over time, the cost of adopting and maintaining this practice gradually lowered relative to the benefits of reproducing it, and so the practice eventually took hold across the field of journalism. As path dependency worked its magic, journalism congealed into a relatively cohesive culture. By the 1920s, most newspapers practiced journalism in the same ways for the same purposes, and most journalists worked for these newspapers. Much like bread rising in an oven, a culture of journalism inflated into existence.

Of course, after the fact, journalists did what anyone might do: they made a virtue of necessity. In textbooks, mission statements, and ethical codes, journalists everywhere trumpeted the way they now practiced news as the way it ought to be practiced and, when done correctly, the way it had always been practiced. A famous example of this is Walter Williams's "The Journalist's Creed" (1906), an early effort by the first dean of the University of Missouri School of Journalism to distill the new field's meaning:

- I believe in the profession of Journalism.
- I believe that the public journal is a public trust; that all connected with it are, to the full measure of responsibility, trustees for the public; that acceptance of lesser service than the public service is a betrayal of this trust.
- I believe that clear thinking, clear statement, accuracy and fairness are fundamental to good journalism.
- I believe that a journalist should write only what he holds in his heart to be true. I believe that suppression of the news, for any consideration other than the welfare of society, is indefensible.
- I believe that no one should write as a journalist what he would not say as a gentleman; that bribery by one's own pocket book is as much to be avoided as bribery by the pocketbook of another; that individual responsibility may not be escaped by pleading another's instructions or another's dividends.
- I believe that advertising, news and editorial columns should alike serve the best interests of readers; that a single standard of helpful truth and cleanness should prevail for all; that supreme test of good journalism is the measure of its public service.
- I believe that the journalism which succeeds the best – and best deserves success – fears God and honors man; is stoutly independ-

ent; unmoved by pride of opinion or greed of power; constructive, tolerant but never careless, self-controlled, patient, always respectful of its readers but always unafraid, is quickly indignant at injustice; is unswayed by the appeal of the privilege or the clamor of the mob; seeks to give every man a chance, and as far as law, an honest wage and recognition of human brotherhood can make it so, an equal chance; is profoundly patriotic while sincerely promoting international good will and cementing world-comradeship, is a journalism of humanity, of and for today's world.

Williams's creed puts the new culture of journalism on full display: professionalism, trusteeship, truth, and independence. Journalists have an important public service mission and strive to fulfill that mission as responsible professionals. Twenty years before Williams wrote his creed, none of these terms could fairly be said to describe journalism. Now, Williams had turned the history of their rise into myth: a story journalists tell themselves about themselves to explain who they are, what they do, and why they do it.

Though most embrace a version of this myth, it is a curious fact about journalists that they find it difficult to talk about their culture in an explicit way. Like native speakers of a natural language, they can speak the language of journalism without being able to express its rules. The first researchers into newsroom culture were greatly impressed by this fact. To them, it meant that journalists reproduced their culture in a relatively unreflective and uniform way. From about 1970 to 1980, no fewer than fifteen observational studies of newsrooms were conducted. To a person, the authors of these studies argued that journalistic culture persisted through unconscious routine. Leon Sigal (1973, p. 101) reports that news routines "take on a life of their own . . . Learned during apprenticeship, reinforced in daily experience on the job, they become 'the way things are done.'" Gaye Tuchman (1978, p. 186) argues that reporters adopt a "natural attitude" toward their work, relying on largely implicit, everyday understandings to guide their activities. Herbert Gans (1979, p. 82) likens news decisions to "quick intuitive judgments, which some ascribe to a 'feel.'"

There is a sense in which these observations are true, and it is one of the reasons that this literature remains relevant even today. Journalists do reproduce their shared culture in an unreflective way, and this can make the culture seem uniform and seamless. But, as with any culture, the opposite is also true. Anyone who has ever been in a newsroom knows that journalists engage in constant argument. They argue over whether a story is newsworthy and, if it is, where it should be played in the newspaper. They disagree about how a story should be written. They negotiate over how many sources must be consulted for a story to be balanced. This contentiousness implies that the culture of journalism is not as seamless or uniform as one might suspect. It implies, in other words, that disagreement may be as vital as agreement to reproducing journalism's culture.

A "second wave" of ethnographic work conducted in the 1980s and 1990s insisted on this point (e.g., Cottle, 2009). In his visits to newsrooms, Charles Bantz (1985) observed that reporters engage in constant conflict and negotiation with one another and with their managers. Nina Eliasoph (1988) discovered much the same thing while working at an alternative radio news station. Seeking to reconcile this observation with the extant sociological literature, she could only conclude that different routines "accomplish different things in different contexts" (p. 315). And the same insight led Mark Pedelty (1995) to argue that at the heart of foreign affairs reporting lies an endless game of managing the contradictions inherent in routines. "Both within and between news organizations," Ronald Jacobs (1996, p. 375) concludes for this generation of scholarship, "there is a significant degree of contestation and heterogeneity."

One way to link these two waves of scholarship is to say that journalists engage in a constant process of justification. As the first generation of research showed, journalists unreflectively do journalism. For the most part, they do not talk about why balance in their stories is necessary; they write balanced stories. Culture comes into play only when they are asked to justify what they have done. If asked, for instance, why I have written a story this way rather than that, I might respond with an appeal to balance: I wished to write a balanced story. If asked why I asked this question of a source rather than another, I might say that I wished to preserve my independence. In this way, the cultural elements that define journalism serve as a reservoir of meaning to which journalists appeal to render their actions sensible. And journalists most often have occasion to turn to this reservoir when they are asked to justify a particular action. Thus, disagreement is crucial for the culture of journalism because it provides journalists an opportunity to reconfirm the salience of the norms and practices that bind them together.

Few researchers have stopped to ask about the limits of justification in journalism. But, if we think about it for a moment, it becomes clear that these limits lie at the boundaries of recognition. Suppose, for example, that I scribbled a few lines from a dream I had last night and tried to publish them as journalism. My editor naturally might express confusion: *this* is news? The limits of journalism lie at my ability to justify my scribbles as news. If I am unable to convince my editor that what I have done is journalism, I have reached the limits of the culture. Whatever I have done in writing down my dream, it is not journalism because I can convince no one else to recognize it as such. One consequence of this fact is that the boundaries of journalism are never stable; they depend on interactions in specific contexts. Having said this, the boundaries do exist, and we know them when we come upon them. They exist at the point where we can no longer recognize an action as a meaningful instance of the practice.

The import of this point will become clear in a moment, but first let me make one last observation about the culture of journalism. Though at the time no one knew it, journalism enjoyed its greatest autonomy from other social fields (e.g., economics and politics) from the 1950s to the 1970s. It was in these years that journalists gained the most freedom to do journalism for journalism's sake, unmolested by owners, sources, or, indeed, audiences. But even in these decades, journalism only ever achieved semi-autonomy. For one thing, it remained strongly shaped by the commercial needs of news organizations, as it had been since the birth of modern commercial news. As fundamentally, however, the political culture in which it was situated had a strong influence on journalism's form and meaning. Media scholar James Carey (1989) made this point over twenty years ago, in a famous comment about newspapers: they are "dramatically satisfying," he wrote, "which is not to say pleasing, presentations of what the world at root is . . . a presentation of reality that gives life an overall form, order, and tone" (p. 21). Carey's meaning is a bit cryptic, so I consulted his original source for this notion, anthropologist Clifford Geertz's essay "Religion as a cultural system" (1973). In that essay, Geertz makes the now famous observation that culture works as a model both "for" and "of" reality. Culture works as a model "for" reality when it serves as a template, guide, or map to action. Think of the blueprint for a house. It is a constellation of symbols put together in such a way that it tells a person how to do something, namely, how to build a house. But a blueprint for a house also presents a model "of" what a house is – it is a structure with at least four walls, a roof, windows, and so on. In this sense, the blueprint for a house, like all culture, "express[es]" one thing (in this case, a house) in "another medium" (1973, pp. 93–4). Carey is telling us that news does the same thing. It expresses one thing (public life) in another medium (the news). In this sense, journalism is intrinsically linked to public culture.

This is a deep insight into the news. It suggests that journalism will always express the dominant sensibilities of the public culture in which it is practiced. In colonial America, for example, public life had a deferential, consensual cast, and colonial news expressed this sensibility. Newspapers of the time strove, as one printer put it, to "please all and offend none." Similarly, nineteenth-century news expressed the associational, partisan sensibility of the public culture. Where colonial printers avoided political controversy, the party press thrived on it. Finally, we can see modern news as an expression of the progressive culture from which it emerged. Its embrace of objectivity, its sense of professional detachment and independence, and its over-riding purpose of informing the public are all expressions of a progressive interest in science, expertise, and persuasion. It is worth pointing out that journalism was not alone in this regard. National magazines, broadcasting, film, advertising – all of the mass media emerged at roughly the same time, and all were shaped by the dominant norms of progressive public culture. Indeed, as James Beniger (1986) argues, mass media were veritably invented out of a felt need by elites to manage mass populations via manipulation of public information. By the end of the nineteenth century, industry could produce enormous quantities of widgets but could not ensure their consumption, and government could invent solutions to public problems but could not guarantee that citizens would go along. Leaders of these institutions required new tools for reaching, organizing, persuading, and managing masses of people. Mass media, including mass-circulation newspapers, became these tools.

Carey's insight gives us a different way of thinking about the challenge faced by journalism. Historians have shown that the profession is a creature of a progressive public culture. This is the culture in which it emerged, and this is the culture in which it thrived. In the past half century, however, this culture has fragmented. Today, we live in a more individualized and personalized culture – a culture far less amenable to elite control. Too many groups compete with one another, too many experts opine on the issues, and people have too many private spaces in which to retreat for elites to formulate cohesive solutions or to manage public opinion toward those solutions. This is not to say that progressive culture has completely unraveled. If anything, technique and expertise are more fetishized today than ever before. Rather, it is to say that a new emphasis on individual autonomy and freedom has fused with progressivism to produce a more chaotic and fractured public life. Well, as public life goes, so goes the news. The wild and woolly world of online journalism expresses the sensibility of this new public culture. The profession, put bluntly, does not. Dressed up as a professional filter for a mass-mediated ball, journalism finds itself dancing to the tune of an increasingly networked world.

Habits, Investments, and Definitions

With this discussion as background, we are now in a position to see how the culture of journalism inhibits change. In my observation, three dynamics within this culture are pertinent. I label them, respectively, habits, investments, and definitions.

As I have mentioned, when the first researchers made their way into newsrooms in the 1960s and 1970s, they were struck by the highly routine and bureaucratic nature of news production. The language of routine implies that news practices are akin to habits, and that journalists reproduce their culture naturally, unconsciously, habitually. Socialization is the key dynamic in this process. Journalists, the argument goes, learn habits through immersion in newsrooms. Warren Breed's (1955) analysis of how newspaper policy is conveyed to journalists is a classic statement of this position. He finds that journalists learn their jobs as if "by osmosis . . . [staffers] become socialized and 'learn the ropes' . . . [by] . . . discover[ing] and internaliz[ing] the rights and obligations of his status and its norms and values" (p. 328). Others have found much the same thing. Lee Sigelman (1973, p. 137) observes that reporters learn how to produce news in a "highly diffuse and extremely informal" manner, mostly by observing more veteran reporters as they go about their business. John Johnstone (1976) describes more formal mechanisms, like the role of the assignment editor, in socializing reporters. Some of this socialization, of course, takes place outside the newsroom – in journalism school, for instance. But most journalists "learn the ropes" of the profession by working in newsrooms.

The taken-for-grantedness of news practices is important to the industry's prospects for change because, as the saying goes, habits are hard to break. This is so for four reasons. In the first instance, their very implicitness makes them difficult to uproot. Even today, after so much of conventional wisdom about journalism has been dispelled, many reporters describe standard news routines as simply the "way that news is produced." This "natural attitude" prevents them from considering how they might respond in new ways to the new environment that surrounds their profession. Second, since being a journalist is closely connected to doing journalism, a change in habit can trigger an identity crisis. Asked to do journalism in a different way, a reporter can come to feel less and less like a journalist. Attending to these identity issues requires time, attention, and reflection – scarce commodities in the contemporary newsroom. Time and again, journalists have told me they wished they had the luxury of thinking during the course of their day. But every day they must get the newspaper out, and to accomplish this feat they must rely on standard routines. In recent years, the task has only become more difficult, as journalists have been forced to do less with more – that is, to fill not only newspapers but websites, blogs, twitter feeds, and the like – all with fewer journalists in the newsroom. Finally, even if journalists do find the time to work through the anxieties and tensions caused by a change in habit, this still requires a degree of trust between news managers and reporters. Reporters have to feel comfortable revealing their feelings about a change in routine and trust that their managers will listen to and act on what they hear. But, if time is a scarce commodity in newsrooms, trust is, if anything, even more rare. Habits, therefore, are hard to break because they are difficult to uproot, and journalists lack the time and degree of trust necessary to work through the issues raised by doing so.

A second dynamic within news culture arises from the fact that news routines are not simply rules which journalists learn. Rather, they are constellations, to borrow from social theorist Anthony Giddens (1979), of "rules *and* resources" (pp. 62–4; emphasis added). Consider the practice of stationing reporters at government agencies. It is true that the practice of "covering a beat" consists of rules. Every reporter knows that covering a beat requires periodic chats with public information officers, attendance at agency meetings, collection and review of publicly available documents, etc. But the practice only becomes effective when it accrues material and symbolic resources. Material resources include such things as office space, rolodexes, websites, and staff dedicated to answering reporters' questions. Symbolic resources include such things as friendships between agency staff and reporters, role conceptions, know-how, status, and recognition. Over time, these kinds of resources pooled around the practice of covering beats, such that the two – rules and resources – tended to implicate and reproduce one another. Applied to the practice of beat coverage, this means that the rules governing the practice naturally reproduce resources, just as the accumulation of resources around these practices tends to reproduce the rules.

The fact that news practices contain rules and resources has several implications. For one thing, it implies that the rules embedded in news practices confront journalists less as commandments than as strategies for action or, better yet, resources for problem-solving. My six months as an intern at the *Daily Bugle* illustrate this idea (see the preface for a discussion of this experience). Toward the end of my time at the *Bugle*, I asked the city editor if I could work as a reporter for a few days a week, just to get a sense of what doing journalism felt like. Of course, I knew very little about how to do journalism. Nonetheless, on my very first day, the city editor sent me out to cover a press conference. To get by, I had to rely on others in the newsroom for help in reporting and writing my stories. After a few months, however, I got the gist of things and learned how to report and write basic news stories on my own. But this is not to say that I simply did the same thing every time. I learned, oddly enough, that as a routine matter I could not rely on routine. Sometimes, it was difficult to know which steps were most appropriate in a given situation: should I call this or that person, ask these or those questions? At other times, I disagreed with the city editor about the newsworthiness of a story and had to invent a strategy to persuade him that I was right. And, sometimes, in pursuing a story I hit a roadblock and did not know how to go on. On these occasions, I sought advice from others, retraced my steps, and pursued alternative paths. Throughout, I actively interpreted the rules of practice to solve the problem at hand.

My experience suggests a general point: the rules embedded in news practices are not sufficient guides for action, and so journalists must be creative in applying them to specific situations. This fact illuminates the performative dimension of news production. Different journalists may apply different practices to the same situation, and the same journalist may apply different practices to the same situation at different times – just as the second wave of ethnographic work insisted. Strategies of action are not so extensive as to account for the particulars of every situation. They are not so cohesive that it is impossible to combine them in different ways. People also are differently positioned vis-à-vis one another and the situation at hand. What looks appropriate from one vantage point may seem inappropriate from another. Finally, people have in their possession many different strategies, any number of which may be brought to bear on a given situation. Practices, then, do not determine precisely how they will be practiced.

Because this is so, news practices present journalists with

opportunities as well as constraints. Journalists who are more skilled and creative at using these opportunities (manipulating available strategies) will naturally accumulate more resources (e.g., money, status, autonomy, etc.) in relation to other journalists. This means that not only is the practice of news production improvisational, it is also, by definition, political. As journalists adapt news rules to local circumstances, a pecking order develops. A few journalists become "stars" and accumulate great resources, which they may then leverage into new opportunities. Others obtain fewer resources and have more limited options. The same dynamic, by the way, applies to news organizations: different organizations will accrue differential amounts of resources available in the field of journalism, and so find themselves placed in a pecking order as well.

This becomes important for the prospects of change because the resources journalists accumulate as they adopt conventional practices represent *investments* in the status quo. Consider the situation of a veteran reporter who has spent years working her way up the pecking order of news organizations. She might have started out at a very small community newspaper and, after stops at other papers, finally landed a job at a regional newspaper. The time, energy, and focus it took to master the practice of journalism represent an investment that she would be, quite understandably, reluctant to relinquish. When contemplating changes to her practice, her natural instinct would be to protect and defend. Her conservative posture toward change arises not from an inability to reflect on her practice, but from the exact opposite, a strategic calculation about how much of her investments in practice to put at risk.

The pull of habits and the depth of journalists' investments in the status quo go a long way toward explaining why journalism has failed to adapt. But they do not explain everything. Since 2007, the once slow and gradual decline of newspapers has greatly accelerated. Indeed, entire newspapers, such as the *Rocky Mountain News*, have folded. During an NPR segment on the issue, Doug Smith, director of the Punch Sulzberger News Media Executive Leadership Program at Columbia University, put it this way to the correspondent, David Folkenflik (2009): "It's chaos out there, and there's definitely a sense of terror." This collective "terror" implies that, in recent years, the costs of maintaining the status quo have grown substantially in relation to the benefits of its persistence. This is borne out in the fact that everywhere journalists talk of change today, and the fact that most every newsroom in the country has developed a strategy for change. Yet, even today, no metro daily newsroom has fundamentally altered its standard practices. This produces a curious situation. Apparently, while they can *imagine* new kinds of journalism, it appears that journalists find it exceedingly difficult to *do* journalism differently.

For help in solving this conundrum, I return to Carey's notion (borrowed from Geertz) that news is a "model of" culture. As "models of" culture, news routines enact constitutive rules for what counts as journalism. The notion of a "constitutive rule," by the way, comes from linguist John Searle (1969), who argues that practices like marriage, a trial, or, indeed, journalism have embedded within them rules that take the form "X counts as Y in context C" (pp. 33–4). Such rules bring into being the very reality they name by defining what counts as what in their particular social domain.

As an example, consider a reporter's notebook. We can think of the notebook as a resource attached to the practice of gathering information. Of course, there are rules for performing this activity: what kinds of information to collect, in what form, etc. In this sense, the notebook has embedded within it a "model for" doing journalism, a recipe for how to perform the activity. However, the notebook also contains a "model of" journalism. It presumes, for example, that a journalist is someone who gathers information (hence the need for a notebook). It assumes that a journalist must collect information from a source (most often, someone who possesses newsworthy information) and deliver it to a consumer (someone who might find the information useful, but otherwise would not learn of it except for the efforts of the journalist). In this sense, the reporter's notebook enacts a definition of what journalism is: it is the act of filtering information obtained from one group and disseminated to another (or, in conventional terms, of acting like a gatekeeper of information). This constitutive rule serves as a background context that lends meaning to the reporter's notebook. To feel this rule at work, simply attend a city council meeting with and without a reporter's notebook and compare the difference in the way that others respond to your presence.

Constitutive rules such as "journalism is a filter of information" persist because they coordinate routine interactions between journalists and others. All day, every day, sources, editors, and even readers approach reporters as if they are filters of information. These interactions can reproduce the status quo even as journalists talk incessantly of change.

Consider the situation of a hypothetical reporter. Let's assume he is in his mid-twenties and relatively new to the field. With few investments in the old ways of doing things, he is willing and eager to try new forms of journalism and talks about this subject a great deal with his editors and fellow reporters. Despite his expressed interest in change, however, in the newsroom he will find himself doing journalism mostly in conventional ways. Why? Because at the heart of his daily interactions with others lies the filtering conception of journalism. On his beat, he does the following most every day: scans the meeting agendas of various government institutions; interacts via e-mail with individuals in and around government who might have newsworthy information; contacts officials and experts to obtain quotes and verify facts he would like to include in his stories; and, when time permits, attends government meetings. In each of these interactions, he and his sources act on the assumption that he is a filter (or gatekeeper) into the newspaper, and therefore into the public conversation. This assumption informs everything, from his skeptical attitude, to the types of questions he asks, to the snap judgments he makes about the information conveyed by sources. Throughout these interactions, in other words, his posture toward others is imbued by the filtering conception of journalism. This conception also informs the attitudes and actions of his sources, who work hard to manage how their information and views are portrayed in his stories.

On this view, the impediment to change lies not in what journalists believe, prefer, or say, but in what they do. Their daily practices place them in relationships with others that, like a gravitational force, push and pull them to reproduce the established definition of what journalism is. Put another way, a key inhibition to change is recognition: the ability of journalists, sources, and even consumers of news to recognize new practices as journalism (and individuals as journalists when they engage in these practices). Take, for instance, the practice of blogging. It is one of the most common new practices in journalism. Yet, in my conversations with journalists, most have described blogging as something their editor has asked them to do *in addition to* their journalism. Typical is the comment of this reporter: "I don't mind blogging, but sometimes it gets in the way of my work." Here, the impediment to adopting the new practice is not normative ("We shouldn't do X") or epistemological ("I don't know how to do X"), but ontological ("Why would I do X?"). This journalist did not resist blogging so much as fail to recognize it as a form of journalism. This is a small example of the larger point. In part, journalists find it difficult to adapt because their daily interactions ritually reproduce constitutive rules embedded in the craft.

Summary of the Book

As I have described the situation, three sorts of cultural dynamics inhibit change in journalism. First, news production is structured by deeply engrained habits. Efforts to change these habits trigger identity crises that are difficult for journalists to work through amid the chaos and toxicity of the daily newsroom. Second, journalists have investments in their prior success, investments they are loathe to give up without a tangible benefit. Finally, journalism is defined by what I have called "constitutive rules." These rules define who journalists are, what they do, and why they do it, and they are "constitutive" because they structure the daily interactions of journalists with sources, editors, and readers. Even as journalists increasingly talk of change, these daily interactions reproduce the constitutive rules of the field. In newsrooms, these dynamics overlap, reinforce, and compound one another, but for analytic purposes I discuss each in a separate chapter.

Initially, I had thought to write these chapters drawing on data from all three of the newsrooms I observed. However, I found that doing so risked obscuring the element of time in my story. Events in the newsrooms I visited took place between 2004 and 2009. Over that time, the situation in journalism, and journalists' interpretation of the situation, darkened considerably. Not surprisingly, the increasing severity of the situation led newsrooms to try experiments in 2008 that in 2005 would have been unimaginable. I did not want to lose this aspect of the story, in part because it risked missing the relationship between time and culture. Habits and investments describe journalists as, in various ways, resisting the transformation of their profession. My sense is that this resistance was strongest in earlier years. Until about 2006, journalism remained a relatively settled profession, and many journalists acted as if the Internet was merely a hindrance to their practice. In contrast, today most every working journalist recognizes that the Internet has dramatically altered the landscape of news, and that the profession must change in response to its new environment. Yet, despite this growing awareness, news production remains as stable as ever. The constitutive quality of news practices better captures this fact: that news production remains unchanged even against the expressed wishes of journalists. Part of what this means, I think, is that the constitutive aspect of culture increasingly represents the biggest stumbling block to change in journalism.

To preserve the link between time and culture in this story, I have ordered the chapters chronologically. Chapter 1 sets the scene of the

Internet's arrival by describing the gradual decline of newspapers, and journalists' response to this decline, over the last forty years. Chapters 2 to 4 take up each cultural dynamic in turn. Chapter 2 begins with an exploration of the nature of journalistic habits, and how habits can limit change in newsrooms. This exploration includes a discussion of an experiment that took place from 2004 to 2006 at the *Daily Bugle*, a mid-sized regional newspaper owned by a large corporate chain. At the time, it had a website, but few people in the newsroom, including the new editor, Calvin Thomas, saw it as central to the future of the newspaper. Instead, Thomas tried to reverse the paper's longstanding decline by promoting broader and deeper regional news. His initiative – which by today's standards seems modest – nonetheless sparked enormous resistance in the newsroom. At first journalists were more than willing to try Thomas's new way of doing things. Quickly, however, they became uncomfortable with the new practices, and this discomfort eventually turned into outright refusal. How and why this happened provides a nice illustration of the role of habits in news production, and how even slight disruptions of news routines can trigger strong reactions.

Chapter 3 addresses the role of investments in limiting change. This chapter revolves around an experiment pursued from 2007 to 2008 at *The Herald*, a mid-sized, family-owned newspaper. By this time, its editor, Hank Carlin, had become convinced that the newspaper was dying. To his mind, *The Herald* would never again achieve circulation levels of the past and therefore would never be as profitable as it once had been. So, like many news managers around the country, Carlin launched a "multi-platform" strategy to develop new revenue streams. His idea was to diminish the role of the newspaper in the newsroom and make up the lost revenue in radio, mobile devices, and the Internet. To do this, he asked his reporters to begin producing news specifically tailored to a variety of platforms. His assumption, of course, was that news practices were fungible: reporters could seamlessly produce news for radio, the newspaper, television, smart phones, and online. This proved to be a mistaken assumption. *Herald* reporters had investments in the core skills, practices, and values of the profession, and they saw these investments as deeply implicated in the newspaper. In their eyes, Carlin's effort to diminish the newspaper was tantamount to diminishing the profession. And for what? All that Carlin could say was that his experiment *might* lead to future profits. To reporters, the losses implied by Carlin's strategy were much greater than these hypothetical benefits. Their reaction to his multi-platform strategy shows that resistance to change among journalists can be strategic, calculated, and intentional.

Chapter 4 takes up a curious fact about the situation in daily newsrooms today: everywhere journalists talk about the need for change, and yet nowhere is change happening to any significant degree. In the summer of 2009, I witnessed this process at the *Cedar Rapids Gazette*. It says something about the state of things in journalism that, by this time, the CEO of Gazette Communications, Chuck Peters, and the editor of the *Gazette*, Steve Buttry, insisted that I use their real names, and the name of the newspaper, in my research. At the time, Peters and Buttry were at the forefront of thinking in the industry about the transformation of news. In fact, they initially met at a conference on this exact subject. Peters recruited Buttry to the *Gazette* because he wished to fundamentally transform the newsroom. Transparency was to be an important piece of this process. They had nothing to hide, they declared (and, perhaps, nothing to lose), and so refused the anonymity I offered to grant them in my study.

Over two years, they planned the transformation of the *Gazette* newsroom around a core insight, namely, that content must be separated from platform. The idea was a logical next step from Carlin's multi-platform strategy. The plan was to detach news production from the newspaper so that reporters could be freed to produce content, pure and simple. Editors would then be assigned the task of directing that content to the most appropriate platform (mobile, online, print, and so on). This strategy required a nearly wholesale reinvention of the newsroom. Mostly, the *Gazette* staff was willing, if not eager, to go along. By this time, things had become so dire in the industry that reporters were happy to see their bosses try something – anything – to stop the bleeding. Yet, though they incessantly talked about change, Buttry and his staff found it difficult to practice what they preached. Mainly, this was due to the fact that every day they had to put out a newspaper. This required them to interact with sources, answer editor questions, and/or take calls from readers – and each of these interactions reproduced a conventional definition of journalism. Thus, while they became very adept at talking about journalism differently, they found it exceedingly difficult to do journalism differently. In the end, they succeeded in doing little more than confusing themselves.

Chapters 5 to 6 offer a wider lens. If it is true, as chapters 2 to 4 suggest, that journalists will probably never adapt well to the new environment, then at the very least journalism will likely get smaller. There will be fewer professional journalists working in

fewer professional newsrooms. Chapter 5 addresses this question:
What does this portend for the future of news? What will become of
journalism? Journalists? If many urban newspapers die, then who, if
anyone, will fill the gap in news coverage? In this chapter, I sketch
likely scenarios for the near and mid-term future of journalism.

Chapter 6 takes up Clay Shirky's (2009) observation that, when
revolutions occur, old models die faster than new models are born.
The interregnum produces a period of uncertainty. This is an apt
characterization for the period in journalism we are entering. The old
professional model is unraveling quickly, but new models have been
slow to emerge. This fact has prompted many observers to worry that
journalism may no longer be able to play its traditional functions in
democracy. Many journalists use these worries as an opportunity to
plead for the reinvention of traditional news. Others, however, are
using the worries as motivation to invent new forms of public interest journalism. A canvass of worries about journalism helps us to do
two things at once: to connect journalism's past to its future and to
deepen our understanding of what the future holds for the profession.

I intend this organization of the chapters to give readers flexibility.
Those interested in the chronological story of how and why journalism finds itself on a cliff will find it most helpful to read the chapters
from beginning to end. Others who may be more concerned about
the broad issues raised by the transformation of journalism can move
seamlessly from chapter 1 to chapters 5 and 6. Readers more inclined
to reflect on the culture of journalism, and how it works to inhibit
change, may combine this introduction with a reading of chapters 2
to 4. Overall, my intention is to provide some sense of why it has been
difficult for journalism to meet the challenges posed by the Internet,
and what this is likely to mean for the future of journalism.

1

Backstory

Every great story has a backstory. *Star Wars* would not be *Star Wars* without "A long time ago in a galaxy far, far away . . ." scrolling up the bottom of the movie screen at the beginning. *Superman* would be puzzling without the knowledge that he was born Kai-El on the planet Krypton, came to Earth in a spaceship, and was adopted by a Kansas farmer and his wife. *Citizen Kane* makes no sense at all without Rosebud. Actors consider the backstories of their characters so important that they will make them up if the script fails to provide them. These histories are important because they make characters three-dimensional and believable. By rendering the history of events, they make plots and conflicts understandable and more compelling. In short, they set the scene for what is to come.

The story I tell in the chapters that follow has a backstory too. I began visiting newsrooms in the winter of 2004–5, and most of the action I describe takes place between then and the summer of 2009. But the people I met and the newsrooms within which they work existed long before my entrance. To truly understand this story – the motivations and actions of the people, the conflicts and prejudices at work in newsrooms – we need to learn something of their backstories.

As a start, consider the following article from the *Los Angeles Times*. The headline reads "Newspapers challenged as never before," and the lead asks, "Are you holding an endangered species in your hands?" The rest of the story documents the industry's woes, which include flattening circulation, a sharp drop in market penetration, plunging advertising revenue, and the closure of many newspapers. It is not inconceivable, the author concludes, that the entire industry could simply die. "If we're not careful," he quotes one editor as saying, "we could find ourselves in the buggywhip business; we could phase ourselves right out of existence." Given the industry's recent woes, you might think this story was published in the last few years. In fact, however, it was published in 1976, *twenty years* before the Internet made its way into most newsrooms (Shaw, 1976). That fact is a central part of the backstory to contemporary newsrooms. Journalists were worrying about their future, wondering if the newspaper industry would survive, and working feverishly to reverse their fortunes *for twenty years* before the Internet made its arrival in newsrooms.

They were also dealing with the corporatization of their newsrooms – another crucial element of the backstory to the modern newspaper industry. Corporate chains have been around since the 1880s, but until very recently they played a minor role in the news industry. Through the twentieth century, most urban dailies were family-run businesses. In 1960, for instance, corporate chains owned only 30 percent of daily newspapers. By the mid-1990s however, the proportion of newspapers owned by corporate chains had jumped to 75 percent, and the family-run newspaper had largely gone away. Corporate newspapers were different sorts of animals than family-owned newspapers. Most obviously, in corporate newspapers the bottom line was more often the bottom line. A story, perhaps apocryphal, but often told by journalists, has it that the Bingham family, which owned the *Louisville Courier* through much of the twentieth century, got by on profit margins as thin as 5 percent. In the 1990s, no self-respecting corporate chain made less than a 20 percent profit margin, and many made a yearly profit of as much as 30 to 40 percent.

Such profit pressures changed the culture of journalism in profound ways. In the midst of a long-term decline in market penetration, they were being asked by new corporate bosses to achieve heretofore unheard of profits for their companies. The effort to solve these problems simultaneously caused a great rift in the culture of journalism. Should journalists give readers what they want in the news? What about what readers need from the news? Would giving them what they want be mere pandering? What would it do to the public service mission of journalism? Who should decide these issues – corporate bosses or journalists? Such questions consumed journalists in these years. The very urgency of the questions forced individuals to take sides. On the one side, corporate managers pressured journalists to be more attentive to reader interests. On the other, editors and reporters held fast to their public service mission. By the people involved, this battle was felt to be over the very heart and soul of the profession, and was fought with these stakes in mind. It too is an important part of the backstory I wish to tell.

Long-term decline, commercialization, and corporatization: these are the crucial elements to the backstory of contemporary journalism. The rest of this chapter sketches these elements in greater detail. If you feel that you grasp this history already, you might skip ahead to chapter 2. But for those who are unacquainted with this backstory, sit back and prepare to enter the story of the modern newsroom (just imagine the text scrolling up from the bottom of the paper).

An Industry in Decline

The problem that plagued metro daily newspapers beginning in the 1970s is relatively simple to describe: circulation remained flat while the number of Americans dramatically increased. According to numbers collected by the Newspaper Association of America, average daily circulation for all US daily newspapers from 1960 to 1995 never reached higher than 62,000 and never went below 58,000.[3] It remained, in other words, basically flat. Over the same time span, the American population nearly doubled, from roughly 132,165,000 in 1940 to 281,422,000 in 2000. Of course, not every one of these new Americans was likely to buy a newspaper. Children, for instance, do not subscribe to newspapers; nor do prisoners or people in mental health facilities. For this reason, industry experts use households rather than individuals as the basic unit of consumption for a newspaper. Combine circulation numbers with the number of households over time and the trends are clear (see figure 1.1). While daily newspaper circulation has not increased, the number of households has mushroomed, from 35 million in 1940 to over 100 million by 2000. In 1940, nearly every American household took at least the Sunday newspaper. By 2000, that number had been cut in half – and it has continued to fall in the twenty-first century. Put another way, in the last fifty years, newspapers have lost half of their market penetration.

These trends have not been lost on the industry. In fact, people like Leo Bogart, a pioneer in newspaper audience research, were already worrying about them in the early 1960s. Bogart worked for the Audit Bureau of Circulation, an organization founded in 1916 to track circulation numbers for all manner of print publications. In his post at the bureau, Bogart performed some of the first systematic nationwide reviews of newspaper circulation. In his initial survey, conducted in 1961, he found that 80 percent of Americans read a paper on a typical weekday. Naturally, the industry trumpeted this number to advertisers.

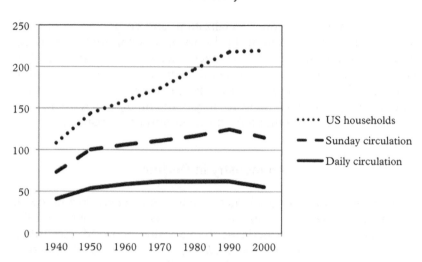

Figure 1.1   US daily newspaper circulation vs. number of households (in millions)

Their product was nearly universally consumed! But, in the ensuing years, Bogart kept counting, and very soon the numbers began to flatten. The bureau spun this relative decline in different ways. They counted circulation among what they called the "active" adult population rather than the total population. They changed their standard metric from circulation to readership. But, no matter how they massaged the numbers, the lines on the graph still went in the same direction: "the growth of newspaper circulation had slowed down, while the number of households had continued to grow" (Bogart, 1991, p. 36). In 1964, Bogart proposed that the bureau convene a "high-level two-day seminar" at which publishers and others would ruminate on the brewing troubles in the industry. His proposal was not accepted, in part because publishers were squeamish about airing their troubles in public. But a decade later, Bogart reports, "the subject of falling circulation and readership [had reached] a crescendo" in the industry (ibid., p. 66). The trends could no longer be ignored.

Why is our Audience Shrinking?

In the mid-1970s, researchers in industry and the academy got serious about diagnosing the decline of the daily newspaper. The Newspaper Readership Project – a joint creation of the Newspaper

Advertising Bureau (NAB) and the American Newspapers Publishers Association (ANPA) – played a prominent role in these efforts. From 1977 to 1983, researchers associated with this project – including Leo Bogart – collected an enormous array of data. They surveyed readers and nonreaders. They asked members of every significant demographic group what they wanted out of a newspaper. They examined different sorts of news content for how well they attracted different kinds of readers. They talked with editors and journalists. They studied the influence on readership of everything from recruitment of newspaper carriers to newspaper design. And they created a "News Research Center" to warehouse these data.

Their analysis of the data indicated that circulation decline was mostly a structural matter, having to do with societal trends that were decades in the making. Suburbanization was the primary culprit. The urban daily newspaper had risen with the growth of cities in the first half of the twentieth century. But in the 1950s people began to move to the suburbs in large numbers, and the population of cities declined. Phyllis Kaniss (1991) reports that, in 1940, the city of Philadelphia contained 60 percent of the area's population, a number that had dropped to 36 percent by 1980. In 1940, 68 percent of people who lived in the area called Detroit home, but in 1980 only 28 per cent of them remained in the city's core. The rest had moved to the surrounding suburbs (1991, pp. 23–5). The same trend was happening everywhere, especially in Southern and Western cities (e.g., Atlanta, Houston, Las Vegas, San Diego, Phoenix), to which more of the country's population was migrating.

Suburbanization had ripple effects for the newspaper industry. At one level, it meant that fewer people were interested in news of city life. What interest did I have in urban crime when I lived 30 miles away? Why should I care what the city mayor was doing (or not doing) when my suburb had its own government? Suburbanization also changed the commuting habits of readers. Suburbanites who commuted to the city for work increasingly drove rather than used public transportation, which meant that they had less time to read a newspaper. Suburbs also siphoned economic activity from cities. Jobs followed people out to the suburbs, and with those jobs went the consumers who once frequented central city businesses – precisely the businesses that newspapers depended upon for advertising revenue. Though the suburban economy grew, urban newspapers were not well positioned to serve the needs of these new businesses. The newspaper offered a scattershot audience spread across the region, while suburban businesses were often interested only in the very specific

audience located in their areas. Overall, the urban newspaper fit awkwardly in an increasingly suburbanized landscape, failing to meet the
interests and needs of audiences and businesses alike.

New suburban newspapers and weeklies emerged to fill these gaps,
and this new competition further eroded the market penetration of
metro dailies. In Philadelphia, for instance, while the circulation of
metro newspapers shrunk from 1.3 million in 1940 to 763,000 in
1988, suburban newspaper circulation rose from 147,000 to 461,000
(Kaniss, 1991, pp. 30–1). In an influential study of the San Francisco
region, James Rosse (1975) found at least four layers of competition
in the newspaper market: the urban newspaper (the *San Francisco
Chronicle* and *San Francisco Examiner*), the satellite newspaper (the
San Jose Mercury News and the *Oakland Tribune*), the suburban
newspaper (the Hayward *Daily Review*, the San Rafael *Independent-
Journal*, the *Berkeley Gazette*), and a fourth layer "of once, twice, or
thrice weeklies, quasi-newspaper shopping guides, free distribution,
partial distribution or throw-away publications, etc." (1975, p. 149).
As the large dailies in the region, the *Chronicle* and the *Examiner*
had some market share at every geographic level, but their penetration in local markets lagged behind the newspaper or weekly that
directly served these communities. The *San Jose Mercury News*, for
instance, had a greater market penetration in San Jose, even though
the *Chronicle* was also available there. The *Oakland Tribune* garnered
some readers in Hayward, but did not enjoy the levels of circulation density obtained by the *Daily Review*. Rosse called the resulting
structure an "umbrella" in which each kind of newspaper thrived in
the shadow of the larger newspapers that loomed above it. These
newspapers did not so much compete with one another as carve the
region into larger and smaller fiefdoms. For the large urban daily, the
ultimate consequence was more competition for the attention of suburban consumers and less overall market penetration. It did not help
that the cost of reaching those consumers was much higher for urban
dailies. The suburbs were stretched across long distances. Reaching
them required more trucks, more drivers of those trucks, more gas,
and more time to reach their destinations.

In several ways, then, suburbanization loosened the grip of urban
dailies on both readers and advertisers. But suburbs alone did not
kill newspaper circulation. They had help from other social trends,
the most important of which may have been the generational shift
away from newspapers that began in the 1960s. Phillip Meyer (2004)
reports that, since the early twentieth century, each age cohort has
read newspapers less than the last. When they were young, roughly

70 per cent of the "Great Generation" read a newspaper on a daily basis. In contrast, only 30 percent of their children read a daily newspaper, and for their grandchildren the number dipped to just over 20 percent. Today, something less than 20 percent of the millennial generation reads a daily newspaper. To Meyer, the meaning of these numbers is clear: "The true source of . . . readership decline," he argues, "is a matter of generational replacement. Since the baby boomers came of age, we have known that younger people read newspapers less than older people" (2004, p. 17).[4] For a long time, industry leaders argued that young people would pick up the habit as they got older, had children, put down roots in a community, and so on. But this never happened. Instead, in each generation, lower percentages of young people turned to newspapers, and, if they didn't read a newspaper when they were young, they never picked up the habit.

The reasons for this generational attrition are complicated, but certainly an increase in information choices is one part of the answer. Baby boomers were the first TV generation. "Generation X" had cable television and its hundreds of channels, and was the first generation introduced to video games. In quick order, access to video games, movies, and music exploded to consume more and more of people's attention. A recent study by the Kaiser Family Foundation (2010) finds that, today, young people aged eight to eighteen consume over seven hours of entertainment media – more time then they spend on any other "activity" except sleep. Clearly, seven hours of listening to music, watching television, browsing the Internet, and playing video games leaves less time for newspaper consumption. But the issue isn't just one of numbers. As David Mindich (2004) found in his interviews with young people, when news is put up against video games and TV shows, it is seen as just another form of entertainment (pp. 47–8). Viewed in this light, newspapers are not nearly as much fun as *Modern Warfare* or the *Oprah Show*. More people will naturally gravitate to information options that take less effort and are perceived as more fun. Perhaps the question isn't why fewer young people read a newspaper, but why any choose to do so at all.

Two other social trends that affected newspaper readership are worth mentioning. The first is the increase in female employment that took place in the second half of the twentieth century. In the 1950s, only 34 percent of women worked, a number that had doubled to nearly 70 percent by the year 2000 (e.g., Toossi, 2002, p. 18). This move into the workforce gave women more freedom and opportunity, and, as the incomes of men flattened and even declined somewhat, it allowed families to sustain a middle-class lifestyle. It did not have such salutary effects on newspaper reading. The increase in female employment accelerated the pace of family life in ways that made sitting down to read a newspaper seem indulgent, if not impossible. Studies conducted for the newspaper industry throughout the 1980s showed a steep decline in women readers. The National Advertising Bureau reported the percentage of daily female readers of newspapers dropped 18 percent between 1970 and 1990 (compared with a 12 percent decline in male readers). Other reports put the decline even higher. "Had we maintained our appeal to women equal to what it was in 1970," one Knight-Ridder report claimed, "we would have seventeen million more readers today" (Harp, 2007, pp. 53–4).

Changes in the public culture also played a role in the decline of newspaper reading. In particular, beginning in the 1960s, public trust in major public institutions declined significantly. Survey data show that Americans' faith in government, corporations, banks, labor unions, lawyers, doctors, universities, and public schools declined in equal measure (e.g., Lipset and Schneider, 1987). Government took a particularly hard hit. Joseph Nye (1997) reports that, in 1964, 75 percent of Americans said they trusted the federal government to "do the right thing most of the time." By the late 1990s, that number had dropped to 35 percent, and was even lower in some polls (1997, p. 1). The reasons for this sustained and pervasive cynicism do not concern us here. Observers have offered hypotheses ranging from increased international economic competitiveness, to a loss of social capital, to the rise of "postmaterialist values." It is enough to note that journalism did not escape these trends. Pew's 2009 *State of the Media* report shows that the public's trust in journalism declined at about the same rate as for other institutions. In 1985, 55 percent of respondents agreed with the statement "Journalists get the facts straight" in their stories, a number that had dropped to 35 percent by 2007. It stands to reason that this loss of credibility contributed to the decline of daily newspapers. When people find public figures to be untrustworthy and the journalists who cover them to be unreliable, they are less likely to subscribe to the newspaper.

The combination of these trends represents a significant structural change in American society. Compared to the situation in the first half of the twentieth century, Americans were working more, becoming more mobile, and living in more scattered suburban communities. They were focused more on private matters and leisure pursuits and less on public matters and formal politics. The urban newspaper fit awkwardly in this changing society, which is why, beginning about

1975, daily urban newspapers invariably lost 1 percent of circulation per year, every year, and lost market penetration even faster.

Changes in the Industry

As journalists sought to make sense of the whirl of change taking place outside their industry, the ground beneath their feet began to buckle due to significant disruptions within the industry itself. These disruptions were primarily of two kinds, which we might label corporatization and computerization. Let's discuss each in order.

Chain ownership was not new to journalism, of course. As I mentioned in the introduction to this chapter, newspaper chains had been around since the 1880s. In fact, the most rapid concentration of the industry occurred from 1910 to 1930, when the number of dailies owned by groups increased by more than 400 percent (e.g., Compaine and Gomery, 2000, p. 22). But the 1980s and 1990s saw a round of buying and selling which, by the time it ended, left three-quarters of daily newspapers – more than double the number owned by chains in 1960 – in the hands of corporations, and an industry transformed (e.g., ibid., p. 12).

A paradox lay at the center of this transformation: newspapers were never more profitable than during the 1970s to the 1990s, precisely the period in which circulation flattened and market penetration dipped. This seems counterintuitive; one would think that fewer readers and decreased market penetration would naturally lead to less in the way of profit. Instead, newspapers became cash cows. Why this happened is a three-part story. Martin Langeveld of the Nieman Journalism Lab at Harvard University has collected data that illuminate the first part of the story.[5] According to these data, newspapers' share of total advertising expenditures dropped from 35 percent in 1940 to less than 15 percent by the early 2000s. Television and direct mail took up most of the slack. In fact, in 1990 television surpassed newspapers as a medium of choice for advertisers. However, there is a second part of the story. According to Douglas Galbi (2001), total expenditures on advertising in the United States began a precipitous climb in the mid-1970s. Galbi finds that, in 1970, just over $19 billion was spent on advertising, a figure that had climbed to nearly $250 billion by the year 2000. Increased advertising expenditures were part of the dramatic growth in the American economy that took place in the second half of the twentieth century. Robert Picard (2008, p. 707), for instance, reports that, from 1950 to

2005, gross domestic product in the United States grew from roughly
$293 billion to $12,445 billion. The third part of the story can now
be easily discerned. Even though the slice enjoyed by newspapers
shrunk, the overall advertising pie grew so much that newspapers
obtained great profits. Picard's data show that, in 1980, the industry
made about $10 billion in advertising revenue; in 1990 it was over
$20 billion, and in 2000 the industry's advertising revenue topped
$40 billion. According to one news executive, so much cash flooded
into newspapers during these years that an owner could make money
even if he were "brain dead" (Paterno, 1996).

These profits made newspapers very attractive to buyers. Some of
these buyers were seeking a safe investment, and no industry seemed
safer than one that faced little competition and generated large quantities of cash. Other buyers were news companies, which saw outsized
profit margins as a way of leveraging their assets more aggressively,
getting bigger, enjoying greater economies of scale, and driving their
smaller competitors out of business. Through the 1980s these buyers
found more willing sellers. Often, such sellers were the fourth or fifth
generation managing a family-owned newspaper, people who were
experiencing financial troubles, or owed inheritance taxes, or were
squabbling with their fellow family members. Other times, sellers
were smaller news companies that saw an opportunity to make a large
profit on their properties (e.g., Morton, 2006). The convergence of
supply and demand set off a buying spree in the newspaper industry.
In 1997 alone, for instance, 125 daily newspapers changed hands.
This meant that, in short order, many of the most prominent family-
owned newspapers – the *Louisville Courier*, the *Des Moines Register*,
the Nashville *Tennessean* – were bought up by corporate chains.

The effects of this rapid concentration of the industry were intensified by the fact that the largest chains that did most of the buying
were publicly traded companies. Dow Jones & Company was the first
newspaper company to go public, in 1963, followed by the Gannett
Company in 1967 and the Knight and Ridder news companies in
1969 (these two companies merged into the Knight-Ridder company
in 1974). By the end of the century, seventeen of the largest newspaper chains – which owned one-fifth of all dailies – were publicly
traded (e.g, Cranberg et al., 2001, p. 25). These companies included
some of the largest and most prominent members of the newspaper
community: the *Washington Post*, the *New York Times*, Gannett,
McClatchy, Lee Enterprises, Scripps, the Tribune Company, and
the like. Generally, they went public to raise cash so that they might
buy more properties and/or protect themselves from unwanted

suitors. But in so doing they made their newspapers subject to the quarterly performance requirements of institutional investors. For these owners/investors, newspapers were – well – investments, whose performance was measured by stock prices, which in turn depended upon quarterly returns, which in turn depended on a steady growth in profits.

The pressure to obtain these profits shook the industry to its foundations. Just as one example, take the job description of editors. In family-run newspapers, they often served as both editor and publisher of the newspaper. This dual role made them responsible for the bottom line, but it also made them unaccountable to anyone else. As one author put it, in those days editors "ruled their world like princes" (Overholser, 1998; see also Jones, 1989; Kwitny, 1990). All of this changed in the new corporate world of journalism. Instead of ruling their kingdoms like princes, editors now were part of marketing committees and management teams. As profit concerns mounted, their job descriptions also morphed. They became responsible not only for the news, but also for marketing the newspaper, developing new products, and meeting the newspaper's obligation to shareholders. In fact, in the form of stock options and other incentive programs, their personal success was often linked to the company's quarterly performance goals. The more the company prospered, the more they succeeded. Almost overnight, it seemed, editors became company men.

These sorts of changes intertwined with a second disruptive force – the computerization of newspapers. It seems strange to say, but, into the 1970s, newspapers were produced using methods that had changed very little since the seventeenth century, and almost not at all since the late nineteenth century (e.g., Smith, 1980, pp. 83–4). It was as if the newspaper industry completely missed the space age. As they had since the 1890s, reporters typed their stories on typewriters and handed the copy to editors. Editors added corrections to the copy – in pencil, no less! Once completed, the copy was sent to compositors for typesetting. Until the 1950s, compositors pinned the copy above their workstation and retyped the stories (including editorial corrections) directly into a Linotype machine. After the 1950s, most newspapers moved to a system in which the copy was typed onto punched tape, which was then fed into the Linotype machine. In either case, once it was entered into the Linotype machine, a leaden version of the copy was created and proofread. Any corrections required the process to be redone, and, once finalized, the leaden type was fitted onto a metal frame in the form of pages. Molten lead was poured over these frames – hence the term "hot copy" – resulting in the creation of a stereotype plate. Each stereotype plate (or page) was then fed into a rotary press – a hulking machine housed in a large, industrial building, out of which copies of the day's newspaper flowed.

As I say, this production system had been essentially unchanged since the 1890s, and many of its essentials had been in place since the seventeenth century. It was labor intensive, time intensive, inflexible, and, by the standards of today, inefficient and costly.

In the span of a few years, however, computers revolutionized this process. With computers, reporters could type stories directly into a centralized system – essentially typeset stories themselves. Editors no longer needed to scribble penciled corrections in the margins of copy. Instead, they could download copy from the central server, make corrections on their desktop computers, and resend the corrected version back to the central server. In the early 1980s, completed copy was printed out on strips of paper and pasted onto life-sized versions of the page. Today, even those pages are laid out digitally, eliminating the need for cutting and pasting. A photograph is taken of each page, from which an "off-set" plate is made. These plates are then fed into the rotary press.

The computer revolution had many consequences, both small and large, for newsrooms. Instantly, it made the newsroom quieter, as the soft patter of keyboards replaced the clickety-clack of typewriters. As reporters and editors interacted more via computer, the newsroom also became a less chaotic place. The days of editors yelling across the floor, or copy boys dashing madly down the newsroom's aisles, were gone. More slowly, computers changed how reporters gathered and reported information. Research that once involved card catalogs and dusty paper file folders increasingly was done using search engines and computerized databases. Stories that once emerged from a reporter's notebook could now be developed by teams of reporters and editors working from files stored on central servers.

The most immediate and dramatic changes, however, occurred where computers met the profit needs of corporate managers. Put simply, corporate managers implemented computer systems to make the process of news production less labor intensive, faster, and more efficient, and therefore less costly. At least initially, most of these gains came on the production side, where computerization eliminated whole job categories, such as typesetters and compositors. This did not happen without a fight. Protesting the elimination of these jobs, unions and guilds went on strike repeatedly through the 1970s and 1980s. But their efforts were for naught. By one estimate

(Squires, 1993, p. 24), between 1975 and 1990, corporate chains reduced their production costs by 50 percent, mostly by using fewer works to produce newspapers. In the process, unions were broken at most of the larger corporate chains.

Other profit gains came on the editorial side. With computers, the work of reporters could be more closely monitored. If a company's performance goals mandated that reporters produce so many stories per month, computers could track these statistics. Computers also allowed managers to use fewer reporters to produce the same amount of news. Beats could be reorganized, for instance, and reporters could be asked to do more reporting faster and with fewer resources. This increased productivity allowed corporate newsrooms to thin the ranks of reporters and yet put out the same-sized newspaper. Layoffs were especially acute during the recession of 1990–1, but the threat of them hung like a cloud over newsrooms through the 1990s.

In what seemed like the blink of an eye, corporatization and computerization dramatically altered the landscape of journalism. The atmosphere in newsrooms became more professional and managerial. Job descriptions and workflows were altered. Relationships between the business and editorial sides of newspapers were blurred. Journalists were asked to do more with less, and with less autonomy. The changes were so extensive, and came so fast, that many observers began speaking of a "revolution" in journalism long before the advent of the Internet.

Industry Response

This revolution in news strongly shaped how journalists responded to the long-term decline of their industry. At the very least, it ensured that journalists would, in fact, respond. There was always the option, after all, of doing nothing. If researchers had it right, and the decline of newspapers was due mostly to social trends outside the control of journalists, then perhaps this would have been the sensible thing to do (or not to do). They could do little about the forces diminishing the status of the newspaper anyway, so why try? This response, or, rather, lack of a response, may seem defeatist, but it came with a silver lining. Freed from the necessity of achieving mass appeal, journalists might instead have focused their energies on the things they – and their smaller audiences – cared about, namely, producing news and information that people need in order to make informed political choices. Many journalists were ready to accept this bargain. As one journalist told a researcher (Kodrich, 1998, p. 86), "Newspapers are losing readership and are not going to get it back." Therefore, he argued, we should concentrate on producing "quality journalism."

I have met many journalists who share this view, and have come across a few newspapers that adopted it as an explicit strategy, at least for a time. But across the industry it was never seriously considered. In fact, as a whole, the industry did the exact opposite: it aggressively sought to reverse its decline and attract readers back to the newspaper. To some extent, journalists supported this strategy. On their view, they could not serve their mission – to inform citizens – if most people, most of the time, were not reading a newspaper. But the aggressiveness with which the industry responded to its decline was shaped mostly by corporate owners, whose outsized profit needs required that newspapers maintain their status as general interest media. A Gannett news executive expressed the conventional wisdom when he told an interviewer, "You can only sell a product that's out of step with its customers for so long" (Bagby, 1991, p. 20).

Corporate managers, therefore, applied great pressure on journalists to commercialize the news – that is, to find out what audiences wanted in their newspapers and give it to them – and this became the predominant response in the industry.

To assist them in this effort, managers brought an army of new consultants into their newspapers. The size of this army is difficult to gauge. I have found no study that tracks the growth of newspaper consulting over time. It is safe to say, however, that the influence of consultants became noticeable in the mid-1970s and common by the mid-1980s. Among the more influential of these consultants were people such as Chris Urban of Urban Associates, Alan Weiss of Summit Consulting, and J. Ann Selzer of Selzer & Company. Trained in survey research methods and organizational and business management theory, they advised management on issues related to organizational efficiency and cultural change. They helped newspapers incorporate new computer systems, for instance, into the workflow of the newsroom. But they also conducted market analyses, which provided corporate managers with information on reader (and nonreader) demographics and the sorts of news to which these groups were attracted. This research filtered into newsrooms and began to influence news decisions.

The consequences of using market research to guide news decisions were predictable. As media economist James Hamilton (2004) argues, market-driven news decisions invariably lead to more soft and less hard news. Definitions of "hard" and "soft" news are fuzzy. Different people draw the line in different places. Generally, however, hard news concerns public affairs, especially news about government. It includes reports from city hall, the police department, the courts, the statehouse, and other governmental agencies. "Soft" news is everything else: feature stories, consumer and entertainment news, lifestyle and health news, and the like. From the 1930s to the 1970s, when journalists enjoyed their greatest autonomy from commercial pressures, hard news dominated the front pages of most newspapers around the country. But, as journalists sought to give readers more of what they wanted in the news, softer news followed.

Hamilton argues that economic logic demands this result. In the first instance, most people, most of the time, prefer softer forms of news. The audience for hard news is relatively small because, for most people, the costs of consuming such news dramatically outweigh its benefits. To demonstrate the point, Hamilton turns to the classic example of election news. From the perspective of the individual voter, the cost of consuming election information includes the time it takes to read or view it and, in the case of the newspaper, subscription costs. Let's assume that consuming this information will increase a given voter's ability to make a good voting decision. We must balance this benefit against the fact that a voter's ability to influence an election is almost nil. That is, statistically speaking, an individual vote has little chance to affect an electoral outcome. "Since [the] odds of influencing the outcome are infinitesimal," Hamilton concludes, the costs of consuming the information will outweigh its benefits for nearly every voter (2004, p. 11). By this logic, the audience for election news is, and always will be, small. The same logic applies to public affairs news generally, which means that most people, most of the time, simply are not interested in hard news.

From an economic perspective, hard news has other disadvantages. It is often more expensive to produce than soft news. This isn't always the case – a reporter can be assigned to write on food as well as city hall – but it is often the case. It is especially true of investigative and explanatory journalism – forms of reporting that take a great deal of time and expertise and so are more expensive than most other forms of news. Hard news is also less attractive to advertisers. Hamilton provides data showing that the audience for hard news skews toward older, white males. Advertisers often wish to attract younger and more female audiences, the former because young people (advertisers assume) have not developed brand loyalties, and the latter because women often control household purchasing decisions. Compared with older, white males, these demographic groups are more interested in softer forms of news. As a general matter, advertisers are willing to pay more to reach audiences who are attracted to softer forms of news.

To sum up: most people, most of the time, prefer softer forms of news; it is often cheaper to produce; and advertisers are more interested in reaching the sorts of people who are attracted to soft news. The ultimate consequence of this logic is that, if news decisions are motivated primarily by market considerations, then newspapers will produce more soft and less hard news (e.g., Patterson, 2000; Stepp, 2002).

This is precisely the message that corporate managers delivered to journalists, often through the new consultants they brought into newsrooms. When suburban readers told consultants that they preferred less news about city hall and the statehouse and more news about their suburban communities, journalists created customized "zoned" editions, each edition filled with news targeted to readers living in different communities. In the late 1990s, it was not unusual for a metro daily to have as many as thirty or forty different zoned editions, with at least one reporter assigned to each zone. News in these zones sometimes focused on public policy, but much of it was of a softer variety: stories about proms and high-school football games, church and school events, prominent small businesses, and local personalities. In the same way, when young readers told consultants that they were interested in consumer and entertainment news, journalists created or beefed up these sections of the paper. Sometimes, these sections became so large that they were turned into stand-alone products, offered free at newsstands around the city. When women told researchers that they were interested in news about home and family life, health and fitness, parenting and career advice, journalists increased the size of the lifestyle, home, and food sections. One former editor told me that, at his newspaper in the 1990s, the food section became so large that it actually spanned two sections of the paper. Everyone told consultants that newspapers seemed staid and boring, and that they had less time to read them, so journalists redesigned pages to make them more interesting and user friendly. They increased the use of color. They expanded the "points of entry" into stories by using more graphics, photos, boxes, and indexes. They reduced the number of stories that appeared on each page and the number of "jumps" from page to page. They tightened writing and included more "quick read" features (e.g., Stepp, 1991). So focused did newspapers become on satisfying reader desires that one observer christened the 1990s the "decade of the reader-driven newspaper" (Bagby, 1991, p. 20).

It is important to acknowledge that many journalists supported this transition. Recognizing that the health of journalism ultimately depended on the health of newspaper companies, some saw it as necessary. Eugene Patterson, editor of the *St. Petersburg Times*, said, "I tend to get a little impatient with the purists down in the newsroom who can't see the problem" (Jones, 1989, p. 24). Others went further, to argue that attracting readers' interest was basic to journalism: "The best editors," Bob Ingle, former editor of the *San Jose Mercury News*, said, "are marketers . . . I want [my staff] to say about me, 'He's a terrific marketer.' Goddamn, that's what we do" (Overholser, 1998).

It is fair to say, however, that most journalists took a more fearful, even hostile, attitude to what they considered to be an unhealthy obsession with readers. Their reaction came less from hostility to soft news per se than from a sense that their professional news judgment was being questioned. In the main, reporters felt that they did not need readers or corporate managers to tell them what was newsworthy. They were professionals, after all, capable of making these judgments without outside interference. Moreover, to them journalism had a higher mission, not only to give readers what they wanted, but also to equip them with the information they needed to play their role as democratic citizens. So, when their bosses began ignoring their judgment in preference for market research, journalists took it as a challenge to their professional autonomy and, more broadly, as a threat to their role in society. Remarking on the state of the industry, one editor put the prevailing fear this way: "The great threat is that all decisions that impact content, staff – everything – tend to be made from the marketing point of view. The threat is of the business strategy dominating the paper" (Jones, 1989, p. 24). Notice that, for this editor, the threat came not from soft news itself, but from the encroachment of the "business strategy" on news judgment. In reader-obsessed newsrooms, many journalists came to feel like mere "functionaries," as one reporter put it, whose news judgment was no longer respected. And so they resisted. As one reporter put it, "If this is the future of newspapers, I want out" (*Columbia Journalism Review*, 1991, p. 15).

The ensuing struggle over control of news decisions left corporate managers and journalists feeling angry, tired, frustrated, and confused. Surveys offer one measure of this growing disenchantment. When John Johnstone (1976) conducted the first scientific survey of journalists in 1971, three-quarters said that they had "almost complete freedom in how they write stories," and 60 percent agreed with the statement that "they have almost complete freedom in selecting the stories they work on" (p. 8). Such autonomy was strongly associated with job satisfaction: the more journalists were left to do their work as they saw fit, the more satisfied they were with their jobs. In fact, 49 percent of journalists indicated that they were "very satisfied" with their jobs and another 40 percent said that they were "fairly satisfied." A decade later (1982–3), David Weaver and Cleve Wilhoit (1986) found much the same in their survey of journalists: most were still satisfied with their work because most remained relatively autonomous in their jobs (pp. 76, 89). In subsequent surveys, however, conducted in the aftermath of the twin revolutions in corporatization and computerization, Weaver and Wilhoit (1996) found a significant decline in job satisfaction. In their 1991–2 survey, just 27 percent of journalists said that they were "very satisfied" with the jobs (pp. 64, 100). The authors trace much of this decrease in job satisfaction to a growing perception among journalists that they enjoyed less autonomy in their work. Newsroom autonomy, they write, "diminished . . . at a startling pace" during these years. In 1992, just over 40 percent of reporters agreed that they had "almost complete freedom" to select stories (compared with 60 percent in 1982), and about half believed that they had "almost complete freedom" to write stories as they saw fit (down from 70 percent in 1982).

An example puts some flesh on the bones of these numbers. Gannett's "News 2000" program, launched in 1991, was one of the first and most expansive efforts by a corporate chain to make its newspapers more reader-oriented (e.g., Gissler, 1997; *Presstime*, 1991; Underwood, 1993). In large part, corporate executives created the program because they no longer trusted the news judgments of editors and reporters. As one executive put it, too much was at stake to trust the "gut feelings" of journalists.[6] Moving forward, corporate managers wanted to ensure that news decisions would be based on hard data collected through marketing research. After months of collecting these data, the corporate office came up with what it called a "10-part news pyramid." This pyramid was meant to serve as template for the news produced by all of Gannett's eighty-two newspapers. At the foundation of the pyramid rested "community interest." To corporate officers, declining circulation was prima facie evidence that journalists no longer knew what interested readers. So the very first task they set before editors and reporters was to conduct local marketing research to discover what readers wanted in the news. On this foundation, journalists would then build up toward the other elements of the pyramid, which included a respect for First Amendment values, diversifying the workforce and representing the diversity of the community, providing a compelling presentation of news, giving people information they need, a focus on emotion, offering consistent quality and value, responding to the immediate needs of the community, being interactive, and, finally, being responsive to change.

Reporters could not disagree with these values, especially the goal of serving their communities better. But the fact that they were being asked to work from a template designed at central headquarters grated. For example, regardless of what particular communities wanted, the template required stories to be shorter and to include more graphics, boxes, and photos. What if their readers preferred long-form narrative? Journalists were also worried that market research was displacing their own expertise. Who knew the community's needs better, they believed, than the reporters who were on the ground in the community every day? On their view, Gannett editors sat in meetings poring over data and making decisions about news content that should properly be made by journalists. Finally, journalists were angry that more resources did not follow the new expectations. Layoffs often were made just as reporters were asked to cover more of the community, and it was not unknown for editors to quash story ideas simply because they were too expensive.

Some editors and reporters supported the program and believed it made their newspapers better. "My job," said Mark Silverman, editor of the *Louisville Courier-Journal* in the mid-1990s, "was to make a newspaper with a marvelous tradition better." A reporter for another Gannett newspaper said of his experience, "When I came through the door, I was as big a skeptic as anyone . . . But I'd call myself a convert. The bottom line is, I think this is a better newspaper because [of News 2000]. More importantly, I think our readers think it's a better newspaper." Some evidence supports this conclusion. After News 2000, Gannett's newspapers certainly looked better; they had sharper layouts and crisper designs, used more color, and included more sections. Gannett's newsrooms were more diverse and more diverse voices appeared in its papers. Moreover, many readers seemed to notice, and appreciate, the changes. "Gannett shows that you can produce a quality newspaper and still make . . . a lot of money," one reader told a reporter. In fact, circulation declines at some Gannett newspapers slowed in the years after initiation of the program, and a few actually increased their market penetration, especially in the coveted suburbs.

Overall, however, News 2000 caused fear and anxiety across Gannett's newsrooms. Reporters were alarmed at the new profit requirements and, as layoffs mounted, were justifiably concerned for their jobs. While the news hole increased, they noted that soft news took up much of the new space. Many argued that their newspapers had "lost their edge." As Sid Gissler puts it, post-News 2000, Gannett newspapers "seem[ed] less feisty on the front page and more muted and parochial on the editorial page." But, mostly, reporters were indignant. Journalism by template offended their professional sensibilities. "It's cookie-cutter journalism," one reporter said. "We're scored by how well we fit a formula predetermined out East." They bristled at the increased oversight of their work and the corresponding loss of autonomy. As part of the diversity goal of News 2000, for example, reporters were required to "mainstream" their stories by including more minority sources. This seemed like a worthy goal, but, to ensure that reporters followed the new rule, management counted the number of such sources in each story, and these numbers became part of each reporter's annual performance evaluation. Reporters recoiled at this level of intrusion into their work habits. As one journalist at *The Olympian*, the Gannett newspaper in Olympia, Washington, put it, for many reporters the program was "absolutely oppressive."

As other corporate chains developed similar initiatives in the 1990s, the same fears, anxieties, and struggles gripped their journalists. The result was not a complete abandonment of traditional roles, values, and responsibilities. In some newsrooms, journalists successfully resisted the encroachment of market imperatives, at least for a time. And, in any event, much of the daily news still emanated from the same sources (e.g., the courthouse, city hall, the police department) and was written according to the same formulas that had been in place for decades. In the face of these outside pressures, in other words, journalists did not acquiesce. Rather, the result was a more combative and argumentative environment. As corporate newspapers pressured journalists to expand circulation, and the lines between the editorial and business side of news became blurred, editors and reporters found themselves in something of a war of attrition with their corporate bosses, a daily struggle over control of the news.

A Changed Culture

The battles fought during this struggle roiled the industry for two decades before the onset of the Internet, and they changed the

culture of journalism in important ways. Most obviously, the constant battles with management made journalists more suspicious of
their corporate owners' motives. The relationship between journalists
and newspaper owners had seldom been what one would call healthy.
But in corporate newsrooms it became downright toxic. To journalists, the infusion of "bean counters" into the newsroom was doing
nothing less than ruining the news. James Squires (1993), former
editor of the *Chicago Tribune*, ends his book *Read All About It!* with a
chapter titled "The death of journalism." What was killing journalism? To Squires, the answer was simple: the corporatization of news.

> During the last decade [the 1990s], the culture of the press has changed
> from that of an institution dedicated to the education of the public
> to that . . . of entertaining consumers for a profit. At the same time,
> the new corporate owners of the press have taken the responsibility
> for "news" content out of the hands of trained, experienced profes-
> sional journalists . . . and put it in the hands of trained, experienced,
> professional business managers. (1993, p. 211)

On Squires's telling, journalists were engaged in a pitched battle
between the avarice of corporate owners and the time-honored tradition of public service journalism. Many others shared Squires's view.
Here is Leonard Downie (former editor of the *Washington Post*) and
Robert Kaiser's (associate editor of the *Washington Post*) rendition:

> For most of the first two centuries of American history the country's
> newspapers were deeply rooted local institutions . . . The growth of
> chain ownership transformed the nature of the newspaper . . . Control
> shifted from the towns or cities where the papers . . . were located to
> distant headquarters . . . Increasingly . . . decisions about the news-
> papers' . . . budgets and news coverage are shaped, if not dictated, by
> corporate executives and headquarters . . . Today's new patterns of
> corporate ownership have fundamentally altered the nature of news
> organizations by changing the incentives and rewards that guide their
> proprietors. (2002, pp. 23, 26)

Gene Roberts (former editor of the *Philadelphia Inquirer*) and Thomas
Kunkel (former deputy managing editor of the *San Jose Mercury
News*) told the story more simply: "All signs indicate [that journalism is moving away] from [its] essential obligation . . . as shareholder
concerns supplant concern for the public" (2002, p. ix). In *Breaking
the News* (1996), James Fallows lists several factors that have contributed to the ills of journalism, changes in politics and technology
among them. Then he writes of corporate owners:

Reporters have come to think of themselves as employees trapped in a "sunset industry." Like steel workers or machine toolmakers, many of them feel compelled to scramble and jealously protect their own financial interests . . . Chain ownership brings . . . a counting-house mentality determined to "downsize" newsrooms and cut expenses to satisfy quarterly earnings demands. (1996, p. 70)

By the mid-1990s, suspicion of corporate owners became so great in newsrooms that, when journalists talked about the decline of newspapers, they rarely pointed to structural factors like suburbanization or generational loss. Instead, they blamed their corporate owners who, they believed, were privileging profits over quality journalism, and in so doing were killing the industry.

Journalists also became more defensive and reactive. Since at least the 1930s journalists had seen their public role as important and valuable. But, comfortable in this role and unchallenged in their newsrooms, they wore that identity lightly. In the new corporate environment, they began to press the identity more strongly. Sayings they once delivered almost flippantly – "We comfort the afflicted and afflict the comfortable," "We shine light in dark places," "We speak truth to power" – were now delivered with more insistence. They began to declare their importance to society more loudly, more often, and in more leaden tones: "It is an article of faith among journalists that what they do is essential to democracy," writes Alex Jones (2009, p. 32). "Journalism is so fundamental to [creating community and democracy]," Kovach and Rosenstiel (2001, p. 18) intone, "that . . . societies that want to suppress freedom must first suppress the press." The less corporate owners thought of journalism, it seemed, the more tightly journalists fastened to their self-conception as defenders of democratic life.

Nothing demonstrates the new mood in newsrooms better than the practice, increasingly common, of resigning on principle. Pressed to raise profit margins by their corporate bosses, many editors and reporters instead quit. Celebrated resignations during this period include that of James Squires from the *Chicago Tribune*, Bill Kovach from the *Atlanta Journal-Constitution*, Jay Harris from the *San Jose Mercury News*, and, perhaps most famously, Gene Roberts from the *Philadelphia Inquirer*. Often, these exits were accompanied by renewed warnings about the fate of the profession. "Journalism – real journalism, practiced in good faith – is absolutely essential to a self-governing nation," declared John Carroll, former editor of the *Los Angeles Times*, to his fellow editors after resigning his post. "This is a cause that is larger than us and larger than our newspapers. It gives meaning to our labors." Explaining his resignation to the same audience, Jay Harris said that he "had lived as long as I should or could with a slowly widening gap between creed and deed."[7]

The irony was that journalists never had more reason to be proud of their craft. Nearly everyone with whom I have talked has said that journalists today are better educated, better trained, and just plain better than earlier generations of reporters. Given the pace of change in their newsrooms, they had to be. Working in modern newsrooms required them to be nimble, flexible, and multi-skilled. One editor might organize the newsroom to focus on one kind of news and a year later a new editor might reorganize the newsroom to reflect new priorities. A new boss might hire four new reporters for zoned editions while the next might move these reporters to the living section. Corporate headquarters might launch an initiative in one year and, without waiting for results, launch a new initiative the next. It was not unusual for reporters to be told one year to do more feature writing, the next to do more "news you can use" stories, and the next to do something entirely different. Often, reporters were handed new beats every year, or had their beats redefined to fit the contours of the latest effort to salvage the newspaper. To survive in this new environment, reporters had to be better educated and better trained, more professional in their habits, and more accountable for their work.

However, placed in the pressure cooker of commercial and technological stresses of modern newsrooms, the new knowledge and skills served only to further harden the culture of journalism. Journalists began to make a fetish of their preferred values and practices. That is, increasingly they came to see these values and practices not simply as one way to produce the news, but as how the news is, has been, and should be produced, everywhere and at all times. Nothing demonstrates this better than Kovach and Rosenstiel's *The Elements of Journalism* (2001), a slim volume that is sometimes called a "bible" for contemporary journalism – which seems natural, given that Kovach is often referred to as a "high priest" of the profession. As director of the Nieman Foundation at Harvard University, Kovach convened a small conference of esteemed journalists, educators, and writers in 1997 to worry over the fate of journalism. Out of this conference came a "Committee of Concerned Journalists," which set out over two years to discover journalism's unique contribution to public culture. The committee held twenty-one public forums and heard testimony from over 300 journalists. It also conducted in-depth interviews and surveys of journalists and completed nearly a dozen content analyses of the news. *Elements of Journalism* distilled the committee's findings.

The authors begin by anchoring journalism to values cherished by every member – in a survey, 100 percent of journalists agreed – of the profession. "The purpose [of journalism]," the authors write, "we have found, is the same . . . to provide citizens with the information they need to be free and self-governing." From this singular purpose, Kovach and Rosenstiel build a description of journalistic practice that is, they argue once again, invariant across time and space. They label this practice the "discipline of verification." It includes "techniques" and "devices" like seeking multiple sources for information, being transparent about where and how information is gathered, attributing information appropriately and in context, identifying stakeholders in stories and ensuring that they are given an opportunity to talk, and never adding (or subtracting) significant facts from a story. It also includes rigorous, "prosecutorial" editing, in which editors interrogate every significant fact in a story, "line by line, statement by statement." Journalism is only journalism when it conforms to this discipline – in other words, when it involves using the basic toolkit of professional journalists working in mainstream newsrooms.

Of course, Kovach and Rosenstiel are wrong in their argument. Historically and comparatively, it is easy to show that journalism has had many and varied values, practices, purposes, and procedures (e.g., Hallin and Mancini, 2004; McGerr, 1986; Schudson, 1998). But the historical accuracy of their conclusions isn't the point. We should see their argument less as an effort to get at the truth of journalism than as a maneuver in an ongoing struggle. Like many journalists, Kovach and Rosenstiel believed that technological and commercial forces threatened, as they put it, to "dissolve independent journalism . . . into the solvent of commercial communication and synergistic self-promotion." They wished to protect journalism's independence from these forces. One way to do so was to frame the field's preferred values and practices as obvious and inevitable, and therefore as beyond challenge. This gambit had obvious rhetorical advantages, but it also had the effect of generalizing, and flash freezing, a specific understanding of journalism.

In this inclination, Kovach and Rosenstiel exemplify a tendency that ran throughout their increasingly embattled profession. Pushed on the one side by commercialism and pulled on the other by new technology, journalists increasingly felt that many of their cherished values and practices were under attack. They could not prevent these forces from intruding into newsrooms, not if they wanted to keep their jobs. But they could resist, sometimes actively but more often passively. They could complain, which many did loudly. More generally, they could hunker down to protect their preferred values and practices, in the hope that they might weather the storm passing over their profession and come out the other end with a culture they could recognize and value.

Conclusion

A thought experiment: put yourself in the position of editor of a major metro daily circa 1995. At that moment in time, what would have seemed of more concern, longstanding circulation declines or the web? Given the option of adding more staff, would you be more likely to hire software programmers to work on the newspaper's website or to replace some of the many reporters you had been forced to lay off in recent years? Where were you likely to find higher revenue streams, in a new weekly entertainment section or the newspaper's website? What would seem like more of a threat to the newspaper's future, corporate pressures to hit certain profit numbers or craigslist? If you are having difficulty answering these questions, then I have achieved my purpose. You are now beginning to appreciate the context in which journalists encountered the Internet. At that moment in time, journalists were in a defensive crouch, more worried about protecting and preserving what they knew to be valuable than about embracing a new medium whose significance had yet to be determined.

Allow me just one more example to reinforce this point. It involves an interaction that took place during the 1987 annual meeting of the American Society of Newspaper Editors (ASNE). The annual ASNE meeting is an opportunity for hundreds of editors from the nation's leading newspapers to renew friendships, listen to important people talk about current events, sharpen their journalistic skills, and hear from experts about trends in their industry like the impact of new technologies. It may surprise you to learn that, as early as 1980, editors were discussing the latter topic, and many individuals who sat on these panels predicted elements of what was to come. Here is a sample of comments from panelists during the 1980s:

> There will be new competitors, companies we never dreamed would be in our own backyard. Some of them have already crawled under the fence – companies like Warner Communications, H&R Block, and GTE. (Robert Marbut, 1980)

Well, my view of the ultimate system is one in which the reader or
the viewer or the consumer can speak to us, that there is this very
swift interaction between the consumer and the editor. Because of the
ability to do that, I think the requests for information will be for highly
detailed information. (Max McCrohon, 1981)

In the kinds of systems you are hearing about today, it is possible to
knife past everything except what you [the reader] want . . . never
bother to look at any other kind of information. (James Batten, 1982)

Most likely, [in 20 years] we will be able to order up a customized
newspaper to precisely meet our own needs. Already, the MIT Media
Lab is experimenting with the individualized newspaper, a newspaper
that can be developed for each of us. (Katherine Fanning, 1987)

Editors no doubt listened attentively to such comments, but what
they heard passed through ears conditioned by the reflex to hunker
down. During that 1987 panel, two of the participants flatly declared
that new technologies threatened the very existence of newspapers.
"No matter how much you focus on quality and all the things we do
in our daily jobs," said Norman Pearlstine of the *Wall Street Journal*,
"if you are looking into the future for mass media, I think it is going
to be very tough for newspapers . . . So I think that one of the things
we have to come to grips with is what the implications of the new
technology really are." In other words, the world is changing around
us. We need to adapt, and we need to do it now.

The other members of the panel were having none of it. One said,
"Some of the most important things we will be doing twenty years
from now are things that we do now, and that are our strength if we
do them well." He added:

I find it difficult to see what else you will hold on a subway or a bus
other than a newspaper . . . I think there is a tendency always to look at
technology and assume that we are at some sort of watershed in civili-
zation . . . and while certainly there are always big threats around the
bend . . . I do not have this sort of apocalyptic view which suggests that
sort of fundamental threat . . . It is a newspaper business and we put
out newspapers . . . and if we look too far afield from things that involve
newspapers there too is a threat of some substantial problem.

A second chimed in:

Every newspaper should have a sophisticated group that concerns itself
with the application of new technology to the production and delivery

of the newspaper. But, in the long run, editors would be making a mistake to become too involved in questions about the future of technology. We should concern ourselves with what we know. No matter the technology involved, content will determine success in the future as today. The newspaper that does the most thorough, most honest, most intelligent job of reporting the news will be successful.

A third panelist ended the conversation with this: "There is only one thing to tell the staff. Regardless of how we deliver what we do, the main thing is to concentrate our minds on quality – quality of our writing and editing, quality of our photography and presentation, quality of all that we do." The world around us may change, these editors seemed to be saying, but news is news. We need to protect it and nurture it. If we do that, they reassured one another, we should be OK.

This exchange exhibits the kind of defensiveness that characterized journalists' reaction toward the Internet as it made its way into newsrooms in the 1990s. This defensiveness did not stem from an aversion to technology or a general unwillingness to change. In some sense, journalists who came of age after the mid-1970s had been changing their entire career in an effort to "save" their industry. Rather, it followed from the perception that journalism was under threat, and had been for some time. To most journalists, keeping their eye on this ball seemed more important than worrying about a new technology whose implications were as yet unknown. In this context, it seemed only prudent, as one of the above panelists said, to "concern ourselves with what we know."

Of course, he could not foresee that he was still in the midst of the profession's backstory. For all the talk of revolution in the 1980s and early 1990s, the real story of changes in the profession had only just begun.

2
Habits

I had no idea what I was doing. True, I had worked in a school of journalism for several years, but, as my colleagues there never tired of reminding me, I had never been a journalist. I had never written on a deadline (well, a firm one, anyway), never been challenged by a source, never felt what it was like to make an error read by tens of thousands of people. In fact, before beginning my visits to this newsroom a little over a year before, I had never set foot in a newsroom. As I came to work that morning in January 2006 as a newly minted "intern" at the *Daily Bugle*, I was about as unprepared for the job as anyone can be. I was well aware of my inexperience, of course, but still, I thought, how hard could it be? I was a voracious consumer of news, I'd just spent the last year observing journalists at work, and there was the matter of that PhD after my name. Surely this would be enough to get me started.

It wasn't, but that was of no concern to Roy Olden, the city editor. He had a paper to get out and too few people to help him do it. To him, I was another warm body. So just minutes after sitting down that morning, before I'd even received my badge and computer password, I heard him yell from across the aisle: "David, I have a story for you." I hustled over to his desk. He said, "The mayor is holding a press conference at the library to promote its new wi-fi system. It starts in 30 minutes." Ushering me out the door, he told me to come back with an eight-inch story for tomorrow's paper. Twenty minutes later, I found myself standing in front of the mayor, reporter's notebook (and press release) in hand, not having a clue what to do next.

My main problem, I soon discovered, was that I did not know how to distinguish useful from useless information. Lots of things are said at even the briefest of press conferences. Which was the stuff that should be printed in the newspaper? Not having a ready answer to this question, I naturally put everything I heard and saw into my notebook: what the mayor said, what the librarian said, questions asked by other reporters, what the furniture in the room looked like, the weather that day – everything. For several weeks afterward, this became my *modus operandi*. My notebooks filled up with the minutiae of my day – everything from what sources wore to how the room was configured. My method was, of course, terribly slow and inefficient. First I created a near verbatim transcription of events, then I went back to my desk and pored over the transcript to find a news story, and then I laboriously pieced together eight, or ten, or twelve paragraphs out of this material.

Despite my diligence, I made just about every mistake short of libel an inexperienced reporter can make. I misspelled the names of sources. I asked the wrong questions of the wrong people. I missed deadlines. I continually buried the lead. My mistakes piled so high that even the other interns, some of whom were my own students, began to take pity on me.

Over the next several months, things slowly got better. The panic I felt when assigned a story began to abate. I learned to write punchy leads and one-sentence paragraphs. I learned to write quickly, sometimes with an editor standing over my shoulder. I learned the formulas for different news stories and how to tell which formulas applied to which events. I learned to pluck newsworthy information from the steady stream that crosses a reporter's desk, and to ignore the rest. My notes became less exhaustive but more useful. I learned helpful techniques, like asking for business cards to ensure that I spelled names correctly in my stories. I learned to rely on my own judgment, even going so far as to pitch a few stories to the editor. I learned to take immense satisfaction in small triumphs: getting a source to talk; finding a piece of information no one else had uncovered; writing a story that generated a bit of web traffic.

Several months in, I could feel my orientation to the job change. One day I interviewed a representative of a national gay and lesbian group about a state legislative proposal to prevent gay and lesbian adults from adopting children. It was a "hot button" story, sure to attract a great deal of interest in the community. Earlier on, I would have let this person talk endlessly about his group's views, and every one of his comments would have made its way into my notebook. Now, however, I knew precisely the kind of story I needed to write, and I knew it would include only a brief quote from this source, probably in one of the story's middle paragraphs. So as he talked I found myself ignoring most of what he was saying. Instead, I thought about how I could get him to give me the quote I needed: a short, declarative statement on why gays and lesbians ought to be allowed to adopt children. My view, in other words, had considerably narrowed. Where a few months before I could not make a distinction between bits of information, now I made some very definite journalistic distinctions: I sought specific information that would help me fill out the stories I needed to write. Most everything else escaped my view.

In short, I was becoming a reporter. But what, precisely, was happening to me? A social scientist would say that I was going through a process of *socialization*. The term "socialization" has a long history, stretching back to the earliest days of social science. Today, nearly every discipline has its own definition of the term. In general, however, socialization is a process through which individuals acquire the attitudes, values, and practices of the groups to which they belong. It is how they become recognizably American, or female, or middle class, to name just a few of the groups into which an individual might be socialized. The process can be overt and intentional, as when parents guide their children toward appropriate ways of behaving or an editor spills red ink on a reporter's copy. But much of being socialized happens informally; it happens as a matter of simple immersion into a way of life. It is this immersion that lends habits their taken-for-granted quality. A properly socialized person is one for whom habits are simply "the way things are done."

I never received explicit instruction in how to be a reporter. No one came forward with a "Reporting for Dummies" guidebook. I never took a test or received a certificate identifying me as a reporter. Instead, I immersed myself in the newsroom. Between working on assignments, asking questions of other reporters, going to lunch with new office friends, and rubbing shoulders with other reporters at public events, I became socialized. Over time, I acted and felt more like a journalist. This is not to say that I ever became good, or even competent, at the work. I was only ever partly socialized by the experience. But, as I adopted the habits of journalism as best I could, I came to feel more and more like I belonged in the community of journalists, and I came to see the habits of this community as normal.

My experience, by the way, is not unusual. Journalists everywhere are socialized into the profession in just this way, and so tend to believe that the best way to become a journalist is to practice. At the *Daily Bugle*, I witnessed several young reporters make their entrance into the newsroom. Like me, they were given a badge and a user-name and password for the computer system, and sent off into the world. The practice extends even to journalism schools. The basic course in journalism often begins by flinging students out into the world with the commandment not to come back until they "find a story." The first habit of journalism, it seems, is the habit of not expressly teaching the other habits.

Because socialization in newsrooms is an informal process, it is also haphazard. But its effectiveness cannot be denied. Journalists everywhere share common values and attitudes toward their work and go about gathering and reporting the news in similar ways. Just as one example, when Kovach and Rosenstiel (2001) asked journalists in a survey what values they consider "paramount," 100 percent (!) answered, "getting the facts right" (p. 37). The habit of gathering facts and working hard to get them right is so deeply engrained in the profession that, for most (if not all) journalists, it is simply "the way that journalism is (and ought to be) done."

It is not difficult to see the value of such habits for journalists. Most obviously, habits allow them to work quickly without having to think very much. Once I learned which kinds of sources to talk to in which situations, I could unreflectively apply this knowledge. I did not have to think about whom to call – I knew whom to call. The fact that habits are widely shared also allows journalists to work with minimal supervision. Editors do not peer over the shoulders of journalists as they go about their work. Habits allow journalists to work together in a relatively seamless way. This isn't to say that editors never interfere in a reporter's work or that journalists agree on everything. Anyone who has been in a newsroom knows that journalists incessantly argue with one another. But even their arguments have the character of habit: reporters and editors tend to argue about the same things and to resolve these arguments in the same ways. Ultimately, habits ensure that the work gets done.

That being said, as many critics have noted, journalists' habits can be an impediment to change. In a confidential e-mail, one journalist told me, "Our challenge is [that] we can't break free of the cultural shackles and move the proverbial ship fast enough." Paraphrasing another journalist, Peter Preston (2008, p. 318) writes this of the problem: journalists "treat every change, every innovation, with suspicion and something akin to fear." Stuck in their habits of mind and practice, journalists simply are unwilling to change, or cannot change fast enough, to match the speed of the transformation underway in their profession. In the academic literature, the criticism is often framed as a "cultural clash" between old and new journalists. To the extent that "old" journalists remain mired in old habits, their unwillingness or inability to change has prevented journalism from becoming more innovative (e.g., Bardoel and Deuze, 2001; Hermida and Thurman, 2008).

This complaint boils down to the bromide that habits are hard to break. While this is true as far as it goes – habits are, indeed, hard to break – it doesn't actually go very far. What we want to know is *why* habits are hard to break. At a time when so much of the environment around journalism is changing, why have the habits of reporting remained in place?

That is the question I pursue in this chapter.

My time at the *Bugle* suggests three sorts of answers. First, as my own experience attests, there is little tradition of formal training or deep reflection in journalism. Neophytes learn the habits of journalism by doing, not by learning a set of formal rules or reflecting on what ought to be done. Under normal circumstances, this approach to training is good enough. But it has left journalists unprepared to respond adequately to the new environment in which they find themselves. Socialized to believe that the way things are done is the way things *ought* to be done, journalists have little experience of imagining how journalism might be done differently. Indeed, most efforts to change news practices come not from journalists, but from management. Even today, most journalists I meet fundamentally believe that their traditional values and practices are proper and ought to be preserved. When new practices are introduced in newsrooms, the lack of formal training makes it difficult for them to gain traction with reporters. Typically, once an editor announces a new direction, it is left to reporters to make the practices work.

Habits are also hard to break because a journalist's identity is closely entwined with her practices. Individuals learn *to be* journalists by *doing* journalism. This means that, when they are asked to do different things, journalists can quickly feel at sea. At the *Bugle*, reporters expressed feeling "uneasy" or "weird" when asked to change their practices. Often, reporters translate this sense of unease into moral consternation: "This isn't right!" When such feelings arise, it takes a degree of trust between journalists, and between journalists and management, to work them through. This raises a third dimension to the problem posed by habits: trust is a scarce commodity in most newsrooms these days. Relations between journalists and the organizations for which they work have always been tense. Today, they are toxic. Thirty years of commercializing the news has made journalists deeply cynical about their bosses' motives. In the last five years, massive layoffs and buyouts have only intensified this cynicism. Even if journalists could invent a new way of doing journalism, and a way of training journalists in the new practices, it is not clear that the organizational culture of newsrooms could work through the raw feelings that would surely follow.

An Experiment

My time at the *Daily Bugle* nicely illustrates these themes. Like other large, urban newspapers, the *Bugle* has fallen on hard times. In the 1960s and 1970s, it had been known as a very strong regional newspaper. Many of its reporters during those years went on to prestigious careers at major news outlets. Today, however, a simple, glaring fact defines the paper: since the mid-1970s, its circulation has been essentially flat. According to the *Ayer Directory of Publications*, in 1974 the paper had a daily circulation of 141,957 and a Sunday circulation of 242,834. For 2005, those numbers were about 170,000 and 230,000, respectively. In other words, these numbers have remained constant despite the fact that the city has nearly doubled in population since that time and is now one of the fastest growing cities in the country. Moreover, the newspaper's fixed costs have risen substantially, and it faces significant competition from weekly and local newspapers and from Internet news outlets. To be sure, in 2006 (the year I left the newsroom) the newspaper was still profitable. Exact figures are difficult to obtain, but at the time editors told me that profit margins at the paper were 25 percent or higher. However, these margins have been bought at the cost of the news staff. The numbers fluctuate, but the city desk, which is primarily responsible for filling the front and local sections of the paper, has about fifteen reporters. In the 1970s, it had double that number. Some of the older reporters remember a time when the city desk had a stable of seven general assignment reporters. Now, the paper has no general assignment reporters. Overall, it employs more news staff, but these workers are distributed across more sections, such as weekly AM sections and a free weekly aimed at teenagers. Nonetheless, as my study began in late 2004, corporate executives believed that, given the economic and demographic trends, the newspaper ought to be growing in both circulation and advertising revenue.

At the end of 2004, Calvin Thomas was installed as executive vice president and editor of news to make this happen. Thomas had a plan. He believed that growth in circulation required making the front section stronger, and, to do this, he needed to change the way that reporters gathered and reported the news. To his way of thinking, the *Bugle* simply could not compete with television and Internet news outlets on daily or breaking news. Rather, the paper's competitive advantage lay in the fact that no other news organization in the community had its resources to produce quality, in-depth journalism. Thomas's idea was to leverage these resources to get beyond daily events: provide context, identify trends, and investigate issues. One of his favorite phrases was that his reporters should "break the news" rather than "cover breaking news." In this distinction, Thomas meant to convey the idea that his reporters ought to get out in front of events. They ought to cover committee meetings before the meetings occur; they ought to uncover information that forces other institutions to react (rather than being reactive themselves). Thomas also reasoned that, like every large urban daily, his paper increasingly served suburban readers. Half of the *Bugle*'s circulation came from the suburbs, and the counties that ring the metropolitan area were growing in population at nearly twice the rate of the urban center. Thomas wanted to regionalize the news to capture these markets. This meant that, if an event happened in the city, he wanted his reporters to find out if similar things were happening in the surrounding counties, and to write that broader story. Finally, from market research, Thomas knew that readers were not interested in "process" news. They did not recognize news of the latest city hall meeting, for instance, or of an agency's planning session as important or relevant to their lives (this notion has become conventional wisdom in the news business, hence the explosion of "news you can use" in both print and broadcast journalism). Thomas wanted his reporters to write high-impact stories that would, as he and others were fond of saying, grab readers by the lapels.

What kind of news followed from these ideas? Thomas issued three directives, and these became the guiding rules for news coverage. On the front page of the newspaper (and only on the front page), he did *not* want to see three kinds of stories: government or political process stories; daily, incremental, stories; or soft, feature-type stories. Instead, he wanted the front page to be filled with broader and deeper stories, analytic stories that "took a hard look at," or "brought the news home about," some issue, event, or trend. For his reporters, this meant that they were *not* to fill the paper with daily stories.

During Thomas's tenure, the key buzzwords in the newsroom were "depth, breadth, and impact."

In practice, these directives meant that reporters were not to make daily visits to the agencies that comprised their beats. John Robbie, the *Bugle*'s federal courts reporter, was told flatly not to visit the courthouse any longer: Thomas was not interested in legal process stories. Maria Lopes, the paper's lone statehouse beat reporter, was told that Thomas did not want stories on legislative meetings. Sandy Hickel, the new transportation reporter, was told not to report on, or attend, public meetings held by the Department of Transportation. Anna Short, a long-time education reporter, was told not to cover education hearings. As an example, during the city's negotiations with the teacher's union, the two sides met once a week. Short was told not to cover these meetings, but to wait until negotiations had concluded: "Editors," she told me, "don't want to publish anything that doesn't have a conclusion." Cops reporter Sebastian Bottom was told not to do "murder of the day" stories. City hall reporters Kate Landers and Tom Campbell were told not to cover city council meetings.

This may seem like an odd directive, but it was in keeping with Thomas's initiative. Editors were concerned that, if reporters were allowed to make daily visits to the agencies on their beats, they would continue to produce incremental, daily stories. To prevent this from happening, it seemed sensible to mandate that reporters not make these daily visits.

The Numbers

A count of the content that appeared on the front page of the front and local sections of the paper show that Thomas's experiment failed. Over a year, I coded every story on these pages as a "daily" or an "enterprise" story. As figure 2.1 shows, in the early days of Thomas's tenure, reporters worked very hard to produce more enterprise news for the front page. In fact, in the month of January 2005, they succeeded in producing more enterprise than daily news, and even in February 2005 the numbers were roughly equal. By July 2005, however, the percentage of daily news had grown substantially, and by September 2005 over 90 percent of the news hole was filled with daily news. From September 2005 to January 2006, the percentage of daily stories never fell below 90 percent. I stopped collecting newspapers in January 2006, but there is no reason to believe that the

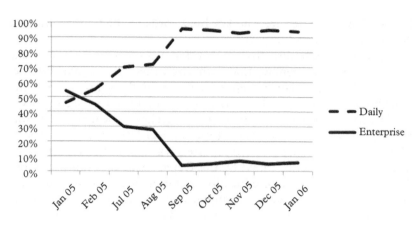

Figure 2.1   Frequency of story type

numbers changed much after that time. Ironically enough, at the end of two years, reporters were producing more daily stories than before Thomas arrived.

It is worth asking how reporters were able to file daily stories without visiting the agencies on their beats. For an answer, I coded the data to ascertain the source of stories that appeared in the newspaper. Here, I mean by source the events that prompted news stories. In typical beat coverage, reporters find daily stories by visiting particular locations and observing events themselves or talking with people who observe events. For this reason, most daily stories are about one-time events. But reporters at the *Bugle* were denied an opportunity to visit key locations on their beats, and so could not gather information about daily events. In this situation, the only other way to produce daily news is to focus on *continuing* events – an event that spurs other events. With a continuing story, reporters learn about the story once and then, from their perch in the newsroom, are able to follow the events it precipitates (press releases and conferences, issuance of reports, etc.) over weeks or months. As figure 2.2 shows, the data indicate that this is precisely how reporters filled the newspaper. While they were explicitly prohibited from attending daily events, Thomas and his editors could not prevent reporters from writing daily news about ongoing events.

An example shows how this worked. When I first talked with Sebastian Bottom, a cops reporter, he assured me that, when summer came and the murder stories "became too good to pass up," the

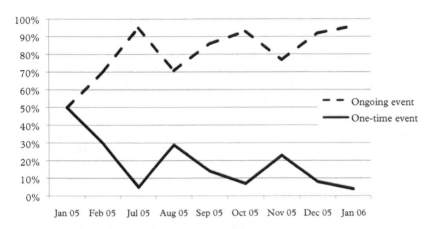

Figure 2.2   Frequency of story source

paper would return to covering the "murder of the day." But then summer came and the rules remained in force. Bottom still was not allowed to visit crime scenes or write about the "murder of the day." His handling of a story about police use of taser guns illustrates how he negotiated this dilemma. In late September 2005 a man died after two police officers repeatedly hit him with taser guns. As per the new rules, Bottom did not cover the man's death. But he did receive permission to cover a public protest over the man's death held three days later. Bottom had been alerted to this protest by an e-mail press release sent out by an attorney for the deceased man's family. Over the next several months, Bottom and three other reporters published ten articles on this story. Bottom published seven of the articles, but on three occasions he was busy with other projects and so other reporters stepped in to write articles. Nine of the ten stories were of the "daily" variety – initiated by a press conference or press release, the publication of investigation reports, meetings of the police board review, and the like. A couple of these stories required a reporter to attend a particular event. But Bottom wrote most of them on the basis of material flowing into the newsroom (via e-mail, faxes, and phone calls), Internet searches, and phone calls to the various parties involved. Only one of the ten articles was an enterprise story. It appeared in early December 2005, two months after the initial events.

To the extent that other reporters followed Bottom's approach, they circumvented Thomas's interest in broader and deeper news. Why did Thomas fail?

Beat Reporting: The Basic Habit

To answer this question, it helps to set a context for his ideas. Thomas was not the first editor to prize enterprise over daily beat reporting. Editors had been making similar arguments at least since the early 1990s, and probably since the 1970s, with the emergence of local television news. It is obvious that no other local news organization can compete with the daily newspaper in providing deep, analytic, local news. Any newspaper ought to have a franchise on this sort of news. Yet, the effort to produce broader and deeper news means altering one of the most basic and longstanding habits of daily journalism: beat reporting.

James Gordon Bennett is sometimes credited with creating the first news beat in the 1820s, when he made a circuit of Washington politics. But the exact origin of news beats is unknown. It is fair to say, however, that they were firmly in place at most large urban newspapers by the 1850s, and by the turn of the century they were a staple of reporting at most daily newspapers. Writing about the news process in 1911, Will Irwin observes that "The city editor keeps men day and night at the police station and emergency hospital . . . he has a man at the local financial center . . . men watch the local centers of government, as the City Hall, the Courts and the Federal Building . . . Probably nine-tenths of the news, and on most days all of it, comes originally from one or another of these sources" (1969, p. 40). One study has estimated that, by the early 1900s, the beat system produced 70 percent of news content at most newspapers (Baldasty, 1992, pp. 96–7).

Through the twentieth century, beat reporting remained the core of daily newsgathering practices. In fact, as I mentioned in the introduction, when sociologists made their way into newsrooms in the 1960s and 1970s, they were uniformly struck by the importance of these routines for news production. Here is Mark Fishman (1980): "The routine work methods of journalists are capable of explaining the distinct character of media news" (p. 14). And Phillip Schlesinger (1978): "Broadcast news is the outcome of standardized production routines" (p. 106). And Leon Sigal (1973): newsmaking and gathering "is routine behavior: a good deal of the news is a product of the coupling of two information processing machines: one, the news organization; the other, government" (p. 4). And Edward Epstein (1973): "The outputs of network news are not simply the arbitrary choices of a few men; they result from a process" (p. 8).

It is not hard to see the advantages of the beat system for news organizations. In the first instance, beats ensure that reporters can reliably find newsworthy information. Indeed, as Fishman notes, in the beat system government does much of the reporters' job. "In routine newswork," he writes, "the detection, interpretation, investigation, and a good deal of the formulation of the written story have already been done by police, city clerks, insurance adjusters, morticians, and the like" (1980, p. 151). For the most part, this information comes at the right price: free. As mandated by public law, government information is public information and is, therefore, free to the public, including journalists. In a sense, this means that government information comprises an important subsidy for news organizations (e.g., Cook, 1998). If journalists did not have access to government information, it is unclear where they would find a comparable supply of reliable, cheap information. But as Cook (ibid., p. 151) notes, the subsidy provided by government goes beyond the simple act of making information available. Every government agency employs individuals whose job is to push the information it collects to journalists. This public relations infrastructure makes the task of gathering and reporting government information infinitely easier. At the very least, it ensures that there is always someone on the other end of the phone who will take reporters' calls and help them find the information they are seeking.

Historically, beats emerged to solve problems peculiar to news organizations. Over time, however, they also became central to the self-identity of daily journalists. Many criteria for what counts as a "good" reporter follow directly from the activities of beat reporting. Consider these notions of what a good reporter is. A good reporter can find information quickly. A good reporter can find stories without help from others. A good reporter can find information no other reporter has discovered. A good reporter has extensive contacts in government agencies. A good reporter manages to gain the trust of sources without losing her independence. A good reporter knows the ins and outs of the agencies she covers. A good reporter holds government actors accountable for their actions. These and statements like them help reporters distinguish between good and bad journalism and good and bad journalists, and they are embedded directly into the practice of beat reporting.

From the moment their careers begin, new journalists are socialized into sharing these notions of what counts as good reporting. At the *Bugle*, new reporters typically start as general assignment reporters for one of the zoned AM editions. From this position, they cover mundane events – everything from BBQs, to school plays, to (in my case) a yearly "largest tree in the city" competition. Such stories are not unimportant, but, in being simple to report and write, they are viewed by other journalists as the most basic of stories. They give new journalists an opportunity to hone their craft and to distinguish themselves by their initiative and hard work. How quickly can they begin finding stories on their own? How well do they source their stories? Eventually, reporters who distinguish themselves move from the AM editions to the city desk, where they are assigned a beat, usually working alongside more experienced reporters. At this point, they have to prove themselves all over again, by finding their own sources in government agencies, by finding their own stories, etc. In this way, journalists move up the pecking order of the newsroom by demonstrating a mastery of practices associated with beat reporting.

Beat reporting, then, fuses the epistemological needs of the profession with the functional needs of news organizations. News organizations use news beats to find cheap, reliable information, and journalists use them to define what it means to be a good reporter. Consider the daily news story. There is nothing natural or inevitable about the fact that reporters must find and report news *every day*. Initially, the requirement follows from the needs of news organizations, which, as Gaye Tuchman (1978, p. 17) notes, have financial agreements with advertisers to present their advertisements daily. Eventually, however, the ability to gather news every day became a key criterion for what counts as a good reporter. Even when everyone agrees that it is a slow news day, reporters are required to find newsworthy information. Not doing so means that a reporter has not done her job – i.e., has failed in a central task that defines good reporting. Not doing so often enough will lead an editor to begin assigning a reporter stories, which, as it encroaches on a reporter's autonomy, is seen by everyone in the newsroom as a significant slight. In this way, satisfying the organization's need for daily stories also satisfies a reporter's need for recognition and distinction.

This brings us back to Thomas's broader and deeper news initiative. In declaring that the organization wanted broader and deeper coverage, he opened a gap – however small – between the organization's needs and his reporters' needs. From the organization's perspective, filling the newspaper with daily stories was no longer useful. Television and online news covered these stories better and faster than the newspaper ever could. Think, for instance, of daily murder stories. By the time the newspaper published a story about this event in the next day's newspaper, it had likely been on TV at least a few times and had been sitting on a local news site for hours. But, in declaring the daily murder of the day story off-limits, Thomas risked troubling the very practices that, for his reporters, defined good journalism. For many decades, crime reporters had distinguished themselves by reporting and writing such stories: by getting the relevant information first, by contacting sources available to no other reporter, by getting information no other reporter could get, etc. In asking for broader and deeper coverage, Thomas inadvertently raised a difficult question: could reporters simultaneously satisfy their own professional needs and the practical needs of the news organization?

How Do We Do This?

When I first interviewed Thomas in December 2004, he showed me a book he had compiled as managing editor at his last newspaper. He called it a "bible," and it contained detailed instructions on how to report every beat in the newsroom. He and his staff had pieced it together over many months, and every new reporter was given a copy. He told me one of his first actions in his new job would be to engage the *Bugle*'s staff in producing its own bible. This never happened. In fact, he did not formally introduce his ideas to reporters until he held a staff meeting six months into his tenure. Over a year later, Thomas had not even introduced himself to most of the staff. One reporter told me that the only words he had ever spoken to her were "Pick up this trash!" as he breezed by her desk one day. During this time, I asked him what happened to the idea of producing his "bible" of reporting. Looking chagrined, he explained that he still intended to do this, but just hadn't had time. Most of his time was taken up with publisher meetings and community events. He tried to do some instruction at the morning news meetings, but only editors were in attendance. Reporters were left to hear about the changes from their immediate supervisors.

When I tell this story to other news executives, they express amazement that Thomas never told his reporters how to accomplish the new goals. They claim that he was simply a bad manager. There is something to this criticism, but it should be noted that the top-down, informal process of change that Thomas pursued is not unusual in the news industry. Writing decades ago about a particular innovation at BBC news, Schlesinger (1978, p. 256) notes, "Internally, there was a lack of consultation about the changes – which . . . can be seen to be the basic style of innovation in news." Schlesinger's observation remains essentially true today. Management created all three of the initiatives in the newsrooms I have investigated. While editors in each case consulted their staffs somewhat, these discussions never extended to the question of whether and how to innovate, and, once initiated, reporters were left to their own devices to figure out how to make the changes work.

The fact that veteran *Bugle* reporters expressed little surprise at not being consulted by Thomas is the best evidence of how typical the top-down style is in newspapers. As I began this project, I was excited at the prospect of watching news production change in a newsroom. Reporters were more sanguine. They told me that they had been through the process many times. A new editor brings his own ideas about the kinds of stories he wants to see in the paper; he reorganizes the newsroom to reflect the new emphasis; the ideas are introduced to reporters with fanfare, but little additional training is offered. Reporters are expected to catch the drift of the new direction as they go along. No formal effort is made to track the success of the new ideas. Reporters more or less go on finding and reporting stories as they have always done. Eventually, the editor leaves for another post, and the process begins again. Reporters with whom I have talked at other newspapers confirm this experience. One told me that he had been through so many of these initiatives that, at this point, if management told him to put a hamster in his pocket, he wouldn't even blink: he'd just put the animal in his pocket and go on with reporting the news.

This prior experience with change explains why *Bugle* reporters cast a jaundiced eye toward Thomas's proposals: in their experience, new initiatives were top-down affairs that almost never led to significant changes in news practices. A consequence of this experience, of course, is that reporters felt they were equipped to deal with any innovation Thomas might propose. "I don't get caught up in the swirl of change," one long-time reporter told me at the outset of Thomas's tenure at the *Bugle*. "I just find good stories and let the editors translate them into the formula of the moment." Another reporter told me, "Things are pretty much the same at every newspaper. I have techniques I can use anywhere to produce different kinds of stories, so it's no big deal." These quotes capture the common sense in the newsroom as Thomas introduced his ideas. He might alter the balance of stories in the newspaper – more accountability news and fewer feature stories – but reporters were convinced that the process of gathering and reporting the news would remain the same.

It turns out, however, that producing broader and deeper news was more of a challenge than reporters expected. On Thomas's arrival, most welcomed his aggressive, hard news style. They felt that the paper had become complacent under the last editor, and were excited to write broader and deeper stories. Their attitudes, however, began to change when they learned that they were not to make daily visits to their beats. This rule presented editors and reporters with several puzzles.

For instance, without daily stories, how were editors going to fill the newspaper? It was a simple matter of numbers. The city desk was primarily responsible for filling the front and local sections of the newspaper. As a general rule, this meant that Roy Olden, the city editor, needed at least six new stories per day: three for the front page and three for the first page of the local section (he might use more, but rarely could he fill these pages with fewer than six stories). Multiplied by seven (for the number of days in the week), this meant that Olden needed at least forty-two new stories each week to fill the front page and the first page of the local section. To get to this number, he had eleven beat reporters and four enterprise reporters available. These reporters were arrayed around institutions that reliably and predictably made newsworthy information available: churches (one beat reporter), state and local transportation agencies (one beat reporter), hospitals (one beat, one enterprise reporter), schools (one beat, one enterprise reporter), city hall and the statehouse (four beat reporters, one enterprise reporter, state and local), police departments and courthouses (two beat reporters), and, finally, nearby county governments (one beat, one enterprise reporter). To produce the requisite number of stories, beat reporters were required to produce three stories per week plus one "weekender" (a story to run on Sunday or Monday). If every beat reporter simply filled her quota of daily news, Olden would have forty-four new stories per week, or just enough to fill the news hole. This numbers game was difficult enough when reporters focused their attention on getting daily stories. Olden had no idea how he would fill the newspaper without access to daily stories.

For their part, reporters were happy to write broader and deeper stories. But how were they to find these stories if they were not allowed to visit the institutions that comprised their beats? Consider the situation of Sandy Hickel, the new transportation beat reporter. Hickel had been a reporter before her stint at the *Bugle*, but her most recent job (which she held for five years) had been as a public information officer for a university. Moreover, she had never covered this beat before and, as is typical, was thrown in with little guidance other than to do enterprise reporting and avoid public meetings. But

where, she kept asking, was she supposed to get information for these
stories if she didn't attend the department's meetings? More veteran
reporters asked the same question. To Bottom, the cops reporter,
covering the murder of the day was important because it gave him an
opportunity to establish relationships with detectives. How was he to
establish these relationships, and presumably learn about the broader
stories, when he couldn't go down to crime scenes? Tom Cybill aptly
summarized reporters' answers to these questions. As editor of the
investigations team, Cybill was largely removed from daily reporting.
In fact, he had not heard of the new rules before I mentioned them
in a conversation two months into Thomas's tenure. Yet, when I laid
out the logic of Thomas's plans and asked him, "Can you do enterprise reporting without also doing daily reporting?," his answer was
swift and unequivocal: "You can't." His reasons were twofold. On
the one hand, he argued, "You are going to do daily news anyway,"
because the newspaper had to be filled. On the other, reporters
typically come across enterprise stories in the course of their daily
routines. Trying to do the one without first doing the other was, to
Cybill's mind, impossible.

Thomas was rarely in the newsroom to explain how it might be
done. Without this instruction, reporters began to chafe at their loss
of autonomy in making news judgments. A meeting in mid-March
of 2005 between the managing editor, Zeb Campbell, and a group
of reporters illuminates the growing tension. While Campbell talked,
Anna Short sat on the edge of her seat with a sour expression on her
face. Seeing her mounting frustration, Campbell asked if she wanted
to say something. This prompt led Short to launch into a minutes-
long complaint. She understood that Thomas wanted broader and
deeper stories. "But how much?," she asked. And did this mean
that she was never to cover an education meeting again? "[I don't]
feel that [I can] go on my beat and determine on my own what
meetings to attend and which not," she told Campbell. "This," she
concluded, as if to confirm Campbell's assessment, "is very frustrat-
ing." Campbell offered some rough guidelines to assist her and the
others in making these decisions. Later, Short dismissed them as
"speaking in generalities." Roy Olden, the city editor, tried to offer
more specific suggestions. He said that Short and the other reporters
ought to get ahead of meetings by receiving and writing about their
agendas beforehand. The idea, he said, is to explain so well what
is about to happen that the newspaper sets the public agenda – it
makes the news and becomes a player in town – without having to
cover meetings themselves. Later, as the "specialties team" met in

their area to decompress, Short remained confused. "I didn't learn anything new," she said, as others nodded their heads. Or, as Bottom angrily told me, "They [meaning, his editors] haven't given me any techniques to make this happen. Meanwhile, they don't want me to go down to crime scenes."

Top editors were aware of the problem, but had no language for helping reporters develop answers. One day, I asked Jeremy Schmidt, the assistant managing editor for visuals, about these issues. Thomas hired Schmidt because he was known in the news business as a forward thinker. I asked him how reporters were supposed to accomplish the new goals. He said: "Reporters have to step back and reflect on what they can add to a story – what kind of questions need to be addressed to broaden a story, to take a hard look at the issue." Yes, I said, pressing him, but what are these questions? Can they be distilled into a new set of 5-Ws? Schmidt leaned into me and said, "This question is crucial for newspapers because they have to sell . . . the value-added they give . . . is precisely their ability to go broader and deeper." Yes, I persevered, but how do you do this? He didn't know, but said that an article on the "new 5-Ws" would be an excellent contribution to the profession. Later that day, I asked Olden if there was a new set of 5-Ws for doing broader, deeper reporting. He stopped his multi-tasking (at that moment, he had been writing an e-mail, looking over copy, and drinking coffee) and gave me a hard look. "That is an excellent question. Let me think about it." A few minutes later he passed by my desk on his way to his next meeting and said "Breadth, context, and impact." I wrote the words down quickly and turned my head up to say, "These are not specific questions" – but it was too late. He had disappeared into the conference room.

One scene nicely illustrates the growing confusion in the newsroom. In March 2005, a mugger began a series of home robberies in an affluent neighborhood. He had a special penchant for women's purses, which he would brazenly snatch by walking through the back door of homes and taking them off the kitchen table. When the first robbery occurred, Clark Brown, the cops 'n' courts editor, correctly told his reporters not to cover it. The newspaper was no longer doing such daily stories. But the purse snatches continued. Eventually, there would be over a dozen. Local TV news ran with the story. For two weeks, TV monitors in the newsroom were tuned to local TV reporters breathlessly describing the latest robbery of what they had dubbed the "Hillwood Mugger." Still the newspaper ignored the story. Reporters merely shook their heads. "If this isn't a news story," one of them told me, "I don't know what is. We ought to be all over this story."

During this time, a group of female reporters began talking to one another about the newspaper's disinterest in the story. Why aren't the cops reporters covering this story? They could not imagine any good journalistic reason. So they determined that it must have to do with gender discrimination: being male, the cops reporters and editors simply did not understand the importance women placed on their purses. The group met with Campbell, the managing editor, to voice their concerns. Because it had not been in the newspaper, Campbell did not know about the robberies. But he assured the women that the lack of coverage had nothing to do with gender discrimination. He then reminded the group of the new directive to produce broader and deeper news. They went away unconvinced. Eventually, Bottom produced an enterprise story that showed crime in this affluent neighborhood was far below the crime rate in other, less affluent neighborhoods. Other reporters appreciated this story, but never understood why the daily robberies weren't legitimate stories as well.

"This Feels Weird"

If you ask a journalist what a reporter is, she will describe what a reporter does: a reporter is someone who gathers facts, packages these facts into stories, etc. In journalism, identity and practice are tightly fused. It should come as no surprise, then, that *Bugle* reporters felt the new rules as a challenge to the self. This feeling is implicit in Short's comment that she did not "feel that [she could] go on [her] beat and determine on [her] own what meetings to attend and which not." Prevented from routinely visiting sources and events on her education beat, Short felt less and less like a "real" reporter.

By the sixth month of the new regime, many reporters shared Short's unease. During this period I stopped by Maria Lopes's desk to ask how things were going. In reply, she described a scene that took place in the statehouse pressroom. Though Lopes was working on an enterprise project, most of the others were, as usual, hanging out while they waited for news to happen. Then word came of an interesting development in a committee meeting down the hall. All of the other reporters immediately fled the pressroom and ran down the hallway. Lopes, however, stayed put. Her enterprise story had to be filed the next day, and anyway she had been told not to cover legislative meetings. "That made me feel really weird," she said. She felt like she was writing for a magazine rather than a daily newspaper. Some months later, Chad Lowe was put on the same beat and expressed a similar feeling. A few weeks in, he told me that other reporters were accusing the paper of "abandoning" the statehouse. He defended the paper's new direction, but admitted that he didn't feel much like a daily reporter.

Other reporters expressed similar views. Maureen Holly said that she "felt weird" about going to state education board meetings and not reporting on the meetings themselves. Sebastian Bottom, the cops reporter, experienced a particularly telling moment. The year before, Bottom had won a company investigative journalism award for a series on state trooper chases on the region's interstate highways. Apparently, such chases often cause accidents. During the early morning budget meeting one day, Bottom popped his head into the conference room and announced, "There's been another [trooper] crash today." After Olden told him to follow up on it, Bottom rushed back to his desk to call his editor, Clark Brown (who was driving to the office). While he cradled the phone to his ear, he busily gathered his things and then began to walk down the hallway. He abruptly stopped when Brown asked him about the enterprise story he was supposed to work on that morning. Bottom said, "It's basically done," but Brown told him to wait. This annoyed Bottom no end. For over half a century, a reporter's legs had been more important than his brains (e.g. Alsop and Alsop, 1958, p. 5). Rushing to accidents, this is to say, is just what reporters do. At the *Bugle*, this was no longer true. After Brown arrived and listened to Bottom's appeal, he decided that Bottom ought to finish his enterprise story. It was more important than spending the morning at an accident that may or may not produce news. He then handed the trooper story to an intern and asked her to follow up by phone. Later, Bottom seethed, calling Brown's decision "idiotic" and saying that the newspaper had reverted to "desk-top journalism." Under the new regime, Bottom didn't feel like he was doing journalism anymore. Anna Short put the matter this way: "I just want to feel like a professional . . . [like I] can make a professional news judgment [about what to report]." Like other reporters, Short wanted to feel like a reporter ought to feel, which entailed, at the very least, control over basic decisions as to how to cover her beat.

Sometimes, however, the pull of habit was simply too strong for editors and reporters to resist. One day in April 2005 Bottom was in the newsroom when news of another murder came over the police scanner. At first, he did not do anything about the story. It was a "murder of the day," and he had been told not to write such stories. But he soon learned more details about the murder. Apparently, a couple had picked up an undocumented immigrant in a local bar and brought him home. The next morning, the husband thought the episode was over. However, for several weeks his wife continued to see the man, even going so far as to hide him in their bedroom closet at night. One morning, the husband came home early, only to find the immigrant in his house. Surprised, the immigrant promptly hit him with a bat and killed him. Neither Bottom nor Brown could resist this story. It was too good to pass up. Brown sent Bottom out to the neighborhood to interview the neighbors. His story appeared in the next day's newspaper. This kind of thing happened on several occasions. One evening a story ran on local TV about a man who had been killed with a sword. In line with the new direction, the *Bugle* did not report it. Learning of the story the next morning, an editor asked one of her reporters to follow up. After watching this interaction, I asked the editor why she wanted to follow up on a story that obviously contradicted the new direction of the newspaper. She responded that there are some stories that are just interesting. "We got beat on these stories last night," she said, "so we're going to do something on them." She agreed that this was a traditional way of looking at the news, but said, "The first part of a newspaper is news, and that's what we publish."

On another occasion, the FBI announced that it had asked the Mexican government to extradite a local man whose wife had been killed a decade earlier. At the time, the man had been a prime suspect but had never been charged with the crime. Apparently, the FBI now felt it had enough evidence to charge the man with her murder. Editors assigned several reporters to cover various angles of the case, going so far as to send one down to Mexico to talk with the man's neighbors. When I asked why they were devoting so much attention to a story that clearly violated the new directive (it was not even a recent murder and had no direct relevance to readers), the enterprise editor told me, "It has all the elements of a good story. It's a whodunnit, a romance, and a local story all rolled into one."

When not giving in to their impulse to follow "good stories," editors and reporters felt stranger and stranger. Take Liam Nelson, a reporter on the public safety beat. Nelson's typical week went like this: he pitched enterprise stories on Wednesday because editors held their weekly planning meeting that day. He worked on them Thursday and Friday and wrote on Monday and Tuesday. During this time, he was almost always pulled off his enterprise story to write two to three daily stories. When Wednesday rolled around again, he had done little daily reporting on his beat that might lead to his next enterprise story. "There's no time to fill the well," he said. By this he meant that he had no time to interact with people from whom he might discover leads for new enterprise stories. In this vacuum, Nelson began to find story ideas on the Investigative Reporters and Editors (IRE) website. The online presence of a non-profit organization dedicated to investigative reporting, the IRE site lists hundreds of story ideas for every journalistic beat – from healthcare to public safety. For Nelson, the IRE site functioned as something of a virtual source. Cut off from daily interaction with his sources, and having little interaction with other reporters, Nelson relied upon the IRE site to help him generate story ideas. For a time, the practice worked. After two or three of these stories, however, Nelson began to have qualms about this method of generating enterprise story ideas. He felt like he was cutting corners. He was not reporting news as it ought to be done. When he came to this conclusion, like many other reporters in the newsroom, he threw up his hands in frustration: you just can't do enterprise news without first doing daily news.

Even top editors expressed a sense that the new practices left them feeling strange. One morning in early May 2005, editors found themselves scrambling to cover a scandal that had hit the statehouse. By mid-morning, several of them huddled in an office to determine who was covering what. As they discussed options, someone asked if the legislature was doing anything else that day. "Yes, they're passing the budget," someone else immediately said, prompting this quick reply from the statehouse editor: "Oh, we're not covering that anyway." The group burst into laughter at the idea that they weren't covering the budget signing. "Well," she continued, somewhat defensively, "we're not doing committee stuff, honestly." This prompted more laughter. Prior to Thomas's arrival, a story about the legislature passing the budget not only would have been done, it would have appeared on the front page. In the context of a highly stressful day, the laughter can be seen as a way of deflating tension. But it is also a register of a broader unease. In this moment, editors contemplated exactly how far they had come from conventional journalistic practices: they weren't even covering the budget signing anymore! As if reading the collective mind, the managing editor said, "But we considered some of these budget stories as front page stories this week." He meant to imply that the paper was not too far removed from old habits – at least editors had considered these stories. However, at that moment the governor began a televised press conference on the scandal and the issue was dropped. Though it remained largely unspoken, for editors and reporters alike, unease about whether the news they produced was "good" or 'serious" or "professional" remained.

Eventually, reporters began to translate this unease into moral terms. John Robbie, the federal courts reporter, was one of the first to do so. Robbie had been a reporter for fifteen years – seven at the *Bugle*. In the newsroom, he had a reputation as something of a character, but also as a gifted, committed reporter, someone to whom younger reporters turned for tips on how to cover their beats. When Robbie's editor first told him not to go down to the courthouse every day, he simply refused. When I asked him about it, he mentioned many of the practical constraints other reporters had remarked upon. He told me, for instance, that the courthouse is a pretty insular place with lots of rules restricting journalists' access to stories. This context required him to be there every day so that he could cultivate relationships with judges, clerks, and others. In other words, if he did not practice his daily routines, it would be impossible for him to find the enterprise stories editors wanted. For the next few weeks, Robbie kept pitching daily stories and his editors rejected every one of them. About this time, I had lunch with him to get a sense of how he was doing. Not surprisingly, he was distraught. But, as he explained the reasons for his distress, Robbie no longer talked about the difficulties of doing enterprise reporting without also doing daily reporting. Instead, he reminisced about a time when reporters could gain reputations for covering a beat really well. He talked about getting stories that no one else got, and about the status such reporting lent to the journalists who pulled it off. And he lamented the loss of a time when reporters had enduring relationships with readers who picked up the newspaper specifically to read their favorite reporter's copy. As I listened to Robbie, it became clear that he did not perceive Thomas's new initiative as impossible; he thought it was wrong. Indeed, as I say, Robbie never tried to produce more enterprise news without daily attendance to his beat. Instead, in April 2005, he quit.

Many other senior reporters quit as well. Shelly Warren left in February 2005. Stan Henson left the next month to take a job with another newspaper. Liam Nelson took a job at a weekly publication. Fed up with being micromanaged on her beat, Anna Short retired. Two business reporters left. Of course, turnover in newsrooms has always been high, never higher than today. And it is unclear that every *Bugle* reporter quit due to moral qualms about the direction of the newspaper. Yet, in the newsroom their leaving was interpreted in just this way. Reporters told me that too many people felt like they could not write "good" stories any longer. At the end of the exodus,

Bottom remarked that more people had left in the past year than had taken early retirement a few years before. And, he observed, most of them were taking jobs at inferior newspapers or quitting the business altogether. Whatever the specific reasons in each case, in the newsroom reporters strongly felt the losses, and most attributed them to the changes Thomas had implemented.

Organizational Culture

Nothing in what I have described so far automatically spelled the doom of Thomas's experiment. Changing habits is always hard, and people can feel uncomfortable doing things in new ways. But many people, and even organizations, push through this discomfort. Why did this not happen at the *Bugle*?

In answering this question, it is important to realize that editors and reporters did not directly confront the challenges posed by Thomas's directives. In the first instance, they confronted one another. Bottom, for example, did not try all by himself to solve the problem of how to cover the cops beat without visiting every murder scene. He worked on this problem with his fellow cops reporters and his editor, Brown. Together, they developed interpretations of what Thomas had asked them to do. These interpretations mediated their understanding of the situation. Their interpretations, this is to say, defined the problem, and these definitions implied particular solutions. So what sorts of interpretations did editors and reporters conjure in the *Bugle*'s newsroom?

One comes from Cybill's suggestion that doing more enterprise and less daily news was not practical. The paper had to be filled every day, and the only way to fill it was with daily news. On this interpretation, journalists were not responsible for failing to produce more enterprise news. Rather, responsibility lay with the demands of daily news production. Moreover, in abiding by the demands of news production, journalists were simply being practical. This suggestion, of course, had the effect of framing Thomas as impractical. Many reporters took this view to argue that Thomas simply was not thinking through the ramifications of his orders. Toward the end of my time in the newsroom, for example, I had lunch with a very disgruntled Sebastian Bottom. He told me that he felt like "a machine strapped to a computer, answering the phone robotically." And he said that, under Thomas, the *Bugle* had become a "1950s newspaper ... We should be out there with cell phones ... we should be blogging . . . we run AP stories about blogging taking over journalism . . . Don't they read their own paper?" Here, Bottom defines himself as dependent ("a machine strapped to a computer") on a system over which he had no control, and at the mercy of managers who were at best confused and at worst incompetent ("Don't they read their own paper?"). While Thomas obsessed over enterprise reporting, Bottom implied, the world of journalism was passing him – and the news-paper – by. In this situation, Bottom had no choice but to do what was required, i.e., fill the newspaper every day.

John Robbie raises a second interpretation of what was happen-ing in the newsroom. To him, Thomas's plan for the *Bugle* was not "good journalism." Within the concept of "good journalism," Robbie packed such things as getting the news first, working a beat every day to wring new stories and new story angles out of it, and gaining special access to sources. Good journalism revolved around the basic practices of daily newsgathering. Correspondingly, a "good" news-paper offered a supportive and nurturing environment for this kind of reporting.

This interpretation was especially persuasive to *Bugle* reporters because it fed into a longstanding sense that the news had been stead-ily commercialized in the past thirty years. Those whose careers went back to the 1970s recalled the dramatic change that occurred when the newspaper was bought by a corporate chain in the early 1980s. Steve Tinton, for instance, whose career at the *Bugle* stretched back to the 1960s, told the story in terms of "before" and "after." "Before" corporate ownership, when the newspaper was still family owned, reporters and editors were free to do "good" journalism even if doing so did not generate high profits. "After" corporate owners took over, new levels of bureaucracy were introduced to wring as much profit as possible from the newspaper. Staff levels dropped. Editors began to micromanage reporters and business types began to microman-age editors. Ever since, Tinton argued, the newspaper had had little regard for "good" journalism. On Tinton's account, Thomas's actions were just one in a long line of slights to reporters and "good journalism" that had begun a decade or more before. Thomas's plans were another iteration of the "do more with less" mentality that defined corporate journalism.

Other reporters elaborated the same basic account in the context of the newspaper industry's current woes. At our first meeting, Anna Short recalled a time decades before when the editor presided over "legendary" news meetings, and the conversation was always about the next great story. Today, she told me, management wants to plan everything. They "package" the news "in pieces, with sidebars and pull quotes" and won't let reporters write about anything that doesn't have a conclusion. This "drives reporters crazy," she said. On this account, Thomas's actions were of a piece with the massive industry layoffs, corporate belt-tightening, widespread confusion on the part of industry managers, and a general disregard for "good" journalism that currently gripped the industry. The newspaper, and Thomas in particular, had little commitment to reporters or to "good" journalism.

For their part, editors accounted for what was happening in the newsroom by pointing to perceived inadequacies of reporters. To them, reporters were not producing more enterprise news because they did not possess the skills to do so. Thomas himself offered this account. About six months into his stint at the *Bugle*, I mentioned the difficulty reporters were having in doing more enterprise reporting. In response, he said, "Most reporters are not able to think in a sophisticated way about the news," and that those who could not do this "are going to leave." Roy Olden, the city editor, said much the same thing: "Some reporters on my staff simply don't have the skills to do the kind of reporting Thomas wants." Olden expressed frustration at having to ask reporters "sixty questions about every story" and to tell them how to do their jobs. "I want my reporters to be self-reliant. That's the way I was as a reporter . . . [but] some of my reporters are not up to that." Clark Brown, the editor for the cops 'n' courts team, said that many reporters on his team "just don't have the skills . . . they have a difficult time imagining what the story is at the outset and framing it accordingly," and so are inefficient and unproductive.

In a theory of situated learning, Etienne Wenger (1998, p. 185) argues that the "ability to explore, take risks, and create unlikely connections" – essentially, the ability to exercise collective imagination to learn new things – requires a sense of community and belonging. To take the risk of imagining together, individuals must feel that they share a common purpose, that their interests and identities are aligned. The interpretations I have outlined show that reporters and editors at the *Bugle* lacked this sense of belonging. In fact, over Thomas's tenure, reporters felt increasingly separate from the news organization. On their view, Thomas was not one of them (he was incompetent – i.e., not a "good" journalist). Moreover, he, and the news organization generally, lacked commitment to reporters' preferred values and identities. Of course, journalists have long had divided loyalties between their profession and the organizations for which they work. And these loyalties have sometimes conflicted with one another. But what I witnessed at the *Bugle* was more of a radical separation. As they sought to understand the situation that confronted them, reporters and editors drew a stark line between "us" (journalists) and "them" (the organization). These symbolic boundaries made reporters and editors unwilling to explore how they might produce more enterprise and less daily news. As I left the newsroom in August 2006, it was clear that reporters and editors were unwilling to work together on much of anything.

Four months later, in December 2006, the company reassigned Thomas to a smaller newspaper in another part of the country.

Conclusion

Habits are, indeed, hard to break. Routines of beat reporting have formed deep grooves in the practice of journalism. They speak to basic uncertainties in the daily newsgathering process and inform reporters' sense of self. In the case of the *Bugle*, redirecting these grooves took more imaginative resources than reporters and editors were able to muster.

It is important to recognize that Thomas pulled only a single thread from the web of purpose and practice that defines beat reporting. He did not wish to change everything about the way his reporters gathered and reported the news. For instance, he did not tell them to stop serving the public. He did not tell them to stop seeking the truth, hold the powerful accountable, or put aside techniques of verification. In 2005, the Internet had yet to make great demands on news practices. In my time at the *Bugle*, the newspaper's website was little more than an afterthought. Reporters were not asked to make constant web updates to their stories, to write 140-character "tweets," to blog, or to do any of the other things that, very soon, would be required of them. In 2005, Thomas merely asked them to stop attending so closely to the public agencies they covered: stop writing daily "process" stories on city and state politics; stop filling the paper with coverage of daily crime; focus less on city happenings and more on regional trends. To his mind, he had good reasons to ask for these changes. To be sure, not all of his reasons were journalistic. Many of them were market-driven. Still, of the many changes Thomas might have implemented in his newsroom, he asked for relatively few.

Yet reporters and editors found even these changes too much to bear. The changes rubbed harshly against conventional practices. They troubled preferred identities. Most importantly, they exacerbated a longstanding and growing discord in the newsroom. An entire generation of reporters and editors had spent their careers battling against the steady encroachment of commercialization. They perceived Thomas's experiment through this lens – as another effort by management to make more money at the cost of doing good journalism. This lack of trust sowed suspicion in the newsroom, and this suspicion made it difficult for reporters and editors to think creatively about how to solve the problems posed by Thomas's initiative. In the midst of this discord, reporters found comfort in the habits of beat reporting. They may never have figured out how to produce broader and deeper news without attending daily to their beats, but they knew how to produce a daily story.

And that is what they did.

3
Investments

With all the talk in the last chapter of journalists' habits and routines, it can seem that producing the news is a mindless activity. The rules of practice are so engrained that reporters simply and unreflectively follow them. But then I think about the career of R. W. Apple, the celebrated political reporter for the *New York Times*. Bombastic and hypercompetitive, Apple enjoyed a career that spanned forty years. According to many accounts, in that entire time he never failed to let other reporters know that he had scooped them, that he knew more and could write faster, that his rolodex of powerful people dwarfed their own, that he made more money than they did. This attitude understandably made other reporters angry. Trillin (2003) tells the story that, while covering state politics in Albany, other statehouse reporters constantly complained about Apple, so much so that eventually they agreed anyone who mentioned his name would have to put a quarter into a drinks fund. At the same time, Apple was one of the very best political reporters of his generation. He produced more and better stories than almost anyone around. In a memoir, James Reston (1991, p. 317) says of Apple, "He didn't invent the [Vietnam] war but taught a whole generation how to cover it." Such prowess understandably made other reporters alternately envious and admiring. "They realized," Trillin concludes in his profile of Apple, that "upon sober reflection . . . he *was* superior. That was the part that was the hardest to take – that he was so damn good."

Reporters like Apple show that reporting the news is not merely a matter of habit and routine. Apple did not just follow the rules, and he certainly wasn't mindless as he went about his job. Instead, he was strategic, calculated, and improvisational. He arranged, ordered, mixed, and combined the rules of news production as he saw fit. He did it because he could. The rules of practice are not so extensive as to account for every situation, or so codified for it always to be clear which rule applies in what situation. And he did it because he wanted to. He wanted to be the best reporter around, and that meant he had to distinguish himself from other journalists. Eventually, he achieved his goal. His creative manipulation of practice took him to the height of his profession.

Apple's career illustrates an important conceptual point: habits engrained in practice are not simply *rules* journalists follow, they are also *resources* journalists compete with one another to acquire (e.g., Giddens, 1979, pp. 62–4; Sewell, 1992). From the beginning to the end of their careers, journalists work to hone their craft, to garner the appreciation of their peers, to get better jobs, to be paid more. From his earliest days in the profession, it was clear that Apple wished to achieve this sort of distinction. To this end, he expended a great amount of time, energy, and attention on acquiring the necessary skills. He worked his way up through the hierarchy of newspapers, from editor of his high-school newspaper, to the *Newport News Daily Press*, to the *Wall Street Journal*, and, ultimately, to the *New York Times*. Within the *Times*, he had yet another ladder to climb: from the local desk, to Albany bureau chief, to covering Robert Kennedy's 1968 presidential campaign, to, finally, Washington, DC, bureau chief. Along the way, he acquired more skill at producing news and translated this skill into better, and more high-paying, jobs. Apple, like any ambitious reporter, invested his time and energy in acquiring the resources that might lead to greater success.

What has this point to do with change? Suppose that, at the pinnacle of his career, Apple had been confronted with wrenching change of the kind journalism is now experiencing. Naturally he would have been hesitant to give up his investments in the very practices that made his success possible. After all, he spent decades of his life acquiring these resources. He might, this is to say, have resisted change not because he was mired in habit. Whatever else Apple was, he was not mired in habit. Rather, he might have resisted change because he had investments in his practice. From his perspective, the costs of giving up investments in the practices he had mastered might simply have outweighed the benefits of change.

This observation leads to the central theme of this chapter. Much of the resistance to change in newsrooms is not due to a mindless embrace of habit. It is, instead, intentional, strategic, and calculated. Today, it is clear that the future of journalism lies online. But, as every working reporter knows, few, if any, news organizations

actually make a profit from their online ventures, and no news organization has shown that the web can support a staff of any size. Given
these facts, to many mainstream journalists a quick move to the web
seems like a recipe for innovating themselves out of a job. It does not
help that web-based journalism often seems hostile to the very practices they have spent careers mastering. Online journalism seems to
reward the quick update, not the long-form story, the blog post, not
the investigative series. Having honed their skills in a previous age, it
is difficult for journalists to get excited about producing a daily diet
of blog posts, story updates, and breaking news of car accidents and
salacious crimes. Moreover, even if they were happy to produce this
news, they would find little distinction in doing so (except, perhaps,
the distinction of keeping their jobs). There is no Pulitzer Prize for
best blog post of the year.

The argument I am fleshing out here is similar to Clayton
Christensen's (1997) description of the "innovator's dilemma."
Christensen analyzes industries that have been beset by a "disruptive
technology," one so profoundly transformational as to present an
existential threat to established companies. Managers of these established companies fail to adapt to the new environment, Christensen
argues, precisely because they are rational decision-makers. He
observes that new technologies often offer lower profit margins and
are not valued by established customers. If managers are interested in
sustaining current profits and growth, they will quite reasonably fail
to innovate because, at least in the short term, the costs of reallocat-
ing a company's investments to respond to a disruptive technology
often far exceed their benefits. Hence, managers fail to adapt, but,
and this is the dilemma, in failing to adapt they risk the future existence of the company: "The logical, competent decisions of management that are critical to the success of their companies are also the
reasons why they lose their positions of leadership" when a disruptive
technology comes along (1997, p. xiii).

It is not surprising that Christensen's book has circulated widely in
the news industry. Newspaper managers face exactly the conundrum
he describes. Upwards of 90 percent of their revenue comes from an
old technology (print). Their most loyal (read: older) customers are
not fans of the web. And, as yet, there are few profits to be made in
online journalism. The situation in which they find themselves perfectly fits Christensen's dilemma. But in this chapter I wish to expand
the argument further. If we think of journalistic skills as resources
and investments, the same logic applies to reporters and editors.
Journalists face a situation in which they have invested a great deal

of time and energy in acquiring traditional skills. These skills remain highly valued by the profession, by their loyal customers, and by the organizations for which they work. Like everyone else, they realize that the future of news lies in online journalism. But from their perspective they see no reason to embrace that future too soon. Why would they willingly choose to reallocate their investments in favor of new practices whose value remains in doubt?

A Plan to Save *The Herald*

The situation at *The Herald*, a mid-sized urban newspaper, illustrates the role of investments in forestalling innovation in newsrooms. I visited *The Herald* in the summer of 2008. In part, I chose this newspaper because it is one of the few family-owned urban newspapers still around. The Keaton family founded the paper in 1894. Since that time, it has been run by four generations of Keatons, many of whom continue to reside in the city and are active in local civic affairs. Today, the company's portfolio has diversified. It owns television stations and a paper printing company, and has holdings in insurance, real estate, and financial services. But the newspaper remains at its heart, and is seen by the family less as a business than as a key part of its legacy.

I also chose the newspaper because it had a recent history of journalistic excellence. Like most urban newspapers, *The Herald* has seen better days, but, unlike many of those papers, those days at *The Herald* were not that long ago. Until the 1980s, it was essentially a small-town newspaper. It had a small staff of mostly local reporters, a small circulation, and a parochial attitude. But in the early 1980s a new editor "brought the paper into the twentieth century," as one reporter who was around at the time put it. He hired "big city" editors and recruited reporters from across the county. By the early 1990s, the paper was hitting its stride. "These were the glory years of the paper," another reporter told me, a time when the staff mushroomed to 170 people, daily circulation climbed to 144,000, and the paper won a great many awards. Many veterans of those days remain in the newsroom, and they have fond memories of the 1990s. "There was lots of time for projects, bigger pieces," one reporter reminisced. Another recalled that she was sent to Russia as part of a long investigation of a local nuclear power plant. And still another marveled that every four years the paper sent him to New Hampshire to cover the presidential primary. In the late 1990s,

Columbia Journalism Review named the newspaper one of the top ten in the country.

The glory days ended in 2001, when the newspaper had its first ever round of layoffs. These layoffs prompted its long-time editor to quit. The publisher then hired Hank Carlin, a veteran newsman of nearly thirty years who had been an editor at several other newspapers. In the 1990s, Carlin gained a measure of notoriety as an advocate of "public journalism" (e.g., Charity, 1995; Glasser, 1999; Haas, 2007), and he had a reputation as an innovative leader who was willing to take risks. Nonetheless, in the next seven years, Carlin presided over a continually shrinking newspaper. Staff levels declined to fewer than one hundred; daily circulation went down to 88,000. When I arrived in the newsroom in July 2008, evidence of decline was everywhere. Carlin was thinking of giving up color comics in the Sunday paper. He was also in tense negotiations to end the paper's contract with the Associated Press. Days before my visit, the publisher announced that the paper's size would shrink from 48" to a tabloid style 46". The "A" and "B" sections were sometimes combined because the advertising department could not sell out the "B" section. Whole areas of coverage were now being ignored. Once the newspaper covered an affluent neighboring county with a bureau of fourteen reporters and two photographers. The entire bureau was closed in 2007. Once there were four public safety reporters; now there was one. Once there was a "local government" team of reporters; now one reporter covered both city and county government. Once the paper had a strong business section; now that section had been folded into the "B" section, and many of its reporters had been laid off.

All the talk of the paper's "glory days" prompted me to take a look in the archive at a week's worth of coverage in July 1998 – exactly ten years before. The difference, I must admit, was incredible. In 1998, the front page offered about the same number of stories as in 2008 – four to six per day. But in 1998 another four to five local stories often appeared in the front section's inside pages. Moreover, in 1998, the regional or "B" section of the newspaper was humongous. By my count, in the week from July 21 to July 28, 1998, the newspaper offered readers an average of eight original stories in that section, compared with the one or two per day during the same week in 2008. The additional reporting (upwards of fifteen more news stories per day in the "A" and "B" sections) was supported by an enormous amount of advertising. The Saturday auto section in 1998 contained ten pages of auto ads (compared with no pages at all in 2008), and the Sunday paper had over twenty pages of classified ads. On a typical day in 1998, the front section contained four to five full-page display ads. In 1998, the newspaper was lucky to have one such ad, and on many days contained none.

Though *The Herald*'s decline was years in the making, the summer of 2008 marked a critical juncture in its fortunes. At an all-hands staff meeting held shortly after I arrived, the publisher revealed that, in the first six months of 2008 alone, retail advertising was down 8.7 percent, auto ads were down 15 percent, classified ads were down 21 percent, national ads were down 10 percent, and circulation was down 15 percent. These numbers were so grim they prompted a reporter to ask, "Is the newspaper dying?" The publisher paused for an excruciating 30 seconds, obviously chewing over the question, and then said: "We're still the best way to get the message out. I don't think I have a great answer. Are we dying? . . . No . . . But there's no answer. There's no guarantee." Carlin told me that, unless something changed soon, his budget would be slashed by another $800,000 in a few months. This would prompt another round of layoffs in the twenty-one to twenty-five person range. "I'm confident," he said, that "unless we make progress quickly . . . we will lose one-third of our staff in the next six months."

Carlin avoided despair by focusing on his plan to reverse the newspaper's downward course. He told me that the company as a whole had no strategic vision moving forward. To his mind, the Advertising Department in particular was resistant to change, and was of little help in fashioning a forward-looking vision for the company. But the publisher, Lance Keaton, gave Carlin leeway to chart his own course, and that is what he chose to do. In its essentials, his plan was simple. Carlin had taken a look at the numbers and found that, over the past twenty years, circulation at *The Herald* had declined by an average of 1 percent every year. This was true even during the paper's "glory days." The award-winning (and costly) coverage reporters remembered so fondly did nothing to stem the loss of circulation. On the plus side, the Internet had not accelerated the decline either. From these trends, Carlin concluded that he could not save the newspaper. Nothing he did – nothing that had been done in the past two decades – was likely to stop its decline. Borrowing some numbers from the Newspaper Association of America, Carlin gauged that circulation would bottom out at about 60,000 – the newspaper's "natural state" given the size of the local economy. Revenues would inevitably drop along with circulation. Given these facts, Carlin felt he had only one option if he wanted to maintain the newsroom at anything like its current size: he had to replace ever-shrinking newspaper revenue with other revenue streams.

Thus was born what Carlin called his "multi-platform" strategy for saving the newsroom. In the past, most of the newsroom's investments in staff, technology, and processes were devoted to the paper. Moving forward, the newsroom would view the paper as but one "platform" among others for its "products." These other platforms included the web, broadcasting, mobile phones, and other print products. In short order, Carlin planned to siphon resources from the newspaper and put them to work for the newsroom's other platforms. He began to make this transition in 2007, when he convinced the publisher to build a small radio broadcast studio in the back of the newsroom. The idea was to have reporters record 30-second and 1-minute synopses of the news, and to give this content to local radio stations in exchange for half of the advertising revenue. Carlin also reallocated staff – eleven people in total – to produce content tailored specifically to the newspaper's website, and to redesign the website to take advantage of this new content. He had other ideas in various stages of development – from producing new print products, to syndicating content, to creating mobile applications for the newsroom's content. In the future, he surmised, the newspaper would provide about 60 percent of the company's revenues. He planned to make up the 40 percent with these other revenue streams. We "must begin liberating content from the albatross of the failing business model in print," he told me. "Print," he said, "is dead." He called this the "liberation theology" he was introducing into the newsroom.

After months of planning for this shift, Carlin was set to proselytize his new theology to the staff in July 2008, just as I arrived in the newsroom.

The Field of Journalism and the Newspaper

Carlin liked to end his talk of change with his staff by saying, "Our core values will remain the same." By this he meant that, while the newsroom would create new processes to distribute its content across many platforms, its basic values were non-negotiable. Reporters would still produce objective, fact-based news with hard-nosed, shoe-leather journalism. Carlin intended this message to reassure his staff. The newsroom was going through great changes, and would go through more. But the fundamentals of journalism, he argued to his staff, were universal. We will still be journalists, he insisted, doing journalism.

Carlin's intuition to couch change in terms of traditional values was the right one. As we learned in the last chapter, in the midst of change reporters can lose touch with their professional identities. Carlin's invocation of tradition went some way toward reaffirming his staff's sense of self. It also had other benefits. By appealing to time-honored practice, Carlin flattered investments which all journalists have in their craft, but which, perhaps, were felt especially strongly by *Herald* reporters. In the 1980s, editors at *The Herald* launched a conscious strategy to elevate the newspaper's standing within the profession. To do this, they and their reporters sought to acquire and display the kinds of skills – in writing, storytelling, interviewing, and research – that were recognized as valuable within the profession. As one example, they aggressively sought to win journalism prizes. In fact, during the 1990s, it was not uncommon for the newsroom to spend upwards of $50,000 per year just on the applications for such prizes. The result was that the paper became known for its "projects": long, complex, beautifully written and photographed stories that were sure to catch the eye of other journalists. Of course, these stories were expensive to produce. But, in an indication of the autonomy enjoyed by the newsroom in those days, the editor didn't care. He instructed his staff to produce news according to journalistic values, not according to the business needs of the newspaper. What was good for the economic health of the newspaper, or even what their customers cared to read, was less important than journalists' own sense of quality journalism.

As the newspaper gained a reputation in the profession for producing high-quality journalism, it attracted reporters who had similar ambitions. Sidney Culler, the local government reporter, said that when he interned at the newspaper in the mid-1990s he was deeply impressed with the quality of the journalism. He saw the paper as a "mini-*New York Times*," and held its investigative team in especially high regard. To Culler, they were doing journalism as it ought to be done. Eventually, Culler obtained a job at a small-town newspaper, but he always had a desire to get back to *The Herald*. When a position opened a few years later, he jumped at the opportunity. To him, the best part of working at the newspaper during this time was the constant attention to quality and the time and space it allowed him to hone his craft.

Through the 1990s, the newsroom attracted more reporters like Culler, and, once they got there, they tended to stay. In 2008, the average *Herald* reporter had been at the newspaper for fifteen years, but many reporters had worked there for twenty years, and a few could trace their careers as far back as thirty years. This longevity was due in no small part to the fact that *The Herald*'s newsroom is unionized. According to union rules, each reporter accrues years in service within a particular job category (e.g., photography, local news, and so on). If and when layoffs occur, editors have two choices. They may lay off reporters with the fewest years in service across all categories, or they may choose to focus layoffs in one category or another, again starting with reporters who have the fewest years in service. When the first layoffs hit *The Herald*'s newsroom in 2001, the editor took the first path, which meant that the youngest and least experienced reporters were laid off first. After several rounds of such layoffs, only the most senior, experienced reporters remained behind. As the managing editor, Todd Thompson, told me, this meant that the layoffs succeeded in getting "rid of the very same people who could change the quickest" – or, put another way, the layoffs successfully retained people who were, like Culler, most invested in traditional practices.

Few newspapers are unionized anymore, and so few have as many veteran reporters as *The Herald*. But the structure of the profession virtually guarantees most journalists will have, to varying degrees, the same sorts of investments as *Herald* reporters. Until very recently, the typical career path in journalism looked something like the following. A recent journalism school graduate could expect to start at a small-town newspaper, work long hours, make little money, and have very little status in the profession. Over a period of years, she would work her way up through a hierarchy of newsrooms: from the small-town paper to the city paper, from the city paper to the big regional paper. At each stage, she would face the appraisal of other journalists, who would assess whether she "had the goods" and was a "real" journalist. If she passed these reviews, her prestige in the profession would grow, as would her paycheck. Along the way, she would also work her way through a series of increasingly prestigious beats: from the night cops beat to the day cops beat, from the cops beat to the city hall beat, from city hall to the statehouse, and so on. At the end of her journey, she might reach the apex of the profession, the big national daily, with the high pay and high status that distinction bestows. This was not the only career path a journalist might have followed, of course, and not every journalist aspired to work at a big national daily. But most career paths had something like this form: a relatively organized set of steps upwards through the profession. As reporters climbed this ladder, they naturally accumulated a growing investment in their success.

It is worth pointing out that journalism has had this sort of cohesive, internal structure for only a brief time. American journalism is roughly 350 years old. In that entire time, it has been autonomous from other social domains for only about fifty years. In the early days of the American Republic, journalism was a side-occupation of printers (e.g., Humphrey, 1996; Sloan and Williams, 1994). For much of the nineteenth century, it was little more than a satellite of the political party system, and so took its cue from politics rather than from anything intrinsic to journalism (e.g., Kaplan, 2002; McGerr, 1986). Late in that century journalism lost its connection to the party system, only to find itself at the mercy of the economic needs of press barons (e.g., Baldasty, 1992; Schudson, 1978). It wasn't until the 1950s that the profession gained a measure of autonomy from economics and politics (e.g., Schudson, 1995b). Only at this time were reporters able to take their cue more from one another than from other social fields. By the 1970s, journalism had reached what one scholar refers to as its "high modernist" phase – the zenith of its independence from other social domains (e.g., Hallin, 1994). More than at any other time in its history, journalists produced news according to values intrinsic to journalism. As we learned in chapter 1, by the 1980s commercialization was already whittling away at this independence. Even if we assume today that journalism retains a vestige of its autonomy from commercial pressures (and many journalists don't), the profession has been independent for only about fifty years.

Though relatively new, however, the fact that journalism developed a complex inner structure had important consequences. To see these consequences clearly, it helps to borrow a few insights from a "field" theory of journalism.[8] A social "field" is precisely the kind of organized, insular social space which journalism became in the mid-twentieth century. Much like a natural field (think gravity or electromagnetism), at this time a set of "properties," as scientists call them, coalesced in journalism to give it greater integrity and sharpened the boundary between the inside and outside of the profession. These properties are the core values and practices (objectivity, balance, fairness, and the like) referred to by Carlin. In effect, by calling out these values and practices as essential, Carlin was saying that he wished to maintain journalism's integrity even in the midst of profound change. This is not surprising, as Carlin himself had been socialized into the profession at its "high modernist" peak.

Besides setting the boundaries of the field, journalism's properties – its core values and practices – perform other roles. Much like gravity, for instance, in a gravitational field, these values and practices push and pull journalists toward one another. The result of this pushing and pulling is that journalists tend to think and act more like one another than like anyone outside the field. And, as they come to think and act like one another, journalists begin to take their cues for success from other journalists. R. W. Apple's actions, for example, were strongly shaped by his determination to be recognized as a "good" reporter by other journalists. This intense focus on one another made journalism something of an insular, almost myopic profession. In its high modernist days, journalists were concerned more to gain status among other journalists than just about anything else.

There is one key difference, of course, between a social field like journalism and a gravitational field: the individuals in a social field choose to inhabit that space. It is true that journalism's core values and practices push and pull journalists toward one another. But individuals must choose to play the game constituted by these values and practices. If journalism privileges objectivity as a preferred value, for example, then a "good" journalist will embrace the pose of objectivity, if for no other reason than to be recognized as a legitimate journalist by others in the field. In this way, the force exercised by the field is one that journalists freely take on. Why do they do this? The simple answer is that they wish to be successful, and to be recognized as successful by other journalists. But success in a field like journalism is a relative term. A journalist can only be more or less successful compared with other journalists. This fact leads to the development of an internal hierarchy in the field – the kind of structure that allows us, for example, to say a reporter for the *New York Times* is simply *better* than a reporter for the *National Enquirer*. And it is this hierarchy that leads to strategic thinking on the part of journalists. Reporters who wish to climb the ladder of success make strategic investments in the field's preferred practices as a way of distinguishing themselves vis-à-vis other journalists. As they accrue investments in such practices, the practices come to seem more valuable and more worthy of protection.

These insights from field theory help us to see that journalistic practices are not only habits that journalists learn, they are also resources journalists compete to acquire. Reporters at *The Herald* had spent years and sometimes decades acquiring skills recognized as valuable in this field. And, since they were at *The Herald*, it is clear that their investments had, to a great degree, paid off. *The Herald* was a nationally recognized regional newspaper that had won numerous journalistic awards. Journalists understood its newsroom as a place where they could practice their craft with little interference from others. Given these facts, Carlin was right to frame his talk of "relentless and merciless change," as he sometimes called it, in terms of journalism's core values and practices. His reporters had such deep investments in these practices that they might not have understood talk of change in any other terms.

That being said, Carlin was wrong to believe that the newspaper is separate and separable from journalism's core values and practices – that he could disinvest in the newspaper and not at the same time disinvest in journalism. The field of journalism grew up in and around commercial newspapers, and its core practices and values are deeply entangled with this medium. This is easy to show. Think, for instance, of the notion "journalists ought to get the facts right." This is a cardinal value of the field, one that is put into jeopardy daily by the permanency of print: a published error is visible and enduring evidence that a journalist has violated this rule. Because this is the case, newspapers have developed complex processes for ensuring the accuracy of their stories. In newspaper newsrooms, reporters are required to verify every significant fact in their stories, and once the stories leave reporters' hands they travel a circuitous route through a series of editors before they appear in the newspaper. At each step, editors check their accuracy. Print reporters see little distinction between these processes and the underlying value. To them, the processes merely make the value concrete.

Herald staffers were therefore highly skeptical of Carlin's claim that he could take resources away from the newspaper and not jeopardize a highly prized value (for a similar reaction by journalists in another newsroom, see Robinson, 2011). Fewer resources devoted to the newspaper would mean that each reporter would have less time to fact-check their stories. It would mean that fewer editors would read each story. It would mean that the editing process would happen quicker. All of this would inevitably result in more published errors, and therefore in a weaker embrace of the value.

For example, the night before an "all-hands" meeting at which Carlin once again insisted to his staff that he would not jeopardize their core values, Greg Nelson, a twenty-year veteran in the newsroom, was asked to fill in as the night city editor. The regular person was out for some reason and, with all of the layoffs in the newsroom, there simply was no one else to do it. Nelson agreed, but he was deeply chagrined. "I have no training to do this," he told me, and "I shouldn't be doing it." Nelson meant to impress upon me that a good newspaper doesn't have someone with no experience whatsoever serve as the night city editor. Nelson connected this lapse to Carlin's reallocation of resources: "While the newspaper devotes more resources to the web, things like [this] go to the side." Translated: while we devote ourselves to the web, central values and practices of the newspaper are being ignored.

"Watchdog" journalism is another example that illustrates the deep connection between the newspaper and the field of journalism. The notion that journalists ought to hold public officials accountable has been a cherished value in the field since the early 1900s. Since that time, it has been a common way for a journalist to obtain status. Early in their careers, many reporters work on beats with lots of breaking or soft news. They might work the night cops beat, for example, which involves reporting on daily crime stories. Or they might work on a neighborhood beat that has them writing stories about bake sales and PTA meetings. As a reporter gains status in the newsroom, he or she will be given more high-profile beats (e.g., day cops, courts, city hall, the statehouse), and these beats will engage them in doing more watchdog journalism. In other words, news beats are hierarchically organized in part according to the privileged status of watchdog journalism.

Carlin risked destabilizing this hierarchy by taking resources away from the newspaper. For instance, as a cost-saving measure, he combined the city government beat with the county government beat. Simply because of the new beat's size, Culler, the new city/county government reporter, could not do much watchdog journalism. "I'm just spread," Culler told me. "When it comes down to it I have forty hours and I only work those hours." The result: more perfunctory news, less watchdog journalism, and more worry on the part of Culler and other reporters that Carlin no longer valued "quality journalism."

We could recount other examples, but I think the point is made. In framing the newspaper as one platform among others, Carlin missed the fact that the newspaper is not simply a technology. Rather, it is a set of social processes that is entangled with the wider field of journalism. To the extent that journalists have investments in this field, they also have investments in these social processes, and therefore in the newspaper.

A Reinvention of TV Journalism

Compared to the newspaper, *The Herald*'s reporters had many fewer investments in the Internet. It is useful to pause for a moment and put the new medium in perspective. By 2008, journalists had been playing with the Internet for roughly fifteen years. As I detail more fully in chapter 1, in that entire time, online news – at least as practiced by mainstream news organizations – was strongly shaped by the gravitational pull of the newspaper. Even in the most innovative newsrooms, most things associated with online news – from design, to content, to business model – were made to fit the sensibilities, needs, and interests of the newspaper. This meant that, even as talk of change and transformation mounted in the early 2000s, reporters' daily practices changed very little. They continued to cover the same beats, to talk to the same people, and to tell the same stories in much the same ways. As one *Herald* reporter put it to me, "My life has changed only to the extent that I sit in my chair worrying about change . . . and then I do my job." Even in 2008, the only difference the Internet had made for most reporters was that web editors now posted (journalists call it "shoveled") their stories online, usually the night before the stories appeared in the newspaper. Since they had little to do with this process, most reporters ignored the newspaper's website.

This situation might have continued if not for the fact that the process of posting stories online the night before led to a troubling result: the website kept scooping the newspaper. With the stories being posted the night before, readers had access to them earlier, and at a cheaper price (free), than they could get them in the newspaper. In other words, the website was eating away at the value-added of the newspaper. Everyone I talked with recognized the problem, but it says something about the depth of journalists' investments in traditional values and practices that in 2008 – fifteen years after the debut of online news – few newsrooms had addressed the issue.

Carlin had done more with his newspaper's website than most editors. He had insisted, for instance, that his reporters post to blogs long before this became common in other newsrooms, and in fact one of his reporters had won a national award for "best blog" of the year. But even Carlin had done very little to solve the underlying problem posed by the newspaper's website. Like every other news site of a mainstream newspaper, his had been scooping the newspaper for years. Circumstances had changed enough, however, that in 2008 Carlin was intent on solving this problem. As he set about this task, he had a wealth of data at his disposal. Thanks to the power of modern computer databases, he could track and aggregate every movement of every user's experience on his news site. Here is what this information told him. The largest wave of users came to *The*

Herald's news site between the hours of 7 and 8 a.m. A smaller wave of users visited again at noon, and then a smaller one still visited at 5 p.m. After 6 p.m. traffic on the site dropped precipitously, not to pick up again until 7 a.m. the next day. In every instance, most users came to the news site's front page (few arrived via links from other websites), and, perhaps most crucially, most stayed an average of less than 30 seconds.[9] This information told Carlin that most people were visiting the news site at work, and that they generally stayed only long enough to catch the headlines. Throughout the day, they came back briefly to see if anything new had happened but, again, stayed only a short time and rarely clicked through to read beyond headlines. After work, they went home and did not visit the site again until the next morning when they booted up their work computers.

This was a very different way of consuming news than reading a newspaper, and it posed two basic problems for producing online news. First, Carlin had to find a way to update the site's content in the hours just before 8 a.m. This was not done best by posting stories intended for the newspaper at 8 p.m. the night before. Not only did this practice drain energy from the newspaper, it also ensured that the website would be populated by "old news" at the precise moment when its largest audience was searching for the most recent news. The site's content also had to be continually refreshed through the day. Users checked the front page several times a day in search of new information. If the site remained static hour after hour, users would likely stop making these routine checks. Again, the conventional newspaper story was not a good solution to this problem, if for no other reason than that reporters could not produce enough stories to continually refresh the site.

To Carlin, the solution to the first problem seemed obvious: create a new position for a "mobile journalist" who would be responsible for gathering and posting the most up-to-date content before 8 a.m. Carlin assigned Will Thurmond, a veteran cops reporter, to this new position, and Lannie Walsh, a reporter for one of the zoned editions of the paper, as his backup. When I arrived in the newsroom, Thurmond and Walsh had been doing their new jobs for several months. They described their typical day to me like this: every morning, one of them arrived in the newsroom at 6 a.m. and immediately made a round of phone calls to various government agencies (sheriff's office, fire department, police department), checked for breaking news (mostly car accidents), and updated the weather and traffic information. They then headed out to the most promising breaking news story to collect audio and video. At 7 a.m., a newly assigned "web editor" arrived to update the site's content again (primarily weather and traffic) and to assist Walsh and Thurmond in posting any stories they might have gathered while in the field. They usually spent one or two hours in the field, and then returned to the newsroom to write web versions of their stories and post the audio and video they had collected. Thurmond and Walsh then made another round of calls, checked and updated weather and traffic, and, if they had time, followed up on the stories they had covered earlier.

In essence, without intending to do so, they had reinvented local TV journalism. Like TV journalists, Thurmond and Walsh had learned an important lesson: at 6 a.m. no other kind of information is routinely available except weather, traffic, and crime. Government agencies do not open until 9 a.m., and usually do not do anything newsworthy (like hold a meeting) until later in the day. Moreover, few government workers are sitting at their desks ready to be called and interviewed at 6 or 7 in the morning. Thurmond and Walsh talked with dispatchers or listened to automated voice messages during their first round of calls. The occasional early-morning crime or traffic accident was their only hope of gathering substantive news at that time of the day (which is why, as a cops reporter, Thurmond was assigned to the job). But even on these occasions they acted more like TV than newspaper journalists. As they explained it to me, Thurmond and Walsh's first responsibility was to shoot video because video was "sticky" – i.e., it kept people on the site for more than 15 seconds. Thurmond told me that, in the midst of shooting video, he had little time to do anything more than basic reporting. He gave the example of a double homicide he had recently covered. As a cops beat reporter, he would have stuck around the crime scene for a long time. He would have interviewed the detectives and gone door to door in the neighborhood in search of information. As a mobile journalist, he had no such luxury. He had to shoot video of the scene and capture audio quotes from the detective, and then get back to the newsroom to post this material as quickly as possible. These practices put him in direct competition with the TV folks.

Thurmond and other reporters in the newsroom reacted negatively to the fact that the news site essentially mirrored TV journalism. To them, it was a clear indication that standards in the newsroom were declining. During an editorial meeting, Wendy Mahorn, the city editor, expressed dismay as she contemplated the latest data on website traffic. The data showed what Carlin already knew: that users preferred to read weather and traffic information, and they were more likely to click on a story about a sensational crime or accident

than any other kind of story. This prompted Mahorn to say that the
newsroom could continue to fill the news site with this sort of material, but "When does this become pandering?" Others around the
table shook their heads in agreement. Another editor said, "Breaking
news is not always breaking news. A car accident is not breaking
news, unless it impacts a lot of people. That's junk!" Another chimed
in: "What is the website for? Is it to run every accident or to be
something meatier?" Greg Nelson expressed the same feeling in a
conversation. "Reporters were once king" in the newsroom, he said.
Now, they take "a back seat to innovation." He went on, "Just look at
Will Thurmond . . . he was a great cops reporter and now they have
him chasing traffic accidents." Thurmond and Walsh were just as
uncomfortable with what they were doing. Thurmond told me that
a downside of the job was that "It feels like I am doing TV journalism." Walsh said that her main concern was to do "good journalism,"
which is hard when she is asked to cover every traffic accident.

Reporters were also confused, and a bit chagrined, that good print
reporters were asked to compete with TV journalists. Thurmond
said he was happy to learn the new tools, but there was no way he
could do the job as well as TV people. Others in the newsroom
agreed. "We should be sharing resources with local TV stations,"
said Nadia Smith, a reporter for one of the zoned editions. "When
you're a [mobile journalist] you don't have time to check records . . .
to do the basic reporting . . . Our [online] content has definitely gone
down." Bob Alexander agreed, saying flatly that "multi-purposing
is bad . . . I don't care [about mobile journalism] . . . It takes time.
I just 'bang' something out – multi-tasking destroys writing . . . I
can't thoughtfully go through the writing process." He would rather
"spend the time to do a good story." Reggie Jefferson, a columnist
for the paper, brought up the situation of Sidney Culler. Carlin had
him learning how to shoot video. "Why have [Culler] take 'half-
assed' video when he can be doing the city council story really well?"
this reporter asked. It didn't make sense to him. "We are not serving
our readers well." Kate Spelling, a Polk award-winning investigative
reporter, said flatly that "mojo journalism" is bad journalism. "We
already have a TV station . . . they're much more geared up to do
that . . . Making print journalists do all that stuff degrades the quality
of everything."

If they were unhappy about the news site's resemblance to TV,
reporters were even less enthusiastic about Carlin's solution to the
second problem posed by the web. Carlin had only a few options to
keep the news site continually refreshed. He could hire more report-

ers, which due to budget constraints was out of the question. He could post content produced by people outside the newsroom (e.g., bloggers, citizen journalists, etc.), but he worried about the quality of this information. Or he could ask his reporters to post information throughout the day. He chose the third option. As reporters gathered information, he instructed them to post it immediately to the web. We "post it," he told the staff, "when we know it." In the afternoon, reporters were to write a "second day" story – a story that spins events forward beyond the basic daily story – for publication in the next day's newspaper. For example, suppose a reporter is working on a story about an upcoming city council meeting. In the morning, he learns that a controversial development project will be on the agenda for the meeting. According to Carlin's strategy, the reporter should immediately publish this information in a paragraph on the news site and invite user response. He should then keep working the story. Throughout the day, as he uncovers new information, he should continually update this paragraph and respond to user comments. At the end of the day, he should collate the information he has found and write a broader story for the next day's newspaper. To assist his reporters, Carlin hired two new "online producers." These producers were responsible for posting online content – audio, video, etc. – that reporters gathered. If all reporters updated their stories in this fashion, the news site would remain dynamic and fresh.

To reporters, this strategy seemed like another slight to "quality journalism." Business editor Terence Bell's reaction was typical: "I understand the benefit of getting information up fast," he told me. But you have "to worry about [its] quality." Has it been verified? Also, Bell was not convinced that information outside of a story is "worth much." Who would read it? "Only real news junkies." To Bell, information wasn't useful until it was put in context. "Are people going to want to see how the sausage is made?" Business reporter Kent Conrad agreed: "I want to write a story complete. I don't want to hang my reputation on three paragraphs." Bob Alexander, a health reporter, echoed Conrad's point: "I'm not against the incremental 'dribs and drabs' approach to updating stories online," he told me. "But many of my stories are complicated . . . I only want people to see my best work." So he didn't update his stories until he felt they were ready to be read by others. Neither did Stephanie Rodriguez, who told me, "I got into journalism to be a writer, not an information gatherer."

In such comments, we see reporters' investments peeking through. To reporters, quality journalism meant the practice of verifying information; it meant lending context to complicated stories; it meant writing stories "complete"; it meant protecting one's professional reputation by only showing one's best work. In the guise of protecting "quality journalism," therefore, reporters also sought to protect their investments in the craft of journalism. In this posture, they simply refused to update their stories. Online editor Gwen Hulman told me that she had to beg reporters to give her stuff, and even then they were reluctant. "They feel like they are doing TV journalism," she said. She related an example that happened just a few days before. It was the middle of the day and, as usual, Hulman was desperate for new content. At that moment, Patricia Cantwell, the public safety reporter, happened by. Hulman asked Cantwell what she was working on. Anticipating the next question, Cantwell cut Hulman off: "I'm sorry. There won't be a story in 10 minutes," and promptly fled to her desk.

His reporters' worries about the decline of the newspaper puzzled Carlin. The fact that "print is a niche element is not my idea," he told me. It is "part of the reality we are confronting. Print is a rapidly declining niche. It will be smaller, more expensive, and reach a much smaller audience. That is a reality." Moreover, despite what reporters said, Carlin didn't believe he was trying to kill the newspaper. "When I say that we will be reducing commitment to print, I'm not suggesting that we go 90 percent web, 10 percent print. That's insane . . . all I'm suggesting is that we have to find ways to use our resources more efficiently." "We are, and will be, a multi-platform news organization," he said.

Compelled by a sense of urgency ("We make this work or some of us won't be here at the end of 2008," he said at one staff meeting), Carlin forged ahead in the face of his reporters' recalcitrance. In June he put together a group of staff members from across the newsroom to study the issue of how the website might be consistently fed more content. Carlin wanted people on this committee who had little "stake in what's come before," so he intentionally chose no one over the age of thirty or who had been in the newsroom for more than five years. Among the staff, this group became known as the "Gang of 8." Carlin gave the group two weeks to sift through any and all information they deemed pertinent. As they went through this material, Carlin gave them two rules: they could not add to or reduce staff size, and they could not recommend that the company kill the newspaper. The second rule was the harder to follow. To these young people, it was obvious that the newspaper was a dying platform and that the company would be better positioned by getting rid of it. As one member of the group put it to me, "Print is dead, and the quicker we kill it and move on the better."

In early July the group presented its findings. Its report began with the thought, "To efficiently run a newsroom that is dedicated to publishing content online, the deadline model for a traditional morning newspaper must be abandoned." In the traditional model, reporters worked throughout the day and finished stories in the mid- to late afternoon. Copy editors, most of whom worked a 3 p.m. to 11 p.m. shift, then edited these stories for publication in the next day's newspaper. According to the Gang of 8, this model created a bottleneck for the copy desk and denied the website much-needed content. Moving forward, the group recommended a new deadline of noon for most stories and the creation of a universal copy desk that would be staffed earlier in the day. This way, edited content would flow to the website continually throughout the day.

The Gang of 8 presented its report in two staff meetings. At the first meeting, the members of the group sat in a row of chairs facing other staffers. The managing editor and assistant managing editor attended the meeting and sat in the front row of seats. After laying out its findings and recommendations, the group asked for questions. A long pause ensued, then someone in the back of the room asked, "Doesn't this plan make the print product more irrelevant at a time when it is still paying our salaries?" Members of the group did not seem surprised by the question, but none stepped forward to answer it either. After an uncomfortable 30-second pause, someone volunteered: "We don't want to say in any way that we would get rid of the newspaper." This didn't seem convincing to the people in the room. Thompson, the managing editor, added this thought: the industry is in a "death spiral . . . we are looking for efficiencies to respond to this problem – what is coming ahead – before the company demands them." This wasn't exactly an answer to the question, but in a way it said everything. The newspaper was a "problem" and in a "death spiral," while the website constituted "what is coming ahead." The newspaper was yesterday and the news site, by implication, was the future.

The Herald's staff could not argue with Thompson's point. In 2008, more and more people in the industry believed that the newspaper was a dying medium and that the future of journalism lay in online news. But, to *Herald* reporters, the news site was still little more than a "black hole," as one reporter memorably put it, a place where quality journalism went to die. They thought this not because the Internet is inherently hostile to quality journalism. Rather, their attitude stemmed from the way in which the new technology was being stitched into the process of news production. To them, quality journalism meant carefully vetted, richly sourced, well-written, hard news. By this definition, chasing accidents and constantly updating the weather report did not constitute quality journalism. Moreover, quality journalism could not be done when a reporter's attention was divided between taking pictures, shooting video, and recording sound. It could not be done on the fly, piecemeal, or in a simple blurb. Quality journalism took time, skill, and craftsmanship, things that the news site seemed intent on destroying. As one reporter put it, the news site is "not quality journalism . . . I chased fender benders when I started out." And, with this thought foremost in his mind, he simply refused to do what was asked of him: "I don't want to do that anymore."

"Let's *Be* the Newspaper"

As the economic crisis in the news industry grew in 2007 and 2008, Carlin spent more time "managing up," as he put it, than talking to his staff. Lance Keaton, the publisher of the newspaper, was deeply worried. I was not given exact numbers, but several managers told me that, while *The Herald's* profits were still in double digits, they were just barely so. This threshold was important because, if profits dipped below 10 percent, penalties on debt carried by the company would kick in, and Keaton wanted to avoid these penalties. Moreover, the Keaton family was reluctant to offset the paper's losses with gains from other parts of the company. They insisted that the newspaper had to stand on its own, and in 2008 it was nearly on its knees. So Keaton was feeling pressure and was increasingly skeptical of Carlin's strategy. You can imagine why. His editor was asking him to invest a great deal of money he did not have in platforms that had never shown a profit. As Carlin put it to me, he was asking Keaton to forego profits he could make today "in anticipation of future profits." Why should Keaton take this route when, with much less risk, he could downsize the newspaper, earn respectable profits, and prevent an economic calamity? Keaton, Carlin told me, would rather the newspaper "become a small-town paper. He [Keaton] asks every day about cutting sports and is wholly behind cutting [the newspaper's contract with the Associated Press]. He would be fine with a paper that covered government and entertainment." Carlin spent a great deal of time trying to convince Keaton that his strategy was worthwhile. Keaton may not make much money at the beginning, but, Carlin argued, by adopting this strategy, he would position the company to make great profits in the future. When Keaton asked about the time frame for these new profits, Carlin couldn't tell him. Two years? Five years? No one, including Carlin, had a clue. Without this information, Keaton was more inclined to take the profits he knew he could make than to bet on the future profits of online news.

Oddly enough, his reporters agreed with him. From the moment I stepped in the newsroom, reporters were keen to remind me that the newspaper brought in 95 percent of the company's revenue – and that this was not likely to change anytime soon. Given this fact, we "should not disinvest in the newspaper," Steve Kline, a long-time politics reporter told me. "The core audience for the newspaper is older people who do not go online . . . [our] first duty is to keep this audience happy by providing them with quality journalism." When I noted that the future of news did not lie with older people, he agreed, but then said: "[Young] people aren't interested in the news, so why cater to them? Let them grow up, get mortgages and kids . . . they'll come back to the news." For Kline, the key was "not to sacrifice the core mission of reporting [by] trying to go after people who aren't interested."

There is a certain irony in the fact that reporters and the publisher were on the same side of this issue. For decades, journalists had been resisting the encroachment of management into the newsroom. Decrying the "commercialization of news," they fended off any effort to impose economic strictures on reporting. Now, reporters found themselves embracing the fact that the newspaper made money. It is easy to see why they might do this. For them, profitability served as a placeholder for more fundamental values. Kline begins his comment above by observing that the newspaper brings in 95 percent of the company's revenue, but he ends with the thought that "the core mission of reporting" should not be sacrificed. Here, revenues are linked to the core mission of the newspaper. Journalists across the newsroom made the same association. For them, the fact that the newspaper remained profitable indicated not only that print is alive, but that their core values and practices remained relevant as well.

This conflation of the newspaper with privileged values of journalism comes across most fully in conversations that took place between members of a "content committee" Carlin formed in the days after the Gang of 8 released its report. Carlin created the content committee to address the question "If you had a blank page, what kind of content would you put into it?" His idea was to keep momentum in the newsroom moving forward by linking conversations about process initiated by the Gang of 8 with new ideas about content. Unlike the Gang of 8, which Carlin filled with young people, all but one of the nine people on the content committee were veteran journalists. Carlin gave them ten days to complete their assignment.

To see clearly how journalists conflate the newspaper with "quality journalism," it is helpful to relate this committee's initial conversation in some detail. Reggie Jefferson, a long-time columnist and informal chair of the committee, began its first meeting by reiterating the group's charge: "If you had a blank page, what kind of content would you put into it?" LeAnne Butler, a reporter for one of the newspaper's zoned editions, immediately responded with "local, local, local." This prompted Bob Alexander to say, "hyperlocal is a charged word" because it implies the use of citizen journalists, and that immediately raises the specter of layoffs. Alexander would like the group to identify "types of stories that the paper can dominate. BIG stories . . . analysis . . . that is our franchise." Brett Williams, a sports photographer, agreed: "We need to dedicate our best reporters to print . . . we need depth, a focus on the best work possible . . . we need more 50-inch stories. No one else does that." Caesar Martin, a photographer with over forty years in the business, chimed in: "We have forgotten that we are the only newsgathering operation in the city. We are trying to be radio, the web . . . *let's be the newspaper.*" This declaration made the group quite animated, and people began to talk over one another. The words poured out of Jefferson:

> We are not spontaneous anymore. We are stale . . . We need big headlines, big pictures, staying on top of the news . . . We are chasing TV by following car accidents . . . We've become over balanced in the direction of crime . . . [We should] shift back coverage to government and politics . . . It's one of our basic duties . . . We do not routinely cover government meetings . . . Maybe our future is as a prestige brand . . . If you really want to get the full, deep story, come here. Maybe that's what we should strive to be. Our niche is as the prestige brand of news.

As Jefferson ended his spiel, Jan Evans, a reporter for the local section of the newspaper, piled on: "The newspaper has been killing itself by writing its own obituary . . . The print product is the most important product . . . We're playing someone else's game with the web [and] TV . . . We need to capitalize on our strengths." Jefferson ended the meeting with this thought: the problem the newspaper faced was a "revenue issue, not a readership issue."

Over the next week, as they met in conference rooms over lunch, members of the committee kept returning to this theme: the print product is valuable – it brings in 95 percent of the company's profits after all – therefore it should be saved at all cost. As they talked, it became clear that they were concerned as much with the durability of their values and practices as with the newspaper's profitability. All the talk of "big" and "deep" stories, of "analysis" and "basic duties," of the newspaper as a "prestige" brand, was code for the values and practices privileged in the field of journalism. "Let's be the newspaper!" essentially meant, "Let's be journalists!"

A day after its first meeting, I caught up with the one young staffer who had been assigned to the committee. Li Penh was one of the two online producers whose job was to assist reporters in posting their content to the web. Like most of the young people in the newsroom, she told me that she "doesn't have an investment in the newspaper" and felt that it "wasn't the future of journalism – so why are we devoting resources to it?" She would much rather talk about different ways of presenting information on the web. Penh did not say a word during the content committee's first meeting. She said that, while she "had heard all the criticisms in small doses at staff meetings," hearing it in such a concentrated fashion "was a bit overwhelming." That night, she went home, listened to Michael Jackson, and had a good cry.

The next morning, Jefferson stopped by the cubicle I had been assigned in order to apologize for what he called the "venting" of the day before. But then he said, "I am a writer. That's what I do. I'm self-selected to do that. The management has told us that writing is no longer enough. But I'm sorry. It's what I do. If they don't value writing, I'll find someplace that does." He and the others on the committee carried this sensibility forward through the rest of their meetings. At the group's second meeting, for instance, Martin reiterated that "No one who has a stand-alone news site is making money," so *The Herald* had to do everything possible to save the newspaper. This prompted Kent Conrad to say, "In the war between people who spend three minutes on the web and thirty-five minutes reading the newspaper, it's a no brainer." Jefferson liked this so much he put it up on the white board. At the end of the group's third meeting, someone asked how they were going to relate their work to Carlin's insistence that the web is the future. "Carlin is going to ask, 'What have you got for me on the web?' and our reply will be 'More newspaper?'" I had been asking myself just this question as I sat in the corner taking notes. But posing the question only led the group to reaffirm its commitment to the newspaper: "Print pays the bills, so it must be our most important product"; "We can do this . . . whether or not it sells a bunch of papers we can look ourselves in the mirror and say that

we are serving an important public mission"; "We have to preserve
our core mission . . . if we don't do anything else we need to do that."
After all, "if we're not doing that, what are we doing?"

The content committee's final report reflected these commitments.
It began with a list of "critical content areas" that, as the group put
it, "absolutely have to be covered": local government, politics, international and national news, and investigative reporting. The group
argued that crime news should be de-emphasized, and encouraged
the newsroom to begin thinking of the newspaper as the "cream" of
the organization. "As the web increasingly becomes the place where
people go to read digests and check headlines quickly," the group
asserted, "many of us felt that print's future might be as the 'class
act,' for lack of a better phrase, of our operation. The print edition
should become the medium for our longer investigative pieces, analysis, commentary, and other kinds of content that show off our local
expertise." Whatever is done, the report concluded, "The last thing
we can afford to do, as an organization, is to take away more and more
print content and give our print subscribers more excuses to leave."

In interpreting their reaction to Carlin's "multi-platform strategy,"
it is tempting to conclude that *Herald* staffers were simply incapable
of thinking outside their habitual practices. There is something to this
notion. Certainly, *The Herald*'s staff felt some of the same unease and
ontological threat as the *Bugle*'s staff. But reactions at *The Herald* had
more of a calculating, strategic flavor. Reporters kept coming back
to this basic argument: since the newspaper brought in most of the
company's revenue, their values and practices were still valuable, so
why change? In making these claims, it is apparent that they resisted
Carlin's strategy not because it challenged their sense of self, but
because they simply saw no purchase in it. On the one hand, moving
to the web seemed to be a good way to innovate themselves out of a
job: "You have to maintain your core audience . . . the mantra is 'the
web is the future' but Joe Schmoe in Koot City isn't on the web . . .
a lot of people are not web first." At the end of the day, this reporter
said, "You have to come back to the barebones fact that the newspaper makes money." Given the fact that the newspaper pays the
bills, an editor told me, wouldn't it be more sensible "to shore up the
newspaper to staunch the tide of readers leaving . . . then . . . wait two
to five years" to see how things are going. On the other hand, to their
professional eye, online journalism did not amount to much more
than chasing accidents and updating the weather. "What I need,"
Chad Potter, the higher education reporter said, "is something more
challenging than doing the same thing day after day." Like most

reporters at *The Herald*, Potter saw himself as a writer. As a writer, he valued depth over speed in his reporting. "I don't just want to start a conversation. I want to find things out and tell people about them . . . I value the old system." Potter admits that he "can't argue with the idea of putting out lots of bits of information, it's just not why I got into the business or what I want to do . . . What if we just tried to be the very best newspaper we can be?" he finally said. "That's a much lowered aspiration for ourselves . . . but what if we did that? Would that be so bad?"

"Still a Newspaperman"

To the extent that he pushed against these arguments, many of Carlin's reporters began to see him as a threat to their investments in "quality journalism." But they misread their boss. Carlin was just as invested in the field's preferred values and practices as anyone in the newsroom. This investment began to show through as the weeks went by. Toward the end of my time in the newsroom, I stopped by Carlin's office to chat. He had just returned from another meeting with the publisher, at which he had defended his strategy for change yet again. He was tired, physically from the exertion required to move his staff and publisher, and mentally from the mounting pressure to show results. For some reason, at that moment I was struck by the fact that I hardly ever saw him in the newsroom. Long-time reporters at other newspapers I had visited told me of times when the editor would stop by their desks, ask what they were working on, and even offer suggestions for making their stories better. I told Carlin that this sort of interaction seemed to be rare these days. He sat back in his chair and replied, "I can't tell you the last time I got to think about the journalism." All his time these days was spent budget cutting, reorganizing the newsroom into new boxes and charts, and "managing up." I asked him if he missed it, to which he replied, "Of course, of course . . ." After a moment's pause, he turned to his e-mail.

I don't know if our conversation had anything to do with it, but that night Carlin posted a new entry to his blog on the newspaper's website. It was titled "Still a Newspaperman." It is worth reproducing in its entirety:

I am a newspaperman.
For some unexplainable reason, I am compelled to say that tonight.
Something is coming, some turn in the media universe, a turn in the

future of my newspaper. A turn that will mean the end of me, of us. There will be reporters. Editors. Something called online producers and multi-media coordinators. Mojos. Slojos and Nojos. Bloggers, froggers and twitters. But there won't be newspapermen.

At 58, I am among the last of a dying race. And what a race it was.

An American archetype.

A newspaperman was a writer. An author. The true, first voice of history.

A newspaperman chronicled the life of his times on old Remingtons with faded ribbons.

A newspaperman wrote on copy paper, one story in one take. If he wanted a copy, he used carbon paper. If it didn't sing, it was spiked.

A newspaperman edited with pencils and always had a ready stack, freshly sharpened, at the start of every shift.

A newspaperman smoked at his desk. And if the managing editor wasn't paying too much attention, he might steal a drink, too.

A newspaperman knew how to eat well and finish off the meal with a stiff drink and a fine cigar – all on the company dime.

A newspaperman wore black slacks, a bit worn. A short-sleeved white shirt and a thin black necktie. A newspaperman owned one pair of black wingtips for his entire career.

A newspaperman had nicknames, raunchy, rude and unashamedly affectionate nicknames, for all of the linotype operators in the basement. A newspaperman reveled in the composing room heat, the smells of melted lead and oily black ink. But the newspaperman was most at home in the newsroom. A loud, smoky, smelly place. Wire machines. Real phones with loud rings. The morning news meeting held in the men's room, the last two stalls on the right, each editor doing his business while conducting business.

The newsroom was a place of boisterous rough housing, crude jokes and tough insults, none taken too seriously, unless they were taken seriously, in which case there might be a bit of a ruckus, maybe a swing or two.

And the characters. The copy editor who barked like a dog. The old city editor who ate reheated fish for lunch. The former war correspondent, hobbling around on one leg, the other lost to drink, not combat.

The newsroom was no place for the meek. The young newspaperman knew that when the managing editor threw a coffee cup at his head, the proper recourse was to duck. There was no HR department ready to take a complaint.

The older newspapermen had their heroes. Ben Franklin. John Peter Zenger. Horace Greeley. William Randolph Hearst. Joseph Pulitzer, maybe. William Allen White certainly. And because he had the heart of a newspaperman, Edward R. Murrow and, later, maybe Walter Cronkite.

For the aspiring newspaperman, heroes were the veterans who welcomed him into the newsroom, all the while expecting he would stay quiet, pay his dues and eventually prove himself under fire. The brightest, most ambitious, most talented young newspapermen were grateful for every day they were able to work next to these great, principled and talented men.

Of course, they were not all men. And in this politically correct world, there are some who think the term "newspaperman" is inherently sexist. But the greatest newspaperman with whom I ever worked was [a woman]. Don't ever tell me [she] isn't a newspaperman. In our world, it was the newspaper that defined us, not gender.

A newspaperman knew the meaning of a deadline. He felt a chill when the presses rumbled at midnight and would look for a reason to be in the press room, slipping an early run paper from the conveyor to give the front page a quick look and maybe also to see his byline in print.

Newspapermen worked hard and played hard. The bartender at the dive across the street knew how many beers each reporter could consume between editions. And after the last edition went to press, the bar lights would be turned up just enough to let the newspapermen read those papers pulled fresh from the press.

The newspaperman was respected in the community. There was a mystique, a glamour that really didn't exist but which the newspaperman happily cultivated. In the movies, the editors were Cary Grant. Or Clark Gable. Or Jack Webb. Or Humphrey Bogart, the greatest of all.

The young newspaperman wanted to be Bogie, standing in the press room, screaming into the phone, "That's the sound of the press, baby." The young newspaperman aspired to challenge authority, defend the defenseless and right wrongs. If he was a Don Quixote with a pen, his windmills were politicians, bureaucrats, crooks and thugs. He thought of his job as a calling and truth was his holy grail.

The old newspapermen have died or are dying. One of my great mentors . . . passed away just a week or two ago. The younger, my generation, are fading, too, facing a future in which journalists serve products and platforms, not communities and their newspapers. The young turks have become the old farts. We pray at the old altars. We worship the old gods. The new media moguls have their shiny new religion. And our passing is seen by them as both timely and just.

But there is more to be lost than warm, rosy recollections. It's not all about nostalgia.

No instrument will ever serve the public interest so relentlessly as the daily newspaper. New media will successfully distribute data and information. "Communities of interest" will develop around niche products. And while print newspapers will survive to serve a small, elite audience, they never again will serve the larger geographic communities that gave them life and purpose. Democracy will have to find a new public square.

Even as I try to articulate a coherent and meaningful future for my newspaper and my craft, even as I struggle to innovate, to experiment, to manage a frightened workforce, I weep for what is lost. Oh, I still hang on to the trappings. The fedora. The rumpled raincoat. I have the aging wingtips and 25-year-old ties. My battered old typewriter can still churn out memos. But the life I aspired to, that has defined me for nearly 40 years, is going, is mostly gone.

It is a sad thing. And tonight, I find myself mourning the fading, disappearing American newspaperman, the bison of the information age. The wooly mammoth and, bless us, the dodo.

Tomorrow I'll try to think again about what happens next.

Herald reporters weren't quite sure how to take this elegy to newspapers, coming from a boss who constantly told them "print is dead." Some of the younger reporters smirked, saying that Carlin's description of journalism sounded like a bad 1950s movie. Others noted with some irony that Carlin wasn't old enough to have been a reporter during the time he described. Still others thought in organizational terms. Was Carlin going to quit? My own sense was that Carlin was letting his investments in journalism show through. Like his reporters, he fervently believed in his profession. He saw his work less as a job than as a mission. He didn't like the language of "innovation" and "platforms" and "products" anymore than they did. He preferred a journalist who hit the streets, who told important stories straight without pulling punches. He liked to think of himself as a writer and author. He lamented the loss of loud, rambunctious newsrooms in which "cub" reporters stayed quiet and paid their dues. At the same time, the post also showed that Carlin saw the future, and it promised to reduce the value of his cherished practices. Like many journalists, he was conflicted about this transformation. Carlin saw it as his duty to lead his newsroom into the future, but he also embraced the values and practices that had been central to his own success. This blog post shows him searching for a way to survive the transition while retaining his investments in traditional practices.

Two months after I left the newsroom, in late September 2008, the budget cuts Carlin had feared came down. They were as bad as he had forecast: $800,000 from the newsroom's budget, which meant twenty-seven staffers from the newsroom. Carlin announced the cuts in an impromptu newsroom meeting. When he came to the end of the list of names to be let go, he added his own. He was stepping down as editor of *The Herald*. "I resigned," he later told me, "because

I just couldn't put my name on the paper that will be left after these devastating cuts." With him went his multi-platform strategy for change. Eventually, *The Herald* launched its new website, but three years after my visit, reporters still gather and report the news in much the same way they always have. They cover the same beats, talk to the same sorts of people, and write the same kinds of stories. Reporters' investments in traditional practices remain intact. The newspaper, in other words, is still the newspaper.

4

Definitions

John Paton is like many news managers these days. Hired in January 2010 as CEO of Journal Register, a company that owns eighteen daily newspapers strewn across Connecticut, Pennsylvania, and Michigan, Paton is convinced that the days of the newspaper are numbered. Borrowing a line from Clay Shirky, he said at a "news summit" conference, "The print model is broken . . . What will work in its place? Nothing . . . You don't transform the broken."[10] Paton believes newspapers have to build something new – and do it fast. To him, this conclusion seems obvious, "but many in our industry just don't get it." Why? "Fear, lack of knowledge and an aging managerial cadre that is cynically calculating how much they *don't* have to change before they [reach retirement]." If we are to survive, he declared, we must "stop listening to newspaper people. We have had fifteen years to figure out the web, and as an industry we newspaper people are no good at it. No good at it at all." Get rid of the newspaper people, and put the "digital people in charge – of everything."

The last two chapters lend credence to Paton's view. Journalists tend to conflate the newspaper with journalism, and they often react with moral indignation when their bosses do not honor their standards of quality. They can also become confused even by relatively small changes and are often suspicious of their bosses' motives. They are wedded to habit and tradition, and they are risk averse. Sometimes, they refuse to adopt new practices for no better reason than that it isn't in their personal interest to do so. Given all of this, it is not hard to understand why Paton wants to get rid of "newspaper people."

At the same time, it is important to acknowledge that many journalists, especially in recent years, have become champions of change.

The crisis in journalism has become so deep, it has dislodged many journalists from their habits and caused them to reconsider their investments. Paton himself is a long-time journalist. He started out as a copy boy and worked his way up the organizational chart from reporter to editor – and now finds himself an agent of change. Many other journalists have had the same experience. It seems that every newsroom around the country has its own experiment in news production, and journalists are actively participating in these efforts. In most places, reporters who might have resisted such efforts have been fired or have quit. In fact, "newspaper people" are leading many of Paton's own initiatives at Journal Register.

And yet real change – on the scale Paton and others yearn for – has not happened. It hasn't even happened at Journal Register. On January 20, 2011, I visited dailylocal.com, the online news site for Journal Register's *Daily Local News* of Chester, Pennsylvania. On this day, the front page of the site featured stories about the weather, local high-school basketball, a car crash, the borough council's vote on a wastewater facility, and the court case of a homeless man accused of strangling three women. On the same day, the *New Haven Register* (nhregister.com), another Journal Register newspaper, located in New Haven, Connecticut, had stories on Senator Joe Lieberman's resignation announcement, a kidnapped baby, a crime spree, the city payroll, and a state healthcare board hearing. Admittedly, this is no scientific sample, and perhaps these newspapers are still in the early days of their transformation. Still, I think it is telling that we could have read the same newspapers on any day in 1970 and found a similar mix of stories. Notwithstanding Paton's eagerness for change, the routine, daily news stories that have characterized journalism for decades, seems to be essentially unaltered in his newsrooms. This is no aspersion on Paton. The same is true for most every newspaper and newspaper website across the country.

This situation presents us with a new puzzle. In the past two chapters, we witnessed journalists *resist* change. Increasingly, it appears that change refuses to come *even when news managers and journalists expressly intend* for it to happen. How can this be? How can it be that the status quo remains even when journalists prefer otherwise?

This is the puzzle I want to tackle in this chapter. As a start toward an answer, I begin with anthropologist Clifford Geertz's famous distinction between culture as a "model of" and "model for" reality (1973, p. 94). Geertz argues that culture acts like a "model for" reality when it serves as instructions for how to accomplish a goal. A blueprint for a house is literally a conceptual model for how to build a house. But culture also has a "model of" dimension. A blueprint for a house not only describes how to build a house, it also offers a definition of what a house is (it has four walls, a kitchen, bedrooms, and so on). The blueprint, in this sense, tells us what counts as a house. Linguist John Searle (1969) refers to this "model of" role of culture as its "constitutive" dimension. He observes that practices like marriage or a trial (or building a house) have embedded within them "constitutive rules" that take the form "X counts as Y in context C" (quoted in D'Andrade, 1984, p. 91). Such rules, he argues, bring into being the very reality they name by determining what counts as what in their particular social domain.

Journalism contains a constitutive rule. This rule is evident when we consider such everyday objects as a reporter's notebook. Among other things, the notebook presumes that a journalist is someone who gathers information (hence the need for a notebook). It assumes that a journalist must collect information from a source (most often, someone who possesses newsworthy information) and deliver it to a consumer (someone who might find the information useful, but otherwise would not learn of it except for the efforts of the journalist). In this sense, the reporter's notebook enacts a definition of what journalism is: it is the act of filtering information obtained from one group (or source) and disseminating it to another (the audience). Or, more conventionally, it is the act of gatekeeping. This constitutive rule serves as a background context that lends meaning to the reporter's notebook. To feel this rule at work, simply attend a city council meeting with and without a reporter's notebook and compare the difference in the way that others respond to your presence.

The constitutive rule of journalism-as-filter anchors journalism to tradition simply by defining what counts as an instance of the practice. It does this in two ways.

First, not everything that might be done by journalists can be justified as an act of filtering information. Take the practice of moderating a conversation. Many advocates of online journalism argue that facilitating conversations between users is a principal role for journalism in an online environment. But, to many journalists, it is difficult to justify facilitation as an act of journalism. After all, what does it have to do with getting information from sources and disseminating it to audiences? When they find themselves in this situation, journalists can become cognitively stuck. It is not that they intend to resist change. Rather, it is that they simply do not know how to go on. Put another way, the impediment to change may not be, as we have seen in the past two chapters, normative ("We shouldn't do

X"), epistemological ("I don't know how to do X"), or strategic ("X is not in my interest to do"). It may be ontological: ("What is X and why would I do it?").

In a recent essay, Ann Swidler (2006) articulates a second way that a constitutive rule like "journalism is a gatekeeper of information" anchors the field to tradition. "The need to engage one another," she observes, "forces people to return to common structures." She means by this that, even when people prefer to act differently, they still need to interact with one another. Constitutive rules coordinate these interactions by telling the participants what counts as what. In the absence of alternative rules, constitutive rules persist because people would not know how to go on without them. To the extent that individuals engage in practices that reproduce constitutive rules, they anchor themselves to tradition even if they wish to do otherwise.

In the case of journalism, there is no more routine interaction than that between reporters and sources. Every day, and often all day, reporters gather information from sources. The assumption that journalists serve as gatekeepers to the news (and, by extension, to public discourse) structures these interactions at every step. It is the reason that sources seek out reporters, and it is the reason that journalists work hard to weigh the relative newsworthiness of the information they receive. After all, what kind of gatekeepers would reporters be if they simply published all the information they received? So long as reporters meet sources, they reproduce the constitutive rule "journalism is a gatekeeper of information." This helps to explain why fundamental aspects of journalism may remain intact despite the explicit intentions of journalists. Even when they prefer to change, the filtering rule informs their daily practices, and so anchors the field to traditional definitions of journalism and its purpose.

Viewed through the lens of constitutive rules, it appears that Paton may be wrong: kicking the newspaper people out and putting the digital people in charge may not bring about the change he desires. Rather, constitutive rules may anchor journalism to tradition regardless of the intentions of newspaper and digital people alike.

Superblogging at the *Cedar Rapids Gazette*

An initiative launched at the *Cedar Rapids Gazette* illustrates this point. Several years ago, Chuck Peters, CEO of Gazette Communications (owner of the *Cedar Rapids Gazette*), began an effort to fundamentally transform the *Gazette*'s newsroom. Though he does not have a background in journalism, Peters is a lot like Paton.[11] Peters trained as a lawyer, and his previous work experience included a stint as president of Amana Refrigeration, where he worked on mergers and acquisitions. It was this experience that initially brought him to the attention of the Gazette communications board, which wished to consolidate the different pieces of the Gazette Company, and to pursue new acquisitions of media properties. But, like Paton and other news managers, once he delved into the numbers, Peters realized that the newspaper's fortunes were quickly worsening. At the time, the *Gazette* was doing pretty well. It was losing 1 to 2 percent circulation every year – in 2009 its Monday to Friday circulation was about 57,000, and that on Sunday, 71,000. But being privately owned, and with a manageable debt load, its profit margins remained in double digits. To Peters, however, what mattered was the trend line. The *Gazette* may have been dying more slowly than other newspapers, but it was still dying.

Initially, Peters had no firm sense of how to change this situation. But in 2001 he began serving on a "Systems Committee" of the Newspaper Association of America (NAA). During this committee's meetings, he told me, "I came to the conclusion that the industry was stuck in 'packages' – ads, editorial, online . . . Everything was locked down into these silos." This thought led him to an epiphany: the way forward was to separate content production (reporting the news) from products (the newspaper). Peters believed that, if reporters were freed from the constraints of distribution platforms, they could be much more imaginative about how to shape and disseminate content. When he raised the idea at the NAA, Peters recalled that he got a "violent reaction" from journalists. But the notion stuck with him, and in 2003 he began to hire new people to help him flesh out this vision.

Steve Buttry was one of those people. By May 2008, when Peters hired him as the new editor of the *Gazette*, Buttry had been a reporter, an editor, and a writing coach for over thirty years. His most recent job had been director of tailored programs at the American Press Institute (API). In that role, he participated in API's "Newspaper Next" project (newspapernext.org), an effort launched by the institute in 2005 to develop new business models for the industry. Adapted in part from Clayton Christensen's theory of business innovation, "Newspaper Next" aimed to provide news managers with tools and processes to help them find and exploit new business opportunities. In line with Christensen's argument that fundamental disruption must be met with fundamental change, "Newspaper

Next" encouraged news managers to think far outside the traditional newspaper model for new revenue streams. Just as one example, the project advised news managers to build platforms for community conversations and sell advertising across the aggregated audiences that followed. Much of what Buttry learned from this project seemed congruent with Peters's ideas. So, when they met in 2007, the two felt an immediate affinity for one another.

Upon his hiring, Buttry knew that his title as "editor" would be short lived. The new newspaper, he surmised, would need something different from a traditional editor. Just how different became apparent when, in August 2008, he released "A vision for the *Gazette*'s future," a memo that outlined a new direction for the newspaper.[12]

Peters's original idea of separating content from platform lay at the heart of this vision. Buttry proposed to create an "Information Content Enterprise" (ICE), a new, wholly separate organization within Gazette Communications. This organization would be "committed to strengthening community in Cedar Rapids and Iowa City and providing information in a variety of forms directly to the public and to client products." ICE formally separated content production at the *Gazette* from the company's newspaper and news site. In working for ICE, reporters would no longer write for the newspaper. In fact, they would no longer be reporters. In Buttry's vision, they would be "superbloggers," individuals assigned to produce content on a particular topic area.

As one example, suppose that the *Gazette* created a superblog oriented to news and information about the University of Iowa Board of Regents. Buttry imagined that this superblogger would produce a continuous stream of content about this subject. She would also link to, aggregate, and curate content produced by "trusted sources," people who would typically be individuals passionate and knowledgeable about the board. And she would engage in conversation with the larger community of people around the board who, while not passionate enough about the subject to produce content, would be interested enough to stay engaged. Together, trusted sources and interested others would form a core community around the Board of Regents, and the superblogger would serve this community.

Working for ICE, superbloggers would post content about their topics in a continual stream on a blog. ICE's clients – including the newspaper and the news site but potentially clients outside the company as well – could then pull content from the blogs and package it in whatever form fit their needs. ICE would enter into service agreements with each client. These agreements would stipulate terms of use and the requisite fees for using the content. Initially, Buttry imagined that ICE would be composed of three core content teams: watchdog, sports, and life and culture. A visual team of superbloggers and a data team of "content wranglers" (working on interactive databases) would assist the core teams.

Of course, with no newspaper to edit, Buttry could no longer hold the title of editor. Instead, he conjured a new title for himself: "information content conductor." In a blog post, Buttry described his new role in this way:

> My new title sounds odd at first (yes, to this old editor, too), but each word tells you something about what we are doing:
>
> Information. We will continue providing factual, independent news and information for the community. While the tasks, presentation and means of delivery will change, integrity and truth will remain the core of everything we do.
>
> Content. The kind of content we provided in the newspaper was pretty simple when I started my journalism career in 1971: stories, columns, editorials, lists and photographs. Graphics became a big deal in the 1980s. The future of content is far more diverse: all that as well as databases, videos, audio, slideshows, text messages, blogs, tweets, interactive multimedia, comments, questions, live chats, interactive maps and more that we can't yet imagine.
>
> Conductor. As much as I have loved the title *editor,* it doesn't describe what I will be doing. Maybe the title will change someday, because I know the work will change as this organization and my job evolve. But for now, *conductor* seems the most accurate term. As a musical conductor does, I will be orchestrating the work of creative people. As a railroad conductor does, I will interact with the public to provide an orderly, satisfying experience. As an electrical conductor does, I need to carry energy in the staff and the community.

Not surprisingly, these new names met with some derision both inside and outside the newsroom. In an online comment, one wag asked if Buttry's new title came with a special hat. But behind the new language lay a strategic vision for a new kind of news organization. This vision had several elements.

A first is the notion that news companies had to be more efficient. Over several decades, many news companies had become unwieldy. For example, Gazette Communications is a relatively small news operation. Nonetheless, at the time of my visit, it printed no fewer than six niche publications and a daily newspaper, managed six websites, and owned a television station and a commercial printing operation. This sprawl produced great inefficiency. The company's niche publications often sought to attract the same audience with the same content, and different parts of the company often duplicated resources. It was not unusual, for example, for several of the company's TV reporters to find themselves standing next to several of its print reporters at a big Iowa state Hawkeyes football game. The sprawl also made it difficult to create shared metrics for success, which prevented the company from knowing if any of the products were meeting company goals. By separating ICE from products, Buttry imagined that the company could begin to get its product house in order.

A second element had to do with the company's content strategy. For several years, the *Gazette* had been trying to go "digital first" – that is, to produce content for its news sites first and serve the newspaper second. But its efforts had met with little success, mostly because traditional routines and workflows were so strongly embedded in the newsroom. Buttry believed that the ICE structure might be more successful. Within ICE, superbloggers would no longer produce content for the newspaper – or for any other platform, for that matter. This radical decoupling of content from platform, Buttry argued, would allow the company to truly become digital first. To demonstrate how this might work, he gave the example of the traditional court story. In the past, he told me, the court reporter would write a story based on negotiations with her editor about the amount of space available in the newspaper, the deadline by which the editor needed the story, and so on. At the end of the day, the online editor might pull the resulting story and place it on the news site. Within ICE, a superblogger could live blog the story all day, link to other information, and curate the best of what was on the web at the same time. As this happened, the online editor could pull paragraphs as needed from the blog to give online readers a constantly updated stream of information. At the end of the day, the newspaper editor could pull the most recent content together into a second day story for the newspaper.

A third element of Buttry's vision concerned the use of metrics to drive content production. Becoming digital first meant that the company would have a wealth of data at its disposal for tracking user movements on the site. ICE would allow news managers to put these data to good use. For instance, suppose that the data showed the most read stories in the newspaper were about dogs. In the past, norms of newsworthiness shared by journalists would prevent news managers from taking advantage of this knowledge. No self-respecting journalist would fill the newspaper with news about dogs.

But in ICE reporters would not work for the newspaper. If the editor of the newspaper discovered that news about dogs sold more copies, he could simply add this to his service agreement with ICE. Because it was bound by its service agreement with the newspaper, ICE would be obligated to provide more coverage of dogs – whether journalists liked it or not.

The most important element of Buttry's strategic vision had to do with revenue generation. Like other news managers, Buttry realized that the company had to find new revenue streams to replace revenue lost by the newspaper. ICE proposed to accomplish this by making each of the company's components a revenue generator. Take, for instance, the marketing department. In the past, its primary responsibility was to market the newspaper to potential advertisers. Under ICE, it would retain this responsibility, but it also would be freed to solicit external clients. For example, it might become a marketing consultant for local small businesses, helping these businesses put up web pages, devise social media marketing strategies, and the like. The same logic would hold for copy editors. In the past, copy editors were charged with editing the newspaper. Under ICE, they would still do page layout for the newspaper, but they would also be free to seek business, as one example, from a local restaurant that needed help publishing its new menu, or, as another, a local retailer that wished to put out a catalog. In the same way, every *Gazette* unit would be required to solicit external clients, and so make a contribution to the company's overall bottom line.

In terms of revenue generation, however, the real innovation of ICE lay in the activities of superbloggers. Buttry imagined super-bloggers as "entrepreneurial" journalists responsible for generating revenue for the company. As he put it in a memo shared with his staff: "Revenue generation traditionally isn't a journalist's job, but helping develop a business model for the future of journalism is every journalist's job today." In his scheme, superbloggers would generate revenue by becoming a "complete community connection" (or C3, as it was called in the newsroom) on their assigned topics. Take, for instance, driving as a topic area. Historically, the newspaper published car ads, covered the occasional traffic accident, and updated traffic reports. None of these activities directly generated revenue. Moving forward, Buttry imagined a superblogger creating a complete community connection around the subject – and building a revenue stream along the way. Imagine, for example, a "driving" superblogger creating interactive maps of gas prices and potholes, issuing text alerts on traffic congestion, and aggregating city red-light camera feeds. Imagine this journalist also building answerbases on every-thing from how to buy a car to how to deal with traffic tickets. And imagine this journalist facilitating discussion forums, curating user-generated photo galleries, and holding contests. All of this activity would take place on a site designed to serve as a one-stop portal for all things driving. In keeping with the decision to separate content from platform, the content from this portal could be shared across the company's TV station, newspaper, news site and other niche publications. More importantly, however, the portal could become a revenue-generating enterprise. For instance, the site might be a place where consumers compared insurance rates and even bought car insurance from the company that gave them the best deal. It might serve as a middleman between repair shops and drivers. A driver stuck on the side of the road, for instance, could use her phone to get text and telephone responses from repair shops that could quickly get to her location. Of course, the site would feature ads for car-related products, but it would go further and take in sales orders for these products. In each instance, the site could take a cut of the revenue generated by these services.

Now imagine *Gazette* superbloggers working in the same fashion on topics as wide-ranging as births, deaths, weddings, home, sports, music, real estate, and so on. Each of these "one-stop" portals would establish a stream of revenue where none existed before. In his mind's eye, Buttry imagined the front page of the newspaper's website looking like craigslist: a powerful search engine coupled with a simple list of portals to various topic areas. He determined that ICE would start with topic areas on which it had a competitive advantage and use these revenues to grow into, as he put it, the "connection to everything people and businesses need to know and do to live and do business in Eastern Iowa."[13] And he established a deadline of April 2009 to complete the initial work of separating ICE from the company's platforms.

Superblogging as a Model of Journalism

In December 2008, Buttry's staff began to work furiously to meet this deadline. Later, they recalled this time as if it were a dream, when they madly devised new organization charts and workflow processes and attended seemingly endless staff meetings. In fact, one reporter joked, they sat in so many meetings that a few people made them into a drinking game. Every time someone said the words "fundamentally change" in one of these meetings, they took a sip from their water bottles. When they weren't attending meetings, reporters went through the anxiety of applying and interviewing for new superblogger positions.

As one might imagine, all this activity caused a great deal of stress. People worried about their jobs, and they wondered if Buttry's experiment would save the newspaper. But, in their recollections, reporters also recalled the time as one of high enthusiasm. Part of the enthusiasm came from an awareness of just how grim things had become. By 2009, the industry was hemorrhaging reporters, stock prices of newspaper companies were plummeting, and a few newspapers had even gone out of business. In this context, many people in the newsroom were pleased to see their bosses "doing something." As one reporter put it to me, "The industry is changing and it's good that we are doing something." Another called the paper's efforts "the best [idea he had] heard for newspapers to survive." One went so far as to say that he was "totally on board" with Steve's plan. "What I'm doing here may not be working and there may be a better way for me [to help the company]."

Some of their enthusiasm also came from sheer relief at having a job. Two days after Buttry's arrival at the *Gazette* in June 2008, Cedar Rapids experienced an enormous flood that destroyed much of downtown. For the next several months, *Gazette* reporters covered this catastrophe and its aftermath. But the flood struck a great blow both to the local economy and to the *Gazette*'s bottom line. In December 2008, the company announced the largest downsizing in its history, shedding nearly 100 positions, including over a dozen reporters in the newsroom. After these layoffs, tension in the newsroom understandably mounted. "Everyone is reading into signs," one reporter told me, "like, who gets the laptops? Who gets the Blackberries?" The sense among people in the newsroom was that, if Buttry's plan could reverse the fortunes of the newspaper, and therefore save their jobs, then they were all for it.

But as they worked through January 2009 to make Buttry's plan a reality, the staff began to come to a realization: no one knew what any of the new labels meant. What was an "information content conductor?" Or a superblogger? Or a content wrangler? At first, the confusion sparked humor and little more. After all, they had a newsroom to transform! But then people began to realize that the new labels had real-world consequences. Just as one example, would Buttry put his new title on his business card? Another: who would pick up the phone if someone called the newsroom and asked for the "city editor?" Over a period of weeks, people became increasingly uneasy that they couldn't answer some very basic questions.

The plight of Jimmy Collins illustrates the dilemma and the mood that began to grip the newsroom. For several years previously, Collins had been the newsroom's librarian. When Buttry was hired, Collins became interested in doing something new, and so applied for a "web curator" position. To his surprise, he got the job, and in February 2009 began managing a website titled "iowanewshawk.com." He soon discovered, however, that he had no idea what a "web curator" was supposed to do, and no one else, including Buttry, could help him. Nonetheless, for two months Jimmy came to work every day and "curated" online news. Mostly, this meant that he scoured the Internet and linked to any and all news about Iowa. As I chatted with him in May, he was becoming increasingly anxious. He had little idea of what he was doing or why he was doing it. The longer this situation persisted, he thought, the odder it would look to his supervisors if they ever took the time to ask. He was becoming paralyzed with anxiety. When was someone going to tell him how to do his job, or, worse, stop by and realize he didn't know himself?

Because most reporters were supposed to transition to the role, the dilemma Collins's situation raised was felt especially acutely by people who were supposed to become superbloggers. Put simply, no one knew what a superblogger was. "For a lot of us," one reporter said, "the idea [of superblogging] was hard to fathom . . . I didn't get it . . . when I first heard the rumblings, I didn't understand." Another said that, after reading one of Buttry's memos, her reaction was, "wait . . . what?" Still another had no answers at all. When I asked her about superblogging, she just shrugged her shoulders, indicating she had no idea what Buttry was trying to do. When they framed superblogging in terms of the organization's needs, the initiative seemed reasonable: "It's a way to have the information side drive more revenue – be able to multiply revenue streams," one reporter explained. But when they thought about superblogging *as journalism*, their minds went blank.

What explains their difficulty? Here is where cultural sociology can help. Let's return to Geertz's distinction between culture as a model *for* and a model *of* reality. Cultural practices like the routines of journalism are "models for" in the sense that they serve as instructions for how to do the practice. They are the rules that journalists follow to produce the news. But news routines also enact a constitutive rule of what, at bottom, journalism is. In this sense, they represent a model *of* as well as *for* the world.

As I mentioned in the introduction to this chapter, the notion of a "constitutive rule" comes from Searle (1969), who distinguishes it from more ordinary, and numerous, regulative rules. It is worth quoting Searle at length on the difference between these types of social rules. Regulative rules, he writes,

> regulate antecedently or independently existing forms of behavior; for example, many rules of etiquette regulate interpersonal relationships which exist independently of the rules. But constitutive rules do not merely regulate, they create or define new forms of behavior . . . Regulative rules characteristically take the form of or can be paraphrased as imperatives, e.g., "When cutting food, hold the knife in the right hand," or "Officers must wear ties at dinner." Some constitutive rules take quite a different form, e.g., "A checkmate is made when the king is attacked in such a way that no move will leave it unattacked." (1969, pp. 33–4)

What Searle seems to be saying is that certain kinds of rules define objects (situations, roles, etc.), so that without those rules the objects would not exist. In Geertz's terms, these rules function as models of the world. Other kinds of rules direct behavior toward or within predefined or independently existing objects (situations, roles, etc.). A constitutive rule tells us what an object is; a regulative rule tells us something about an object. Constitutive rules are ontological; regulative rules are epistemological.

The filtering conception of journalism represents just such a constitutive rule. It is worth remembering that this wasn't always so. In the nineteenth century, the political parties were primary filters of information in public life, and journalism acted more as a political cheerleader. Very slowly, practices associated with the filtering conception began to emerge. By the 1860s, the reporter had been invented. By the 1880s, the notion of the "interview" took hold. During this period, journalists began to source stories on their own, and critics began to call for a more independent press. But it was only in the 1920s that these values and practices congealed around a new definition of what journalism was and what it was for. And, by the 1950s, sociologist David Manning White (1964) had coined a new term for this form of journalism: "gatekeeper." Today, we call this definition of journalism common sense.

What reporters at the *Gazette* began to realize was that, within their standard frame of reference, superblogging didn't make any sense.

When I arrived in the newsroom on schedule in May 2009, I quickly stumbled upon their difficulty. So one day early on I stopped by Buttry's office and asked him about it. I asked, how is superblogging journalism? He insisted that it was, and, in trying to explain how, he gave the example of a journalist reporting at the scene of an accident. In the past, the journalist would have written a story based on information gathered from officials on the scene and interviews with witnesses. In contrast, the first thing a superblogger might do is create a twitter #hashtag and ask everyone on the scene to tweet what they knew about the accident. She might also gather the photos people were taking on their phones and put them into a photo gallery on the news site. This superblogger would also get information from officials and interview witnesses – Buttry intended the "super" part of superblogger to connote traditional reporting practices – but a good deal of a superblogger's time would be spent aggregating and collating information produced by others.

I scribbled down this example and went away to think. A short while later, I realized that Buttry had done what journalists often do. When asked to define what a superblogger was, Buttry described what a superblogger did: superbloggers aggregate, curate, and so on. In the past, when journalists agreed on the definition of journalism, doing just this much was fine. But, as Buttry told his staff again and again, his experiment was an effort to fundamentally transform the newsroom. In this context, describing what a superblogger does (e.g., its regulative rules) is not the same thing as defining what it is and what it is for. Without this key piece of knowledge, reporters were in the position of the person who says, "I can understand your words, but I don't know what you mean!" If superbloggers were gatekeepers, then how was Buttry's experiment innovative? If they were not gatekeepers, then what was the point? What was the goal of superblogging? Who are we when we are superbloggers, reporters asked, and why would we engage in this activity?

This is an ontological problem. Generally, it arises when people cannot justify what they do (regulative rules) in the context of more basic definitions of what a practice is and what it is for (constitutive rules). Elizabeth Bird's (1992) study of tabloid journalism offers a nice example of how this usually works in practice. In an ethnographic study, Bird finds that tabloid reporters are acutely aware of how other journalists perceive their work. For this reason, they take great pains to justify their activities in terms of conventional journalistic rules: we rely on official sources; we gather facts; we publish informational articles – *just like any other journalist.* "They are eager to show," Bird writes, "that in many respects they have not abandoned the methods of objective journalism" (1992, p. 92). In other words, this need for recognition, by themselves and others, leads tabloid reporters to defend what they do (regulative rules) in terms of a traditional definition (constitutive rule) of what journalism is.

Part of what this means is that constitutive rules serve as a kind of boundary for the field of journalism. Even tabloid reporters won't do just anything to produce the news because they realize that some actions will not be recognized as appropriate or legitimate in the journalistic community. After all other justifications have been exhausted – they use credible sources, they gather facts, they write balanced stories, etc. – their appeal must be that how they gather the news is valid *because* they are professional gatekeepers. Recognition, in other words, acts as a kind of ontological "bedrock." And this is just another way of saying that regulative rules ultimately find their justification in constitutive rules.

Lacking any other constitutive rule, *Gazette* staffers sought to understand superblogging in terms of a traditional gatekeeping conception of journalism, and so kept coming up against ontological bedrock. They were not especially hostile to blogging, for instance, but to them it was more a form of expression than journalism. They were happy to curate information, but they could not tell me why it was a valuable journalistic practice. If it saved their jobs, they were determined to tweet all day, but as journalism the practice seemed meaningless. They were happy to superblog, this is to say, even if they could not see its connection to journalism.

Superblogging simply did not resonate with them. It wasn't that they were hostile to it. As I say, nearly every reporter expressed excitement about the prospect of change. Many insisted that they fervently wished this to happen. One reporter declared, "We are not resistant to change," and then said it again for emphasis: "We are not resistant to change . . . we're as comfortable with change as anyone." But, when it came to their feelings about Buttry's specific plan to save the *Gazette*, they seemed to feel very little either way. Even though he proposed to do something much more radical than anything tried in other newsrooms, no one expressed moral indignation at Buttry's plan. I heard none of the "This isn't right!" exclamations commonly uttered in other newsrooms I had visited. At the same time, no one demonstrated much enthusiasm for the plan either. "I'm happy to do it," one reporter said, but "I'm not . . . throw[ing] my heart and soul into [it]" either. Another had few criticisms of the initiative, but said, "It just isn't something I [am] excited about." When I asked one of the editors about the general lack of emotion around Buttry's proposal, he agreed, then said: "Most people are like, 'I'll go along because [you] asked me to' . . . but they are not emotionally invested in it. They aren't passionate about it."

The reason for this lack of emotion, I think, is that reporters saw superblogging as something separate from journalism. *Gazette* reporters had been involved in countless "change" initiatives over the years. At one time, the paper had no fewer than five zoned editions and covered eighteen different Iowa counties. After these editions were scrapped, managers created "innovation teams" that were made responsible for creating new products and practices. One reporter told me that he had applied and reapplied for his position at the newspaper four times in twelve years. But Buttry's plan felt different. How so? Editor Tony Rodriguez explained that, in the past, the question was "how to change what existed." Today, "We're not thinking about what to do with the newspaper." Another long-time reporter said much the same thing. "The changes now are not about the newspaper," he told me. "The new experiment is interested in serving other platforms, so in the sense that the newspaper is no longer the center of attention." As we saw in the last chapter, reporters often conflate the newspaper with journalism. *Gazette* staffers were saying that superblogging had little to do with journalism and, therefore, little to do with them.

Since this was so, reporters did not know how to feel about Buttry's ideas. Should they resist superblogging or should they embrace it? It was tough for them to say. Their experience was like that of encountering an exotic ritual practiced in another culture and being asked to assess whether it was good or bad. Since the ritual lies far outside our own meaning systems, how are we supposed to know? That is how *Gazette* reporters felt about superblogging. They may have wished to change, but it was difficult for them to get excited about superblogging when they lacked a frame of reference for understanding it as a form of journalism.

This made for many awkward, disjointed interactions in the newsroom, none more so than the interviewing process reporters went through to become superbloggers. Since he had no firm sense of what superblogging was, Buttry could not write detailed descriptions of these new jobs. Without these descriptions, it was difficult for reporters to show that they were qualified for the positions. Laura Black, manager of the company's human resources department, participated in many of the job interviews. Later, she told me that they were some of the oddest she had ever witnessed. As she sat in the room listening to the interactions between Buttry and the interviewees, she realized that reporters were just "explain[ing] back what they thought

Steve wanted to hear. 'I can do that job in the new world,' they would tell Steve." Indeed, most reporters with whom I talked told me that, in preparing for these interviews, they merely added blogging to their old jobs. Sam Dennis, for instance, applied for a superblog position centered on his old government beat. When he interviewed for this job, he told Buttry he planned to "do more enterprise work and attend fewer meetings." To this explanation, he appended the idea that he would also do "more linking, posting documents, and the like." That was the sum of his pitch to Buttry, but it was enough to get him the job. To Black, the interactions seemed surreal. How could reporters interview for – and obtain – positions that neither they nor Buttry could define?

To be clear, the problem was not that reporters saw superblogging as nonsense (the opposite of sense). This assessment might have triggered moral indignation ("This is nonsense!") Rather, it was that the practice made no sense at all. Placed in this ontological quandary, many reporters chose to believe that superblogging changed nothing. "Reporting is the same," one told me. "I blog. I tweet. I have my camera. I've learned the value of outsourcing/community involvement." But the only thing superblogging changed, he said, was "how you present" information. Or, as another explained, superblogging was merely a matter of "learning new tools."

One result of this attitude was that reporters mostly turned the new practices to old purposes. Most everyone in the newsroom tweeted, blogged, curated, and/or aggregated, and nearly everyone said that they were happy to do so. "I'm happy to blog . . .", "I'm excited to blog . . .", and "I like blogging" were common sentiments. But mostly they were happy to blog because, as one reporter put it, they saw it as a "form of therapy." He explained that the newspaper had been getting thinner in the last few years. Where once reporters could get 15- and even 20-inch stories in the paper, increasingly it seemed that editors wanted stories no longer than 10 inches, and sometimes even shorter. "This has affected how I think about my blog," he told me. "I'm now able to write longer and more in depth on my blog than in my print stories." Another told me that he likes the idea of a blog because it gives him the "space to write more, longer, and deeper stories." So many reporters thought this way that it led the digital editors to complain. "Some of these people," one told me, "are using [their] blogs to write 25-inch stories!" And they were. But they were not doing it out of a sense of indignation or malevolence. They were doing it because it was a way to make the practice sensible.

In the midst of their confusion, of course, reporters still had to put out a newspaper, and this also reinforced standard definitions of journalism. Sociologists have known for some time that people do not confront social structures so much as *interpretations* of those structures (e.g., Archer, 1996; Emirbayer, 1997; Joas, 1993; Wiley, 1994). At the heart of these interpretations lie constitutive rules for what counts as what in a social domain. This insight has led sociologist Ann Swidler (2006) to argue that constitutive rules anchor social practices by serving as the "infrastructure of repeated interactional patterns" (p. 85). As *Gazette* staff worked to put out the newspaper, they naturally interacted with sources, their editors and readers, and one another. These interactions forced them to return to longstanding definitions of journalism.

The experience of Charlie Adams illustrates this idea. In his mid-twenties, Adams started as an intern at the *Gazette* three years before. At the time of my visit, he was the newspaper's city politics reporter/superblogger. In a conversation, Adams expressed a willingness to change his practices. He liked blogging and was active on Twitter. When I asked about Peters's idea of a journalism that was more collaborative and interactive, Adams did not flinch. He said that something like this kind of journalism was inevitable. In fact, Adams was so enthusiastic about the changes underway, Buttry held him up as someone who "got" the new mindset.

For about six weeks, Adams practiced superblogging on "Hot Beat," his blog covering city politics. He found himself doing journalism mostly in conventional ways. Every day, he scanned the meeting agendas of various government institutions; interacted via e-mail with individuals in and around government who might have newsworthy information; contacted officials and experts to obtain quotes and verify facts he would like to include in his stories; when time permitted, attended government meetings; and, of course, fielded calls and e-mails from people in and around government who were interested in sharing information and pitching story ideas. When I pointed out that he was mostly doing conventional journalism, he gave me a blank stare. "It's my beat," he said, and left it at that.

Even as he grew more comfortable talking about change – and Adams was one of the most comfortable doing so in the newsroom – his interactions with sources ritually re-enacted a traditional definition of journalism. So long as he followed standard practices, these interactions persisted, and therefore so did the constitutive definition guiding those interactions.

The same was true of his interactions in the newsroom. Though Adams posted to his blog many times every day, his editor never read these posts. In fact, although many reporters blogged, to my knowledge, no editor routinely read this work. When I asked Adams's editor why she never paid attention to his blog, she was dumbfounded. The idea had never come to mind. She was too busy interacting with him in ways editors had done for decades. She made sure that he talked with the right people and asked the right sorts of questions. She checked to ensure that he had verified information and correctly quoted sources. And, of course, she made sure that he got his stories done on deadline. Reading his blog did not seem to have much to do with journalism, and so she ignored it.

As the April deadline drew closer, frustration among reporters and editors began to rise. Reporters were asked to apply for superblogging positions but ended up reapplying for their old jobs. Many took up the new practices but mostly turned them to traditional purposes. A few took up their new duties as superbloggers, but, for people like Jimmy Collins, this only led to more confusion. For others, like Charlie Adams, the experience had the ironic result of reconfirming traditional conceptions of journalism.

During meetings, editors began to express their frustration more vocally. "When [we] started to implement the vision," one told me, "[we] couldn't resolve some key questions. [We] kept avoiding the issues." This editor was particularly concerned about establishing standards for superblogging. "To what standard," she asked, "will reporters work? [For example], a city hall blog may be of interest to only 500 people. It would be a great success to attract that number. It would be a disaster for a sports blog." As an editor, she quite rightly wished to hold reporters accountable. But how could she hold superbloggers accountable if she couldn't take a measure of the practice? "We weren't dealing with the big issues," she said, "[and] I was frustrated at the answers we couldn't get."

When I discussed these issues with Buttry, he recited Clayton Christensen's idea that, in a climate of disruptive innovation, no one can know how to proceed because the environment is too uncertain. In this context, the point was not to avoid failure but to fail quickly, and repeatedly, until the right answer could be found. So he was perfectly happy to proceed without firm definitions of roles and responsibilities. To him, this was the only way to eventually get to the right answers. When I mentioned this response to one of the editors, she responded, "There have to be parameters. This is management 101. You have to set boundaries. You have to provide those boundaries." Translated: you have to have some bounded sense of what superblogging is and how to measure it before you can ask people to do it.

By late February, tensions in the newsroom escalated to the point where they came to the attention of Chuck Peters. As Peters looked at the situation, it became clear to him that Buttry had not implemented his plan very well. "Steve hadn't brought anyone along," Peters told me. "He hadn't explained the plan very well to people." Peters had expected Buttry to roll out new plans soon after his arrival in June 2008. But then the flood hit and Buttry became "hyperfocused," as Peters put it, on covering this "story of the century." When in the fall of 2008 Peters asked him when he planned to initiate ICE, Buttry still had no firm timeline, but then came back a week later and declared, "We're going to do it by April!" Peters's reaction: "This did not inspire confidence." By late February, it was clear to Peters that Buttry had caused a "train wreck." When he asked Buttry to explain what he was doing, Buttry gave Peters the same response he had given to others. According to Peters, "He said it was going to be a mess whatever we do so we should just get on with it."

By early March, Peters had seen enough, and called an all-hands staff meeting. At this meeting, he reiterated that dramatic changes were taking place across the news industry, and repeated his determination to separate content production from distribution channels. To show his resolve, he revealed that the company's television station would become part of the ICE reorganization. Finally, he announced that Nancy Teague, the director of the company's television news division, would take Buttry's place as head of ICE.

Just like that, Buttry's experiment in superblogging was over, almost before it had begun.

"You Are Still a Reporter"

The March staff meeting marked the end of Buttry's involvement in the *Gazette*'s experiment, but not of the experiment itself. As I visited the newsroom in May, Peters remained determined to separate content from product. In fact, by adding the television station into his plans, he had, in a sense, doubled down on the idea. Now, ICE would include reporters from the television station and the newspaper, and would have to figure out how to serve three rather than two major platforms (TV, print, and the web). At the helm of this effort stood Teague. When she took the job, Teague had been news director of the TV station for eight years. In that time, she had built up the station's brand as the area's primary source for weather and breaking news, and the station had been number one in its market for the past three years. Peters saw her as someone who could work "fast but not precipitously," who could execute the changes he wanted while "keeping revenue up" and not "break[ing] the franchise." In short, Peters trusted Teague to get the job done, to do it within budget, and to do it in a way that did not cause a "train wreck" in the newsroom.

It is worth briefly discussing how Teague proposed to accomplish these goals. The first thing she did was to get rid of superblogging and the other labels Buttry had invented. There would be no information content conductor, content wranglers, or superbloggers. Teague's title was to be director of content. Editors would remain editors, and reporters would be reporters. Upon assuming her new role, Teague had one-on-one conversations with as many reporters as she could fit into her schedule. At these meetings, she tried "to assure them," as she put it to me in an interview, "that they will be doing much the same kind of thing they have always done." Her message to them was, "You are still a reporter, still producing content . . . You will be doing breaking stuff, daily stuff, and enterprise stuff, just like you've always done." In another conversation, Teague said that maintaining the identity of the journalist was key. People have an "internal need" to be journalists, she told me. "We need to recognize that, honor that." Otherwise, she concluded, "Why would you take this job? Where is the self-fulfillment?"

Of course, many print reporters blanched when they learned that a TV person was now in charge of the newsroom. "They are after the soundbite," one reporter said, by way of describing TV people. "Is that the direction we're going?" he asked. "I'll do what I have to do," but "what worries me is the quality. Are we going to put out a quality product?" But, if the choice was between the longstanding, and recognizable, conflict between TV and print and the uncharted territory of superblogging, most reporters preferred the former. In fact, compared with Buttry, many found Teague comforting. One said that her meeting with Teague "allayed many of my fears." Another came away feeling that Teague was "someone who had the news at heart." Despite her history in TV, reporters responded to Teague because she spoke in a language they could understand.

Without superblogging, the separation of content from product came to look something like media convergence, an idea that stretched back to the early 1980s. Media companies that owned print and TV properties had long wished to converge the two, largely because doing so promised to make content production much less expensive. Instead of maintaining two separate newsrooms – TV and print – the company could have one newsroom filled with people capable of producing content across platforms. As news became digitized, and regulatory rules against meshing TV and print newsrooms weakened, the idea took hold in many pockets of the industry.

Under Teague, ICE became a process of converging TV, print, and web-based reporting. She assigned reporters to beats in each of the following areas: crime, public safety, weather, floods and fires, trials, terrorism, elections/politics, government, sports, and traffic. Their instructions were to write longer (enterprise) and shorter (breaking news) stories, and to incorporate video, audio, and text in such a way that the content could be used across platforms. The content would be housed in a "data repository," an integrated content management system (CMS) that allowed ICE clients to search for and upload material to their respective platforms. The idea, Teague told the staff, was to separate content from products, but to do so in a way that did not "screw up the products."

With the exception of superblogging, Teague retained much of the original ICE structure. As had been planned before, she entered into service agreements with the editors of the newspaper, the website, and the television station. These agreements determined the kinds and quantities of content each platform wished to obtain from ICE. For content ICE could not provide, editors of the respective platforms would have to look elsewhere (e.g., to stringers and users). To describe how this would work, the newspaper editor used the analogy of shopping at the grocery market: "I go with a shopping list and they [ICE] have an agenda they're trying to sell you and ultimately I get what I want and probably [buy] some things I didn't know I needed." At the outset, Teague planned to have her senior editors meet daily with owners of the platforms to ensure that agreements were being honored and, in the case of the newspaper, to plan coverage over days and weeks.

In theory, ICE reporters were supposed to produce a steady stream of content in "raw," "semi-packaged," and "packaged" form. In practice, however, no one knew what these labels meant. What was "raw" content? Were reporters supposed to download everything in their notebooks to the CMS? And how did a "semi-packaged" story differ from a "packaged" one? Did this mean that editors would, in a sense, write stories based upon information they found on the CMS? If so, whose byline would be placed with these stories? No one was comfortable with the idea of editors writing stories. Reporters did not like losing that amount of control over their work, and editors did not want to write stories about events they had not reported themselves. In the face of these difficulties, reporters' lives actually changed very

little. They covered their beats as they had always done. They interacted with their editors, who gave them the same sorts of instructions
they had always given, e.g., "The newspaper needs a 15-inch story on
this trial for tomorrow's edition," or "We need you to cover this accident for the 11 a.m. news." And, of course, they interacted with the
same sources. "When something big happens," the higher education
reporter told me, "I'm not going to get information from the community . . . I'm going to get that information from official sources . . .
If people are being laid off at [the University of Iowa], I won't get the
specific information that everyone wants from the community . . . it
will come from official sources." As another reporter described it, the
separation of content from platform seemed like a "wink, wink" kind
of thing. "We [are] still sitting right next to one another," he said,
and so we coordinate all the time.

When I asked Buttry what he thought of Teague's revisions to his
plan, he was understandably critical. "If the company had been on a
trip [from Des Moines] to Albuquerque" in the original plan, he told
me, "it is now going to Kansas City." Buttry believed that the only
way to enact fundamental change was to adopt fundamental changes.
Half-measures, he believed, would not work because the pull of the
status quo was simply too strong.

As I ended my visit to the *Gazette*, Buttry gave me a ride to the
airport. He was despondent. It had been three months since the
March staff meeting. ICE had been taken away from him and his
status in the company remained uncertain. As we sat outside the
security gate, he confided that he was actively looking for another job.
"I've given up on legacy news companies," he told me. "They just
can't change. It won't happen here."

Buttry may be right about "legacy news companies." If so,
however, their failure will not be due to a lack of will. As of this
writing, the *Gazette*'s experiment continues apace. At a staff meeting
before I left, Teague told reporters, "For far too long we've had a
culture where we're fearing failure." No longer. "We're going to take
the deep dive," she insisted. By the latter half of 2010, the company
had successfully divorced content production from platform, and
Teague was seeking to incorporate more community engagement
in her reporters' beat coverage. As part of this effort, she introduced
"beat blogging" into the newsroom, and she remained committed to
including more "user-generated content" in ICE's coverage of the
community. There had been some staff turnover but, when I talked
with her and a few reporters in the summer of 2010, they remained as
committed as ever to turning the company's fortunes around.

If this experiment fails, it will likely be due not to a lack of will, but to a lack of imagination. Teague agrees with her reporters and their sources that journalism is essentially a practice of filtering: obtaining information from sources (people and institutions), discerning which of this information is newsworthy, and packaging it as news for the consumption of an audience. Their daily judgments and interactions confirm and reconfirm this agreement, so much so that, when they try experiments that reach beyond it, they run into "ontological bedrock." Beyond this bedrock of agreement, it is simply difficult for them to see.

Allow me to indulge in one more anecdote that illustrates this idea. One day, Charlie Adams intentionally got a ticket for jaywalking. He was in a local neighborhood, talking with three people who were angry that police were handing out jaywalking tickets. They thought the actions were racially motivated. So Adams, who is white, walked across the street, and the police promptly issued him a ticket. He thought about writing a story about the experience for the newspaper, but his editors discouraged him. If it happens to a reporter, by definition, they argued, it is not journalism. So he wrote a blog post instead. His editors had no problem with the blog post because, to their mind, it wasn't journalism.

Such incidents produce a kind of "groundhog day" effect in the newsroom. *Gazette* staffers talk incessantly about change, only to return to their desks and seek out the same sorts of information from the same sorts of people, and to use the same narrative formulas to write the same sorts of stories on the basis of this information. As one reporter put it, "I blog [and] I tweet . . . [but] reporting is the same. Gathering information is the same. [It's just] how you present [that] is different."

So it would seem.

5

The Future

Journalism is doing so poorly, it is easy to forget that it once enjoyed great success. In the first half of the twentieth century, every part of the enterprise worked together seamlessly. Reporters wrote stories that attracted large audiences. Their news organizations translated these audiences (through advertising dollars) into revenue. The more audience reporters attracted with the news, the more money their organizations made. More revenue allowed organizations to hire more reporters, who produced more stories that attracted larger audiences, and so on. This was a virtuous cycle for news, and it was more than just a business cycle. Journalism succeeded so well because it meshed neatly with key strands of modern society, with everything from the temporal rhythm of the eight-hour workday to urbanization, to the increasingly bureaucratized, professionalized, and consumerist world that came into being. In fact, it was so powerful that the same virtuous cycle sustained every other mass medium as well, including advertising, movies, music, and the broadcasting industry.

As the twentieth century wore on, this positive feedback loop dissipated. Anyone who has read chapter 1 of this book knows why. Modern society changed. It became more suburban and less urban. Both parents in families began to work and to work longer hours. Entertainment options exploded. Journalism grew out of tune with the rhythms of post-industrial society, and what once was a virtuous cycle turned vicious. Lower market penetration and circulation led to lower revenues, fewer reporters, less news, even fewer readers, and so on. Journalism lost its ability to loop more of one thing (news) around another (audience) and another (advertising revenue). The impact of this process was muted both by time and by the fact that total advertising expenditures exploded for all media in the last quarter of the twentieth century. But, over a period of decades, journalism lost its footing in society.

As I suggested at the end of chapter 1, in some ways journalists' decades-long struggle against these forces of decline left them unprepared to grapple with the Internet. This medium offers a very different set of challenges to journalism from those journalists faced in the past. In the first part of this chapter, I bring forward the story we left off in chapter 1 by describing these unique challenges. They start with the fact that the Internet is a networked medium, and so operates by very different principles than a mass medium. A networked medium is more distributed and fragmented than a mass medium. It allows users more choice about what to do with the information they consume. Using a networked medium, groups may form and dissipate more efficiently and quickly than via a mass medium, and people may collaborate with one another more easily. A networked medium also pivots around a different kind of scarcity than a mass medium. In the age of mass media, attention was abundant and information was scarce (e.g., Lanham, 2006). Specialists controlled most of the information that circulated in public life. But once they distributed this information in the public square, they could attract the attention of millions of people. In a networked medium, information is abundant and attention is scarce. Once it is known by anyone, networks make information available to everyone. In fact, networks produce so much information it is difficult for any organization to attract and hold the attention of many people.

To show just how, and how much, these traits challenge journalism, I borrow from the field theory of journalism I first introduced in chapter 3. "Field" theorists (e.g., Benson, 2006; Benson and Neveu, 2005; Bourdieu, 2005) argue that journalism sits on a three-legged stool: the profession itself, the economy, and the state. As journalism moves online, each of these legs is severely weakened. There is no business model for online news, for instance. It is also not certain that many of journalism's cherished values and practices, especially those related to objectivity, are useful in an online environment. As if this were not enough, the Internet also allows public officials to bypass journalists and contact their constituencies directly, thereby robbing journalism of a crucial state subsidy. As important, the Internet has frayed the relationship *between* these forces. Journalism gained coherence in the pushing and pulling between professionalism, the economy, and the state. Online, the pushing and pulling between these forces is much weaker, and this has weakened the integrity of the field.

None of this means that journalism is dying. It is actually quite rare for a medium to cease to exist – we are still using pencils, after all, a medium invented in the sixteenth century. Going forward, there will still be journalists, and there likely will still be newspapers. Rather, journalism is unraveling. By this I mean that the boundaries of journalism are blurring. It is increasingly difficult to distinguish the inside from the outside of the field. Many new people and organizations have entered the field, and this, in turn, has made it difficult to tell who a journalist is apart from any other news producer, or to identify standards of "good" journalism that are widely shared (and enforceable). Journalism, put simply, is losing coherence as a distinctive social field.

Framing the issue in this way casts a different light on this particular moment in journalism's history. For hundreds of years, people as diverse as government bureaucrats, to university professors, to priests, produced news without the need of journalism. We may come to see the period from the early 1900s to the 1990s as a historical anomaly, a time when journalism briefly inflated into a distinctive social space, when, for a brief time, professional journalists controlled the production of news. And we may be entering a more normal time when news production goes on in the absence of an integrated social field we call "journalism."

This frame also implies that whether journalism is ever stitched back together is, in important respects, not up to journalists. As I say, the virtuous cycle of twentieth-century journalism worked because the newspaper was in tune with modern society. The same will be true of any virtuous cycle for networked news. Today, journalism has come undone. If the past is any guide, it will be put back together only if it comes to resonate with other aspects of a networked society – and this depends on whether and the extent to which networks transform other institutions of public life. Many scholars detect the influence of networks on these institutions (e.g., Benkler, 2006; Bimber, 2003; Bimber et al., 2005; Castells, 2010; Chadwick, 2012; Shirky, 2009). But the Internet is very new, and these trends have had little time to develop. For this reason, the future of journalism hangs suspended, awaiting developments in other social fields.

All of this makes firm predictions about the future difficult. However, it seems safe to say this much: the future of news lies online, and therefore in networks – networks of computers linked together via phone and cable lines, and networks of mobile devices (essentially mini-computers) linked together by wireless routers and satellites. We know that networks present journalists with a different problem than do the mass media. In the age of mass media, the problem was how to attract the attention of millions of anonymous consumers. Online, the problem is how to induce fewer, but more passionate, people to do things together. Networked journalists are adopting new practices to solve this problem. Most of these practices, which include crowdsourcing, aggregation, curation, facilitation, and moderation, invite people to do things in common and leverage the ease of coordination and collaboration afforded by the Internet to amplify the effects of their work. The intuition seems to be this: the more time people spend with a journalist, the more work they accomplish together, the more avenues exist for monetizing this work – more interaction, more work, more avenues for revenue, and so on. We do not know if this formula amounts to a virtuous cycle or whether it can sustain an entire field of journalism. But, whether or not journalism is put back together as a distinctive social field, networks are clearly changing the way news is produced or consumed.

I unpack these ideas more fully below, but I begin where we left off in chapter 1, with the field of journalism under increasing duress.

A Field Unravels

I introduced the term "social field" in chapter 3, where I used it to refer to organized, cohesive social spaces. Social fields are what make it possible for us to know that we are engaged in the practice of art-making rather than politics, politics rather journalism, journalism rather than science. To see its use for thinking about journalism, it will help to fill in a few more details of the concept.

According to Bourdieu, fields arise in the nexus between social forces, or what he calls "power lines," that operate in society. Like gravity or electricity, these "power lines" exercise force on social actors by pushing and pulling them in particular directions. Journalism is a social space defined by the relation of three such forces: professionalism, commercialism, and the state (see figure 5.1). The arrows along the axes of this figure reflect greater and lesser amounts of what Bourdieu calls "capital," or resources, along each power line. When we say, for instance, that a reporter is intent on mastering the skills of reporting, we mean that she wishes to accumulate a fair amount of professional capital, and so move farther along the professional axis of the field. To the extent that news organizations focus on making money, we mean that they strive to move farther along the commercial axis. Journalism's relationship to the state can seem

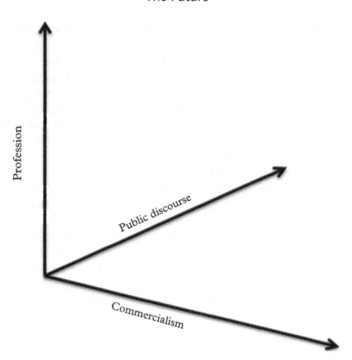

Figure 5.1   The field of journalism

more obscure. But it simply means that the state subsidizes journalism in both direct and indirect ways (Cook, 1998; Sparrow, 1999). An example of a direct subsidy is the Newspaper Preservation Act of 1970, which among other things allowed newspapers operating in the same city to form joint-operating agreements. Unlike the situation in many other countries, the US government provides journalism with few direct subsidies. But it does provide the field with a very important indirect subsidy, namely, information. As we have learned, much news flows from the relationships reporters maintain with public officials. Journalists need public officials because they provide most of the information that goes into news stories. This need allows the state to exercise a powerful force on the field.

If we take these forces together, we see that the pushing and pulling between them inflates journalism into a three-dimensional social space. Three attributes characterize the structure of this space. First, it has boundaries; there is an inside and outside to the field of journalism. For much of the twentieth century, journalists were easily identifiable: they worked for commercial news organizations oriented to publishing news to an audience. Anyone who did not work for one of these organizations was not a journalist. Second, the inside of the field is relatively ordered. Inside journalism, reporters and news organizations occupy definite relationships vis-à-vis one another. This is because the axes of professionalism, commercialism, and the state tend to vary in relation to one another. More professionalism means less commercialism, just as more integration into the discourse of the state means less professionalism. Knowledge of these variations allows us to say, for instance, that the *New York Times* is a more "professional" newspaper than the *National Enquirer*, or that a veteran investigative reporter is a "better" journalist than a new reporter working the night cops beat. When we make such judgments, we mean to say that one organization or journalist possesses more of the forms of capital (resources) preferred in the profession. Finally, the field generally is stable over time. As we learned in earlier chapters, journalists tend to reproduce and develop investments in the forms of capital preferred in the field. These investments ensure that the field persists over time.

By emphasizing its boundaries, orderliness, and stability, it can seem as if journalism never changes. But, as in any social field, journalism has many sources of dynamism. New people enter and exit the field every day, for instance, and journalism abuts many other social fields, like economics, politics, literature, and science. These contacts ensure that new ideas and practices routinely pollinate the field.

In fact, this is exactly what happened in the 1980s and 1990s, when corporations bought up most family-owned newspapers and introduced new economic ideas and practices into newsrooms. When new corporate managers sought to make news production cheaper and more efficient, they pulled against the professional impulses of the field. In turn, this triggered a reaction from journalists, who quite naturally wished to protect their professional autonomy from this perceived encroachment of commercial values.

For the journalists who lived through this period, it often seemed that commercialism was changing the very nature of journalism. But commercialism has been a constitutive force of journalism since its emergence in the 1920s, and journalists have had to manage the inevitable tension between commercialism and professionalism over this entire time. It is worth noting that journalism shares this tension with other mass media, including advertising, movies, radio, and television. All of these industries have a particular structural arrangement that lends them a family resemblance (figure 5.2). For example,

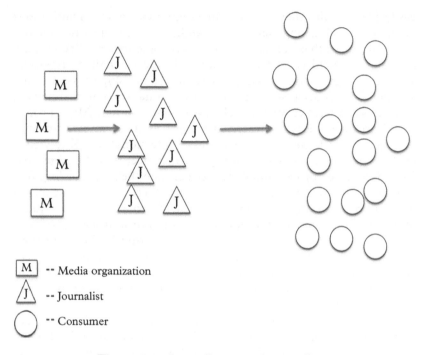

Figure 5.2 Journalism as a mass medium

they are composed of commercially oriented news organizations that rely upon advertising revenues to make money. These organizations hire a small cadre of specialists trained to filter and package information in a variety of forms (advertisements, songs, movies, news). And these specialists push these products out to relatively anonymous and passive mass audiences. With competing demands to make money and satisfy professional dictates, a tension between commercialism and professionalism is built into the very structure of the medium. Specialists oriented to professional values naturally resist, more or less, commercial pressures, just as corporate managers naturally press, more or less, for specialists to produce news in a less costly, more efficient manner. Like movie producers and musicians, then, journalists must always negotiate the inevitable tension between commercialism and professionalism. Doing so is part of the journalistic "game." So, even as commercialism increased in the 1980s and 1990s, it did not fundamentally change the nature of the field.

The same cannot be said of the Internet. As a networked medium,

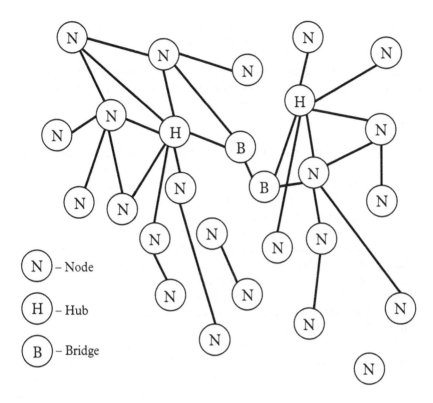

Figure 5.3   The structure of small worlds

the Internet has disrupted nearly every aspect of journalism. When I call the medium "networked," I mostly mean that it takes the form of small-world network structures (e.g., Barabási, 2002; Buchanan, 2002; Schnettler, 2009). In the introduction to this book, I described the basic architecture of small worlds. I won't review that material here. Instead, let me draw a picture (figure 5.3). This visualization of nodes, hubs, and bridges makes it clear just how utterly different is the Internet from a mass medium. A mass-mediated system filters public information through a set of very few, very large, organizations. Increasingly, journalism is entering a networked environment which, if it retains filters (in the form of hubs), nonetheless affords much greater flexibility in who produces information, how it is distributed through the system, and what people can do with it.

If you wanted a capsule description of the problem facing journalism, this would be it: invented as a mass medium, and native to a mass society, journalism is migrating, in fits and starts, to a networked medium. As I say, this movement represents a challenge for journalism not of degree, but of kind. In Bourdieu's terms, it changes the nature of the "game" that is played within the field. To see this clearly, it helps to reflect a bit more on the nature of networks. For our purposes, networks differ from mass media in four essential ways:

1 Compared to mass media, small-world networks create an abundance of information, and the people who produce this information are motivated by a more diverse array of interests. As Benkler (2006, p. 52) notes, the Internet lowers the physical costs of cultural production to such an extent that the primary barrier to production becomes personal motivation. Within mass media, people produce culture mainly for "extrinsic" reasons (i.e., to make money). In contrast, more people may produce culture online merely because they are interested, or wish to impress a friend, or like working with groups of like-minded others, or want to gain distinction within a community, or due to any of a host of other "intrinsic" motivations.

2 The Internet makes it easier for people of like minds and interests to find, coordinate, and do things with one another. As Shirky (2008) puts it, "Our recent communication networks are [essentially] a platform for group-forming" (p. 54). In the age of mass media, people lacked the tools to find and easily coordinate with one another. In a networked age, such tools are more widely available.

3 As I discussed briefly on pages 10 to 11, power laws characterize the distribution of online groups. In simple terms, a power law describes a situation in which, the more popular a member of a network is at T_0, the more popular it will be at T_1, T_2, T_3, and so on. Over time, a power law produces a situation in which a very few nodes (hubs) attract most of the links in a network, and most nodes have relatively few links. In short, distributions in online groups tend to be lumpy in that they skew heavily toward their most popular members.

4 Economies of scale are less important in online economics as compared to mass-media economics (e.g., Anderson, 2006; 2009). The term "economies of scale" means that the per-unit cost of producing a product (a music CD, a movie DVD, a copy of a newspaper, etc.) goes down as more units are produced. For example, the cost of producing one copy of one daily newspaper

equals the entire cost of newspaper production – the cost for ink, labor, paper, administration, and so on. When a second copy is produced, the per-unit cost halves, and, as a third, fourth, fifth, and so on, is produced, the per-unit cost continually decreases. In part, it is their interest in leveraging economies of scale that leads media companies to get so large: the larger they are, the more units they can produce and distribute, the lower the cost per unit of their products, the more competitive they become. In an online setting, the costs of duplicating a product are nearly zero. For this reason, economies of scale are less important for online economics than they were for mass-media economics, and companies therefore have less need to get very large.

This structural arrangement (information abundance, mixed motivations, easy group formation, and less need for economies of scale) represents a deep challenge to each of the "power lines" that define journalism. Its impact on the field's economic axis is easiest to understand – and the most discussed among journalists – so let's begin there. The economics of newspapers in the twentieth century depended on three sources of advertising revenue: national, local retail, and classified. All three categories grew from the 1950s to the 1990s (except for brief periods during the recessions of 1981 and 1991), essentially mirroring growth in the gross domestic product (GDP) of the nation. But media economist Robert Picard (2002) notes two significant facts about this growth. First, in the last part of the twentieth century, newspapers relied more and more on advertising revenue (as opposed to circulation revenue) to sustain very high profit margins. In 1950, the average newspaper obtained about 50 percent of its revenue from advertising and 50 percent from circulation. By the year 2000, the average newspaper relied on advertising for 80 percent of its revenue. Second, classified advertising grew exponentially compared with the other two types of advertising. Picard reports that, while retail advertising increased 177 percent between 1950 and 2000, and national advertising 125 percent during the same period, classified advertising – which includes auto, employment, and retail ads – grew by an astonishing 691 percent! So, in the last decades of the twentieth century, newspaper revenue increasingly came from advertising in general, and classified advertising in particular.

When, in the early 2000s, Internet use began to grow at a rapid rate, these trends set the industry up for a major fall. Classified advertising was the first to go. Internet companies like monster.com, craigslist, eBay, and match.com gave people quick, easy, and inexpensive ways to do what classified ads had once done – allow people to find one another – and thereby decimated the newspaper's classified advertising revenue. National advertising was not far behind. The Internet increased the number of options available to national advertisers for getting their products before consumers. They could set up their own websites, use Google's advertising system, and/or advertise on websites that targeted their specific consumer base. With more choices, national retailers increasingly chose to abandon the regional newspaper. Very quickly, in a span of about five years, the local retail market became the major source of advertising revenue for regional newspapers. Unfortunately, for decades newspapers had taken advantage of their monopoly status to charge local retailers premium ad rates. As their other sources of revenue withered, they were understandably resistant to reduce these prices. For this reason, local retail ad dollars have failed to make up for the loss of the other two revenue streams.

The result has been an astonishing economic collapse. The industry has not experienced year-over-year quarterly advertising growth since the second quarter of 2006. Using numbers from a 2010 Newspaper Association of America (NAA) report, media analyst Alan Mutter (2010) finds that, from 2005 to 2010, newspapers lost 85.2 percent of employment ad revenue, 73.3 percent of automotive ad revenue, 72.8 percent of real-estate ad revenue, and 41.1 percent of retail ad revenue. Online advertising has increased, but revenue from this source accounts for only about 12 percent of the total for newspapers – a number that has remained stubbornly flat since 2007. Given the rapid decline of print advertising revenues, online advertising would have to pick up by about 80 percent to take up the slack (Benton, 2011). In recognition that this is not likely to happen, newspapers have begun to look to circulation – in the form of apps, paywalls, membership fees, and the like – for new revenue. For example, media analyst Ken Doctor (2010) reports that the *Dallas Morning News* now gets 38 percent of its revenue from circulation, 54 percent from advertising, and 8 percent from contract printing. However, as I will discuss more fully below, given that newspapers have tended to keep profits afloat by cutting staff and reducing the amount of news they produce, it is unclear that any but the largest among them (read: the *New York Times*) can grow circulation enough to replace lost advertising revenue.

The Internet has caused a similar disruption of the field's professional axis. Professionalism involves journalism's preferred practices, values, and identities, things like the practice of attribution and the value of fairness. As I discussed in chapter 2, journalists experience these attributes as habits – habits of mind and of heart. As such, most journalists understand them to be ordinary, natural, and even inevitable. But scholars have shown that the profession's preferred habits of mind and heart arose and persisted for the most mundane of reasons: because they were useful. For example, there is perhaps no more cherished set of practices and values within journalism than those associated with objectivity. But journalists did not come to embrace objectivity because it was morally worthy. They adopted it because it helped them to manage particular problems. In a review of the broader literature, Michael Schudson (2001) summarizes four of objectivity's most important functions: it serves as a method of social control in newsrooms; it allows journalists to distinguish themselves from those in contiguous occupations, especially public relations; it is a principal means for recognizing distinction in the field; and, finally, it works as a cultural glue linking generations of journalists over time.

Schudson leaves unsaid that objectivity served these purposes for a specific form of journalism, namely, journalism practiced in a mass-mediated context. After all, journalists did not become specialists until they were designated as such by the mass-media organizations for which they worked. And it is only as specialists that they developed a need to distinguish themselves from those in other specialist occupations. We can extend this thought. It is only when journalism became a professional occupation that a need arose to transmit its myths and traditions across generations of workers. Many other aspects of professional journalism find their source in some problem raised by a mass-mediated environment. It is only because mass media try to reach "the masses" that journalism adopted a generalist style of writing for everyone, and therefore to no one. Further, media organizations are large and unwieldy because they need to leverage economies of scale. However, it is only because they are large and unwieldy that something like objectivity is necessary to ensure a measure of social control in the newsroom.

A networked environment presents journalists with a very different set of problems than does a mass-mediated environment, and the simple fact is that journalism's preferred habits of mind and heart are not nearly as useful for solving these problems. As Yochai Benkler (2006) argues, compared to mass media, the Internet provides people with more choice. They have more control over the information to which they are exposed, more control over what they can do with this information, and more choices of information outlets. The fact of more choice adds up to a dramatically different situation. In a mass-media environment, journalists create value by collecting relatively scarce information and packaging it in the form of an "attention trap" – i.e., the newspaper or TV broadcast. They then sell this attention to advertisers. In the networked environment of the Internet, information is abundant and attention is scarce. According to the 2010 Pew *State of the Media* study, even the best, most information-packed online news sites attract only about 10 minutes per month of their readers' attention, or about 20 seconds per day (e.g., Ostrow, 2010; Redman, 2010). Information alone, in other words, and the practices, values, and identities anchored to a conception of journalism as information, will not solve this problem.

Consider the situation faced by Josh Marshall, proprietor of talkingpointsmemo.com, a very popular and successful online-only political news site. Marshall knows that people have more choice online, and most of these people will not choose to consume information about national politics no matter how well it is reported. Further, he knows that the people who choose to consume this information are already interested, and even passionate about, the subject, and so he is not likely to tell them many things they do not already know about the subject. They are also active users rather than passive consumers of information, which means that talking at them will not likely hold their attention for very long. Finally, Marshall knows that people tend to use the Internet less to consume information than to interact with others.

Knowing these things means that Marshall cannot act like a traditional journalist and hope to attract the attention of users for very long. For example, knowing that his audience has passionate views about politics has led him to eschew the traditional professional value of neutrality. His site exudes the liberal progressive sensibilities of his community. Republican views are always lampooned and Democratic politicians are held to account to the most liberal perspectives in the party. Knowing that his audience is in search of conversation more than information, Marshall has developed an intimate writing voice. In contravention of the Associated Press style book – a guide to news writing that has been taught in every basic journalism course since the early twentieth century – "I's," "you's," "me's," and "we's" pepper his stories. Knowing that his audience wants to do things together and not just consume information, Marshall has invited his community to participate in the newsgathering process. In fact, he first gained fame by relying on his audience to help in the reporting of a scandal involving the US Justice Department – an instance of collaborative journalism that won him a 2008 George Polk award for legal reporting. Marshall has not adopted these new practices because he thinks they are "better" than traditional practices. He has grasped them because they are useful for solving the problem of attracting and holding the attention of an online audience. In so doing, however, he has moved far beyond what it means to be a "professional" journalist.

The Internet's impact on the relation of news to the state has not been as obvious as its effect on the business and practice of journalism, but the impact has been just as disruptive. As I said above, government subsidizes journalism to the extent that it provides reporters with cheap and efficient access to information. This implies that journalism is strongly shaped by the way in which information flows around the state. For example, over the past century, aggregating and distributing information has been so costly, difficult, and time-consuming that only large institutional actors – i.e., the political parties, interest groups, and federal bureaucracies – have been willing and able to pay these costs (e.g., Bimber, 2003; Bimber et al., 2005). To the extent that they congregate around them, journalists take on the sensibilities and character of these institutions. It is no accident, for instance, that, like these institutions, news organizations are large bureaucracies or that, like the people who inhabit these institutions, journalists view themselves as professionals.

Increasingly, however, new digital tools are lowering communication costs. This has allowed new organizational forms, like "meetups," networked interest groups, spontaneous protests, and viral communication lists, to emerge. One example of this phenomenon is the Tea Party, a movement within the Republican Party that has grown in a networked fashion without formal organizations or organizational leaders (Rauch, 2010). Another is President Obama's 2008 presidential campaign, which relied upon thousands of small, self-organizing social networks to raise money and canvass communities (Abramowitz, 2009). According to Bimber (2003), the rise of such networked organizations indicates a transformation of American public life toward a "post-bureaucratic" order.

The rise of this social order has important consequences for journalism. Most obviously, it threatens to rob the profession of a crucial subsidy. In a mass-mediated context, political actors needed journalists to get their issues on the public agenda and manage public opinion (e.g., McCombs, 2004). This is the origin of the "negotiation of newsworthiness" researchers have identified as the heart of conventional communication practice in politics (Cook,

1989). In a post-bureaucratic public life, organizations may go around journalism to pursue their political goals. When, in 2009, the oil company Chevron learned that the news program *60 Minutes* planned to produce a segment on the company's role in contaminating the Amazon rainforest, it did not launch a PR campaign in the media. Instead, it hired a reporter, produced its own story, placed the resulting 14-minute video on its website, and conducted an Internet campaign to place the video at the top of Google searches on the topic (Stelter, 2009). Similarly, when the governor of Hawaii, Neil Abercrombie, wished to announce a new agreement with the state's largest labor union, he did not hold a press conference with reporters. Instead, he tweeted the announcement and linked to an interview he held with himself on YouTube (Temple, 2011). Examples of such maneuvers are quickly multiplying. When the *Los Angeles Times* began to devote less attention to the city's hockey team, the Los Angeles Kings, the team hired its own reporter, who produces and distributes news on the team's website, Facebook page, and Twitter feed. And, when coverage of city government by traditional news outlets shrunk in Portland, the city communication office hired a reporter to cover regional politics (Mortenson, 2011). In these examples, political actors have learned that, in a networked society, once anyone knows something, everyone knows it, so they no longer need journalists to distribute information. To the extent that this recognition grows, traditional news organizations (read: newspapers) will find themselves bereft of a subsidy that has sustained them for nearly one hundred years.

Individually and together, the disruptions taking place along journalism's axes are fascinating. But focusing too strictly on any one of them risks missing the forest for the trees. The ultimate consequence of these disruptions is not that the axes themselves are changed, but that the relations between them are weakened. Remember that it is not the forces, but the relation between them, that constitutes social fields. The field of journalism is constituted, for instance, by the fact that more commercialism inevitably means less professionalism in the news (and vice versa). It is this predictability that lends meaning to the field. But, in online news, such relationships are no longer automatic. Many online journalists are exploring new business models of news with little interest in gaining distinction among traditional journalists. For them, more commercialism does not mean less professionalism because they have no interest in being professional journalists. The same is true for the many organizations that now produce news around the state. Today, the Council on Foreign

Relations, a think-tank, produces as much international and foreign affairs news as any newspaper, and Circle of Blue, a network of journalists and scientists, covers water issues and climate policy as deeply as traditional news organizations. Neither, however, is doing so to gain recognition (or capital) within the profession of journalism. In this way, traditional relationships between commercialism, professionalism, and news oriented to the state no longer necessarily hold.

When the "power lines" that constitute a field no longer vary together, we should expect to see more variation among its members. In the past, a tabloid newspaper such as the *National Enquirer* was different from a newspaper such as the *Washington Post*. But these differences were muted by the fact that they inhabited the same field, and so felt the pushing and pulling of commercialism against professionalism. Journalists at a commercially oriented newspaper like the *Enquirer* still sought distinction among their fellow professionals (e.g., Bird, 1992). And, no matter how professional, reporters at the *Washington Post* had to be aware of the commercial needs of their company. When these forces cease pulling against one another, organizations are freed to spin away from each other, much like planetary objects do when freed from the gravitational force of a star. As this happens, they become more different from one another over time.

Compare, for instance, Demand Media and ProPublica, two online news organizations. Demand Media is a so-called content farm. It deploys an algorithm to analyze millions of web searches on niche topics and uses this information to drive its content decisions. If, for instance, people often search the question "How do you fix a leaky faucet?," then Demand Media will hire a freelancer – to whom it pays as little as a few dollars for the content – to write a brief answer. It will post this answer to one of its web properties, such as e-how.com, and use search-optimization techniques to ensure that the answer comes up high on Google search results. The entire exercise is commercially driven. Computers rather than professional journalists make editorial decisions. The algorithms put in place to make these decisions are purposely written to satisfy commercial goals. And the "content creators" put in minimal effort to write "just good enough" copy. As one former freelancer for the company put it, "I was completely aware that I was writing crap . . . I was like, 'I hope to God people don't read my advice on "how to make gin at home" because they'll probably poison themselves'" (quoted in Hiar, 2010; see also *The Economist*, 2010; Meaney, 2010; Roth, 2009).

ProPublica, a self-described "independent, non-profit, newsroom that produces investigative journalism in the public interest," is different in most every way. It specializes in investigative reporting, a genre that reporters have long held up as the epitome of professional journalism. In the past, even most professional newsrooms invested only a few resources in this style of journalism, mostly because it was very costly and time-consuming. ProPublica's thirty-plus reporters only do investigative journalism. They track the influence of the pharmaceutical industry on medical prescriptions, and whether the military is taking care of its wounded veterans, and who is at fault for the financial industry meltdown. They do this not in a few stories published once in a newspaper but in dozens of stories published over many years. For instance, they have written more than 300 stories over three years on the federal stimulus program alone. Where Demand Media circulates quick, short blurbs to maximize profits, ProPublica produces deep investigations for no profit all.

To the extent that this extreme variation happens, the field of journalism begins to lose meaning. I mean by this that journalists lose a shared sense of purpose in what they are doing and why. For example, even as recently as the late 1990s, it was possible for a new journalist to chart a course through the "game" of journalism. After journalism school, she could imagine beginning at a small-town daily newspaper, working her way up to a city newspaper, then a big regional newspaper, and so on. She could do this because there were settled understandings of the "game's" rules and resources. The forms of capital (the skills and values) she would need to acquire, and the moves she would need to make, were widely known. For new journalists, this game has all but disappeared. Honing the skills and embracing the values of traditional journalism are no longer sure pathways to success in the field. But acquiring new skills is no guarantee of success either. Suppose that she learns how to engage communities using social media tools such as Facebook, Twitter, foursquare, and the like, and these skills land her a job as a "community coordinator" for an online news site. Where does she go from there? There is no ready answer. No one knows how to leverage these skills into a career within online journalism because, as yet at least, there is no "game," with widely recognized rules and resources, to play. This is a nice illustration of the underlying point: as networks weaken the relations of force within journalism, the field unravels. As it unravels, it loses meaning, and people lose a sense of how to go on.

After over ten years of buffeting, the field of journalism now looks more like figure 5.4. Each axis of the field has been deeply troubled,

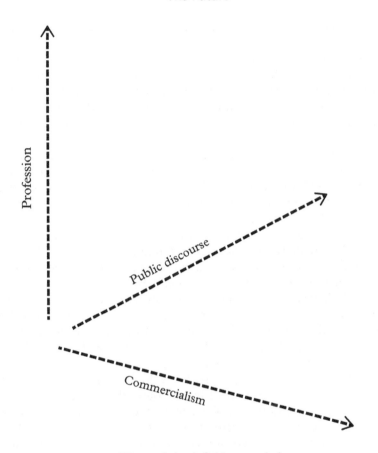

Figure 5.4 A field unraveled

and the relations between them have been disrupted. Instead of pulling against one another, the forces are now pulling apart. This has weakened the boundaries of the field, made it more porous, and allowed organizations in the field to grow more dissimilar. Longtime strategies for successfully navigating the field no longer seem effective, but new ones have yet to be codified.

Virtuous Cycles

The question now is, what will happen next? More properly, does a virtuous cycle for networked news exist? If so, will it stitch the field back together? And, whether or not this happens, how will journalism be changed?

It says something about the importance of the state to journalism that a federal law could obviate these questions. Public officials might conclude that traditional professional journalism is so vital to democracy that it deserves to be directly subsidized by the state. Many observers have encouraged Congress to do just this. For instance, Len Downie, the venerated former editor of the *Washington Post*, and Michael Schudson, a leading academic researcher, have called for the creation of a "national fund for local news" to be managed by the Federal Communications Commission (FCC) and supported by fees on telecom users, broadcast licenses, or Internet service providers (ISPs) (Downie and Schudson, 2009). Others have noted that public subsidies are helping journalists in other countries better weather the challenge of the Internet (e.g., Benson and Powers, 2010). Journalists often criticize such ideas for, among other things, being a violation of the First Amendment. But this has not deterred a House Judiciary Subcommittee from considering just this sort of policy in 2009, or the Senate Commerce Committee from doing the same shortly thereafter. To date, however, Congress has not acted.

It also says something about the state of mind within journalism that many journalists have sought a way around these questions by putting their faith in, of all people, Steve Jobs. The former CEO of Apple Inc., Jobs created a set of technologies that suggest a way of re-creating the conditions of scarcity that once supported journalism. The mini-computers Apple produces – the iPhone, iPod, and iPad – are deeply attractive to consumers because of their elegance and ease of use. But these devices cannot be modified or reprogrammed except in ways approved by Apple. Moreover, Apple has tethered them to applications that are available only in Apple's iTunes store and, again, controls which applications are available in this space. Finally, Apple has entered agreements with the largest content providers (e.g., Time Warner, Disney) to feature their content in its store. Under Jobs's leadership, Apple succeeded in creating a "walled garden" online, a space in which it can control the conditions under which people gain access to information. In a sense, Apple has reinvented mass media for an online world.

But excitement over Apple's "walled garden" is misplaced. On the one hand, the largest news organizations have no need of "walled gardens" online. Instead, they can take advantage of power laws to achieve the same result – that is, to achieve relative dominance in the network. On the other hand, organizations outside the largest few will not be able to take advantage of Apple's "walled garden" strategy under any circumstances. They simply cannot drive enough traffic to their content, whether it is packaged in a newspaper or an app, to remain viable over the long term.

In a discussion of a typical news blog post, media analyst Ken Doctor (2010, pp. 26–7) explains why. Suppose, he writes, that David Pogue, a reporter and columnist for the *New York Times*, publishes a blog post on its news site. Also make the following assumptions: that the post is surrounded by three ads, that the *Times* ad rate is $12 per CPM (which means "cost per thousand" views), and that the blog generates 2 million page views per month. These are all conservative estimates of the actual numbers. But, doing the math, $36 per page for every 1,000 page views, at 2 million page views per month, generates about $2,400 in revenue for that one post. Assuming that Pogue publishes at least one post or story per day, he produces about $72,000 per month in revenue. Use numbers more typical of a regional newspaper like the *Chicago Tribune* or the *Miami Herald*, and the result is very different. Doctor tells us that a blog at a regional newspaper may attract 200,000 page views per month, and that, because these newspapers are less prominent, they can charge only about $8 per CPM. In this scenario, the same post generates only $240, and the same reporter only about $4,800 per month. That amount is not insignificant, but it pales in comparison with the revenue that a reporter working for one of the very largest news sites can generate. These sites, which may number fewer than a dozen, have much more ability to leverage a traditional advertising model online.

We may draw two lessons from this example. The first is that the largest media companies have no need of "walled gardens" to reconstruct the virtuous cycle of mass-mediated news online. Power laws ensure that a handful of popular companies – Doctor estimates as many as a dozen or so, including organizations like Reuters, the BBC, the *New York Times*, News Corporation, and CNN – will drive enormous traffic to their products even in an open system. By the way, this gap is already opening. According to comScore, an Internet ratings company, in early 2011 the *New York Times* was the most visited newspaper news site in the United States, with over 32 million unique visitors per month. Among other newspapers, only the Tribune newspapers attract more than half of that number (24.7 million). The next two newspapers, *USA Today* and the *Washington Post*, attract about 16.7 million unique visitors. As this gap widens, the *Times* will gain greater advertising revenue and use this revenue to hire more "star" journalists. These journalists will produce more high-value content that will drive more traffic, which, in turn, will generate more advertising revenue, more separation from other organizations, and so on. In a world characterized by power laws, the rich almost always get richer.

Part of what this means is that mass-mediated news will not likely disappear in a networked environment. Neither, therefore, will professional journalism. In fact, given that these companies now operate in a global market of roughly 500 million English-language Internet users worldwide, they will be able to pack their newsrooms with the very best journalists. This is not to say that journalism as practiced at these organizations will remain the same. Here is one likely change: because people have more choice online about which information to consume and from whom, online journalism, even as practiced in the largest organizations, is likely to be more intimate and personal than in the past. Many consumers will visit the *Washington Post* to read whatever happens to be on the front page, but many more will go directly to stories and posts written by Ezra Klein, a journalist who works for the paper. And, because power laws advantage the most popular nodes in a network, some of these journalists, like Klein, will obtain a large following, even to the point of becoming brands themselves.

Another difference may be that a feeder system of smaller professional news companies develops around the small group of very large mass-media organizations. For example, the audience for MSNBC's news site may increase, but this does not mean that the company will be willing or able to pay for its journalists to produce high-end, and therefore costly, video stories. Instead, it may prefer to outsource these stories to a company like mediastorm.com. Owned by Brian Storm, a former director of multi-media for MSNBC.com, mediastorm.com produces documentary narratives for a host of clients, including MSNBC, the *Los Angeles Times*, and the *Washington Post*. For these larger news companies, purchasing video stories from mediastorm.com is cheaper than paying full-time journalists to do the same in-house. Similarly, the *New York Times* may wish to outsource its most expensive investigations to an organization like ProPublica, the non-profit newsroom mentioned earlier that employs over thirty journalists to produce long-form, in-depth investigations on a variety of topics. How extensive this feeder system becomes will depend on the market that develops for its services. But its existence may complement the number of traditional, professional journalists working within and around the remaining mass-media organizations.

The second lesson to draw, however, is that, with or without "walled gardens," every other organization will have to learn to survive in a networked environment. Remember that regional newspapers have been losing market share and circulation for decades. Fewer members of each generation read news than the last. The only thing that has sustained these papers is their monopoly on regional and local markets. The migration online does not change these facts. For reasons that Doctor outlines, even within walled gardens most regional newspapers will not be able to attract the requisite traffic to be successful.[14]

These organizations are already getting smaller. Will they die? This is not likely. But, once they dwindle below a certain size, whether or not they cease to exist becomes less important. In every city across the nation, regional newspapers employ the great majority of working daily journalists, and these journalists produce the vast amount of daily news. As they are laid off in larger numbers, not only will the pool of professional reporters for local and regional news get smaller, the amount of news produced on a daily basis will get smaller as well.

The more important question is whether a virtuous cycle for networked local and regional news exists and, if so, what it will look like. Recent developments in cities like Seattle and Chicago shed some light on this question. In 2009, the *Seattle Post-Intelligencer*, founded in 1863, ceased print publication and became an online-only newspaper. In so doing, it immediately downsized from 165 to twenty staffers, and today it employs eleven "newsgatherers" (e.g., *The Oregonian*, 2009; Sharples, 2009). The city continues to be served by the *Seattle Times*, a family-owned newspaper in which the McClatchy Company also holds a 49.5 percent stake. But the *Times* has been downsized as well. A study commissioned by the New America Foundation estimates that, between 2004 and 2009, the newspaper let go of 165 out of 375 employees (Durkin et al., 2010). In fact, according to the 2011 Pew *State of the Media* report, in the decade from 2000 to 2010, Seattle lost nearly 60 percent of its working daily journalists (Fancher, 2011).

Hundreds of neighborhood blogs, community websites, Facebook pages, and online newspapers, magazines, and newsletters have stepped into this void. A recent canvass of local neighborhoods by the City of Seattle Information Technology Department identified 260 news and information outlets in the city's thirteen districts – everything from a Facebook page to a neighborhood blog. And, according to the Washington New Council, at least ninety place-based news sites have sprouted in the region (Caggiano, 2011).

Some of these sites are quite popular. The ten blogs associated with nextdoormedia.com cumulatively attract over 1 million users per month, and approximately 750,000 people visit the West Seattle blog each month. Many others are very small and rarely updated, and more than a few rely on local citizens to produce free content. Still, the New America study tells us that, taken together, these sites employed 104 part- or full-time journalists in the summer of 2010.

Something like the same process is happening in Chicago. While print media, like the *Chicago Tribune*, shed workers at a fast rate, a vibrant network of online news sources has emerged. A study conducted by Rich Gordon and Zachary Johnson (2011) identified 277 separate online news sources in the Chicago area. Some of these sources were online versions of print or broadcast operations (such as the *Chicago Tribune*'s website). But most were micropublishers and niche publications staffed by a few of employees and focused on narrow topics. Many were not news organizations at all. For instance, Gordon and Johnson found that the City of Chicago, the City Transit Authority, and the Field Museum were central players in this emergent information network. In fact, more sites linked to these organizations than to the sites of traditional news companies like the local newspapers or broadcast stations.

We should acknowledge that these cities are distinctive. They have a highly educated, technologically literate workforce and an expansive digital infrastructure. Thanks to the downsizing of local newspapers, they also have a critical mass of professional journalists in need of work. Not every community has these advantages, but certainly most large urban areas – from San Diego to Boston – do.

What do events in Seattle and Chicago tell us about the future of networked news? One thing they tell us is that networked news faces what I call a "Goldilocks" problem. In both cities, the information system is highly distributed and fragmented, and most sites are very small. This means that the audience for the smallest neighborhood and niche sites is not large enough to generate much revenue. There are not enough people interested in what happens on a particular city block, street, or neighborhood to drive much traffic to these sites. Yet, across the region the information environment is quite diffuse and abundant. Thousands of people produce information on a wide variety of topics. This abundance makes it very difficult for sites to distinguish their content. A study (Hindman, 2011) of local news content done for the FCC, for instance, finds that "local news is a tiny part of Web usage; collectively, local news outlets receive less than half of a percent of all page views in a typical market" (p. 11).

So, although in 2010 West Seattle blog posted six-figure revenues using a display ad model, the blog faces a highly fragmented environment in which profits will be difficult, if not impossible, to obtain. Already, a regional media company, Fisher Communications, has launched its own 43-blog network in Seattle. This competition makes it is unlikely that even a site like West Seattle blog can produce enough content to grow a large audience or, for this reason, to build an organization of any scale.[15]

It appears, this is to say, that the online market for local and regional news is both too narrow and too diffuse. It is too narrow to support hyperlocal sites and too diffuse to support larger sites of any size. This problem is complicated by the fact that many people produce and distribute news in this environment, and not all of these people, perhaps not even a majority, are professional journalists who wish to be paid. Some of these people produce news to help their organizations fulfill other goals. Still others do so for a host of "intrinsic" reasons: because they are interested, because they are seeking companionship, or because they wish to gain status among their peers. As the saying goes, it is hard to compete against free. When others are willing to do what you do for little or no money, survival, much less growth, becomes very difficult.

The question facing local and regional news sites is not whether they can find a business model. There are lots of business models for digital news. One media scholar has developed a list of twenty-one different subsidies for online news – everything from government money to wealthy benefactors (Rosen, 2009). Rather, the question is whether these sites can discover a virtuous cycle. For instance, because of the success of sites like Minnpost, Voice of San Diego, and ProPublica, a non-profit business model has attracted much attention in recent years. In this model, news organizations rely on grants (whether corporate, foundation, government, or individual) to fund news production. But, while these sites have used this model to persist, they have not grown very much, mainly because non-profit news lacks a positive feedback loop: producing more news that attracts more readers does not necessarily translate into more grant dollars. Failing to find this connection, it is not surprising that most non-profit news organizations, including the three mentioned above, are seeking to diversify, to cobble together a combination of donations, grants, subscriptions, and advertising dollars, so that they may grow.

Niche publishing – another popular online business model – faces a similar problem. In this model, a journalist produces information on a narrow subject that is of such quality consumers are willing to pay for access via membership or subscription fees. For example, Michelle Leder, a seasoned business journalist, created footnoted. org, a website devoted to information contained in SEC filings. This information is of such value that a small community of investors is willing to pay for access, and Leder has made a nice living from subscription fees. However, by definition the community of people willing to pay for this information is small, and will remain small. There are only so many investors interested enough in information from SEC filings to pay for it. Despite its sustainability, therefore, the model lacks a growth cycle. This may explain why Leder sold her site to Morningstar, a financial firm interested more in her audience than in the prospects for the site itself.

Absent a virtuous cycle, no business model can serve as a template for how to grow a news business online. And, without this template, networked journalism will not gain traction. Sites will come and go, but the field as a whole will not congeal into a relatively integrated social space. But if a virtuous cycle for networked news exists, it will be found in the relationship between news and the rhythms of a networked society. As I canvass the field, only two potential virtuous cycles fit this criterion. Each capitalizes on a different feature of networked society.

We might call the first an "aggregated network" cycle (e.g., Fourcher, 2010; Gluckstadt, 2009; Niles, 2010; Rainey, 2010). This cycle takes advantage of the ease of coordination in a networked society by linking together numerous hyperlocal sites into larger networks. It then aggregates audience across the sites and monetizes this audience by selling advertising across the network. For example, most of the hundreds of bloggers in Seattle drive fewer than 10,000 unique monthly visitors to their sites. But, if these bloggers formed a network, their aggregated monthly audience might number in the millions. They could then sell advertising across the network and divide the resulting revenue proportionally. The cycle would look something like this: more bloggers equals more audience, equals more ads, equals more revenue, equals more bloggers, and voilà! – a virtuous cycle is born.

This virtuous cycle is not without problems. The most obvious is that each online ad brings in only pennies, so the network will have to sell an extraordinarily high volume of advertising for each blogger to make a living. This problem will be exacerbated if competition between networks erupts and divides up the audience. It is also not clear that an audience of sufficient size for hyperlocal news exists.

A survey by the Pew Research Center for the People and the Press found that only 20 percent of American adults use online tools to stay informed about their communities, and only 10 percent have read a community blog in the past year (e.g., Mutter, 2011; Palser, 2010). Many initiatives, from tbd.com to LoudonExtra, have tried and failed to solve these problems. But its economic potential – by some estimates, the advertising market for hyperlocal news approaches $100 billion or more – ensures that it will continue to attract interest.

Crowdsourcing is a second candidate for a virtuous cycle in online news. According to Jeff Howe (2007), the writer for *Wired* magazine who coined the term, crowdsourcing is the act of outsourcing work once done by an individual to a group. It takes advantage of the fact that networks make it easy for groups of people to collaborate with one another (e.g., Bimber, 2003; Shirky, 2008; Tapscott and Williams, 2006). For instance, the work of taking photographs, once done by professional photographers, may be outsourced to a crowd of amateur photographers, who can take many more photographs and work together to identify the best of the lot. The work of devising T-shirt logos, once done by professionals, may be outsourced to a crowd of T-shirt wearers. The work of scientific innovation, once done by individual scientists working in the isolation of their labs, may be outsourced to a crowd of scientists working collaboratively in a networked environment. The same might be done in journalism: once accomplished by individual reporters, the work of producing news might be outsourced to a crowd.

To the extent a news site can prompt such collaboration, it may stimulate a virtuous cycle. The cycle begins with catalyzing user interaction. The more people interact with one another, the stronger their relationship becomes to a site. The stronger their relationship to a site, the more often they return, and the longer they stay. The "stickier" the site becomes, the more collective work people produce on the site. The more work they accomplish, the more valuable the site becomes, both to its users and to its owners. For owners, the simple fact that people chat with one another means that the site will rise in search-engine results (more pages equals more prominence). If the crowd produces more than talk, then the owner of the site has been rewarded with content produced efficiently and virtually cost-free.

Many news organizations have experimented with this model. Gannett's "mom" sites (e.g., "Cincymoms" at the *Cincinnati Enquirer*, "IndyMoms" at the *Indianapolis Star*), on which crowds of moms produce content on everything from diapers to best parks in town, is one example. The crowdsourced January 2011 issue of *Forbes* magazine is another. In June 2009, *The Guardian* launched a crowdsourced investigative project of over 17,000 public documents, and in 2011 *The Atlantic* launched OpenWire, an online space in which the magazine's editors invite its community to crowdsource the news.

If these initiatives seem like one-off experiments or ancillary to the main work of producing news for a site, they are. I know of no news organization of any size that relies solely upon crowdsourcing to produce news. There are likely many reasons for this difficulty. For one thing, crowdsourcing is not an easy process to catalyze. It takes a core group of committed amateurs willing to devote long hours to the enterprise, and it takes journalists who know how to catalyze and maintain this commitment. Such people simply may be in short supply. For another, the process of crowdsourcing is not predictable or controllable. If the crowd does not want to write news about city hall, then no news about city hall will be written. And if the crowd wants to talk and write about the latest in swimsuit fashions, then that is what it will do. It may be that few journalists are willing to allow so much unpredictability to invade the newsgathering process. Given the amount of time and attention it requires, it is not obvious that a wholly crowdsourced news site is economically viable. Will anyone beyond the core group of users routinely visit the site? Will the group be able to consistently produce compelling content? Underlying such questions is another: Are we witnessing the transformation of public life into a "post-bureaucratic order"? As Carey (1989) reminds us, journalism expresses public life. Networked journalism will thrive only in the context of a broader networked society. Journalists likely will not discover answers to the particular questions they face unless and until an answer to this broader question emerges.

In the meantime, a great number of experiments in journalism are underway. In fact, the Knight Community News Network (kcnn.org) lists over 1,000 online experiments in news production, and there are surely hundreds, if not thousands, more. The reasons for this explosion of innovation are twofold. First, the cost of trying is very low. Anyone with a Wordpress blog and a dream can set up shop. Second, the potential impact of even the smallest of sites is very large. Josh Marshall's Talking Points Memo, which employs as few as a dozen people, drives as much traffic as a mid-sized regional newspaper staffed with hundreds of people.

These experiments indicate that, regardless of whether journalism is ever put back together as an integrated social field, the process for news production is changing. This is so for an obvious reason: a

networked environment presents journalists with very different problems from those encountered in a mass-mediated environment. For
instance, in a mass-mediated environment journalists were faced with
the problem of attracting and holding the attention of a heterogene-
ous, anonymous mass audience. They approached this problem in
several ways. They remained neutral toward the issues they covered
for fear of seeming biased toward a segment of their audience. While
many acquired subject-area knowledge, the profession privileged a
"generalist" sensibility that could explain complicated information
to people with little knowledge of the issues. They wrote in a "for
everyone and therefore for no one" style.

The corresponding problem in a networked environment is nearly
the exact opposite. In this environment, journalists must first appeal
to a small number of highly passionate people. These are people who
return most often to a site to chat with one another, make comments
on posts, and write posts themselves. According to power laws, they
will accomplish as much as 80 percent of the interaction that takes
place on a site, and they are absolutely vital to hyperlocal or crowdsourced journalism. Their work opens the way for other, less interested, folks to engage with a site. For online journalists, the problem
is not how to appeal to a mass audience, but how to attract this small
group of passionate people.

An early experiment in crowdsourced journalism, Assignment
Zero (assignmentzero.com), shows how working through this
problem leads journalists to adopt new practices. Conducted in
2007, Assignment Zero combined the efforts of amateurs and professionals to crowdsource the phenomenon of crowdsourcing. The
professionals served as editors for the project. Initially, they acted like
editors have done for decades: they made assignments and badgered
reporters to get their work done. Some of the 500-plus amateurs
who were attracted to the project – mostly those who wanted to
become professional reporters – took this cue and went out to report
their stories. Most of the other amateurs did not. These people were
motivated by a desire to interact with their collaborators. In other
words, they desired relationships, not information. So they e-mailed
their editors incessantly to engage them in conversation and became
frustrated that the site did not provide a space in which they could
meet and talk with their peers. Eventually, after a tense meeting, the
professionals realized that their job was to act less like editors than, as
Lauren Sandler, one of the editors on the project put it, like someone
"throwing a house party . . . You program the iPod, mix the punch
and dim the lights and then at 8 o'clock people show up" (quoted in

Carr, 2007; also see Howe, 2007). In other words, the editors realized that relationships are crucial when trying to attract and retain the attention of highly passionate people who are not motivated to become professional journalists. To create these relationships, they began to imagine themselves as throwing a party. The skills of throwing a good party include such things as inviting the right sorts of people, distributing invitations, making the space inviting, mingling with guests, and the like. Put in journalistic terms, they include the art of making connections with people and helping them make connections with others. They also take in listening and responding to users, facilitating conversations that take place on the site, and designing an experience that makes the site seem comfortable and familiar. None of this involves digging up scarce information, holding public officials to account, having a good narrative eye, or writing well and quickly – i.e., practices traditionally valued in the field. But, faced with a new need, the editors at Assignment Zero found themselves gravitating to new practices.

Journalism may never again be an integrated social field. As I said in the introduction to this book, there will always be news, but journalists may not produce it, and, if they do, they may not work in journalism. Moreover, much of the future of the journalistic field is not up to journalists. Rather, it depends on dynamics within the broader public culture: whether and the extent to which institutions of government become networked, whether and the extent to which civic institutions take a networked form, and so on. It is impossible to predict how this story will play out, and so it is impossible to predict what will happen to journalism. But even now it is clear that the practice of news production and consumption is changing. The networked environment of the Internet poses new problems to news producers. These problems require new solutions – new practices and norms, new principles and identities. And these solutions are changing the way that news is produced, distributed, and consumed.

6
Worries

One day, over lunch with a long-time journalist, I was describing the future of news as I saw it when he stopped me in mid-sentence. "Let me ask you something," he said. "Are you comfortable living in a country where your children, thirty-five years from now, won't have access to an impartial account of events?" I sat for a moment trying to think of what to say. "I'm serious," he said. I knew he was. Journalists had peppered me with similar questions in every newsroom I visited. When they were gone, they pressed me time and again, who was going to speak up for the powerless? Who was going to watch corrupt politicians? Who was going to do the investigations and dig up the information? When they asked these questions, I often imagined them as Colonel Jessup, the Jack Nicholson character in the movie *A Few Good Men*. When a reporter insisted to me that journalism has a "core mission" to serve the public, and then asked this question, "If we don't do that, then who will?" I heard Jessup declare, "You want me on that wall!"

No one expresses this sensibility better than Alex Jones. A former media reporter for the *New York Times* and currently director of Harvard University's Shorenstein Center on the Press, Politics, and Public Policy, Jones wrote *Losing the News* (2009). In this book, he vividly articulates journalists' concerns, returning again and again to the connection between news and democracy: "One must ask whether a genuine, vibrant democracy can thrive without ... traditional, objective journalism" (p. 33); "If a fundamental confidence in the 'iron core; disappears ... then one of the most important supports for our democracy will weaken" (p. 100); "The very profession of journalism ... [may be] passing ... should that [happen] we shall be the poorer for it" (p. 195). Translated: "You want [us] on that wall!"

Those in few occupations think of themselves in such grandiose terms. You won't find out-of-work software developers worrying that the loss of their jobs spells the downfall of democracy. Then again, the software development industry is not mentioned in the Bill of Rights. Americans have always associated journalism with democracy – in different ways at different times, but associated them nonetheless. The two are so intimately related that people sometimes use journalism as a barometer for the health of democracy. This is what Alex Jones and my journalist friend are doing. As journalism unravels before their eyes, it seems clear to them that the downfall of democracy cannot be far behind.

Is their worry justified? In a word, yes. "This is what real revolutions are like," Clay Shirky (2009) observes. "The old stuff gets broken faster than the new stuff is put in its place." Chatting with, of all people, Alex Jones, at a Shorenstein Center event, Shirky expounds on this point: "A bad thing's happening. People aren't taking seriously the idea that this is going to get worse for the foreseeable future. Increasing corruption is probably baked into the current environment." We're facing "a long trough of decline in accountability journalism," and our goal needs to be to "minimize the depth of that trough, and hasten its end" (Zuckerman, 2009). A gap has opened up in the space between the unraveling of journalism and whatever comes next. Contemplating this gap, journalists have become quite concerned. Shirky is telling us that we should be worried too.

The question is what to do with these worries. Many of the journalists with whom I have talked turn the worries in to a defense of traditional journalism. This is certainly Jones's intent. He wants to "save the news," he writes at the end of his book, which means, to him, "finding a commercial model that will sustain professional journalism . . . with traditional values and standards" (2009, p. 200).

While understandable, this response is not especially helpful. In the first place, it is unrealistic. As I showed in the last chapter, traditional journalism, especially at the local and regional levels, simply fits awkwardly in an online environment. No amount of handwringing will change this fact. The response may also be misleading. The wish for a return of traditional journalism implies that journalism is changing, but that democracy is not. On the vision sketched by the worriers, democracy will always need professional journalists to filter information for a relatively apathetic public. Even if this was once true, it has not always been true, and, moving forward, it may no longer be true. It may be that networks are changing democratic practice every bit as much as they are changing journalism. In this circumstance, democracy may need a different kind of journalism to play a new role in public life. Worriers' investment in the past risks obscuring this possibility.

In recent years, many news entrepreneurs have responded in a different way. They are as worried as any traditional journalist, but they have avoided the impulse to reinvent the past. Instead, they have used their worries as motivation to build new, networked forms of public service journalism. A review of these innovations suggests that, in the future, journalists will not act as solitary sentinels of democracy. Rather, they will collaborate with crowds to perform journalism's democratic function. Whether this new role of engaging crowds will amount to a fundamental transformation of journalism is difficult to say. Partly, as I argued in the last chapter, it depends on whether and how networks change the norms, practices, and institutions of public life. Were a fundamental change to occur, however, worries about the loss of traditional journalism would, ironically enough, have helped to catalyze a wholly new sense of journalism's purpose.

A canvass of worries about the loss of journalism is important because not everything about the future will be positive. Some aspects of traditional journalism will be lost that we would prefer not be lost. A review of worries is also useful because of the responses they have engendered. These responses add additional detail to the future of news we sketched in the previous chapter and set a context to help us understand events as they unfold.

Journalism and Democracy

Journalists don't often think of themselves as "theorists." In fact, they generally see themselves as the exact opposite: pragmatic, hard-nosed, feet-on-the-ground sorts of people. But I have found that most carry around with them a theory, a relatively organized set of ideas that inform who they are, what they are doing, and why they are doing it. I have also found that the theory is not far from the surface. If you scratch a journalist in the right way, say, with a series of naïve questions, it is easily elicited. Take my lunch partner worried about the absence of "impartial" news. If I were to ask him why we need "impartial" accounts of events, he would no doubt say: so that the public will be informed. If I were to ask him why the public must be informed, he might respond that it is their responsibility to make good judgments about the issues reported in the news. If I then asked him why people needed to make good judgments about these issues, the answer would be obvious: so that the public may guide the behavior of public officials. And there you have it: a rudimentary theory of journalism and democracy!

According to this theory, journalism mediates the relationship between government – as represented by public officials – and the public. Reporters take information from government (in the form of documents, interviews, press conferences, and so on) and transform it into news. They deliver this news to the public, which uses it to form judgments about the issues of the day. Journalists then aggregate the public's judgments into "public opinion" and convey this opinion to public officials. With public opinion in hand, journalists hold public officials accountable for serving the "public interest." In this way, a modern, complex society can make a democracy "of the people, by the people, for the people" work. By extension, if journalists do not play their prescribed role – if they are not there to take information from public officials, or if people no longer consume the news – then democracy is in danger.

As I say in the introduction to this book, this theory of journalism expresses the progressive culture from which it sprang (e.g., Hoftstadter, 1963; Gans, 1979; Schudson, 1998). It is in this culture that the large, bureaucratic, and technocratic institutions of modern public life found their *raison d'être*. Society needed large public institutions because progressives sought to tackle public problems on their largest scale. These institutions needed to be bureaucratic to promote efficient management and control. And technocrats were necessary because public problems were perceived to be so nettlesome that they required expert knowledge to solve. Journalism "expressed" this culture, as James Carey (1989) argues, in the sense that it mimicked the progressive faith that government should tackle large public problems, that it could manage if not solve these problems, and that expertise was key to the whole enterprise. Journalism also expressed these cultural beliefs in its very structure and organization: journalism itself became large, bureaucratic, and technocratic.

It is difficult to overstate how fervently journalists embraced this self-conception. In another place, James Carey eloquently put it this way:

> The god term of journalism – the be-all and end-all, the term without which the entire enterprise fails to make sense – is the public. Insofar as journalism has a client, the client is the public. The press justifies itself in the name of the public. It exists – or so it is regularly said – to

inform the public, to serve as the extended eyes and ears of the public, to protect the public's right to know, to serve the public interest. The canons of journalism originate in and flow from the relationship of the press to the public. [For journalists] the public is totem and talisman, and an object of ritual homage. (1987, p. 5)

Given the centrality of this self-identity, it is no wonder that recent events have caused journalists such anxiety. Public officials no longer automatically accept that journalists represent the public. With the Internet, they may go around journalists to reach their constituencies. Moreover, majorities of the public no longer believe journalists provide them with an impartial rendition of events, and many of these people have exercised the freedom made available by the Internet to congregate with like-minded others who share their political views. Even more simply ignore the news altogether. The theory, in short, is in a shambles.

Critics will stop me at this point to argue that the theory never corresponded well to reality. A large literature exists demonstrating as much. Murray Edelman (1988) calls news reporting a "construction of political spectacle," in which political elites vie not to inform the public but to define reality. W. Lance Bennett (1983) argues that news reports are personalized, dramatized, and fragmented. Far from informing the public, he says, the news more often leads people to adopt "familiar stereotypes . . . and rigid modes of thinking" (p. 98). In a book titled *Democracy without Citizens*, Robert Entman (1989) observes that the press is so hamstrung by political elites on the one side and commercial elites on the other that it has little ability to truly inform the public. These criticisms are not new, of course. Walter Lippmann (1920, 1922, 1925) already made most of them in the 1920s, the precise moment when the theory was formed. "The vast elaboration of the subject-matter of politics is the root of the whole problem," Lippmann writes. "News comes from a distance; it comes helter-skelter, in inconceivable confusion; it deals with matters that are not easily understood; it arrives and is assimilated by busy and tired people who must take what is given to them. Any lawyer with a sense of evidence knows how unreliable such information must necessarily be" (1920, p. 38).

Generations of scholarship have shown Lippmann to be right. In fact, the theory breaks down right from the start. Most people, most of the time, do not follow the news. The average citizen is simply not interested enough to pay attention, and anyone who is not paying attention cannot, by definition, be informed about the issues. The small percentage of people who faithfully pay attention pose a different problem for the theory: they are high news consumers, to be sure, but they also tend to possess fairly fixed views on public issues. By a process psychologists refer to as "confirmation bias," these views lead them to pay more attention to news that confirms their prior opinions and to discount the rest. The news does less to inform than to reconfirm the views of these individuals. A middle group of people can be occasionally interested in the news, and their views are not so fixed that they are immune to new information. However, they tend not to pay very much attention, only enough to discover "information cues" – small bits of information which they find in headlines or the first paragraphs of news stories – that allow them to make snap judgments. Statistically speaking, public opinion is determined by this middle group. As expressed in survey data, the views of apathetic and ignorant people tend to be random, and so cancel one another out. The views of highly informed people rarely change. It is the middle group, where views fluctuate, that moves public opinion in one direction or another. But their opinions are not so much informed as formed by the news. Political elites know as much, which is why they work hard to shape the information cues by which this group makes sense of the issues. The news is a crucial information cue. Much of the practice of political communication involves managing the news, in the first instance by setting the news agenda, and in the second by convincing reporters to frame issues in ways that support one's political position. In so doing, political elites hope to provide the information cues by which the middle group of interested but not very informed Americans processes the issues – and thereby move public opinion closer to their views.

All of this is well established in the literature on public opinion, political communication, and journalism (e.g., Bennett and Entman, 2001; Delli Carpini and Keeter, 1996; Iyengar, 1991; McCombs, 2004; Neuman, 1986; Patterson, 2003; Zaller, 1992). Little of it supports the theory that journalism either informs the public or holds public officials accountable for acting in the public interest. Public officials are more interested in managing public opinion than being led by it. Few members of the public act like the rational consumers of information imagined by the theory. And journalists typically act less as representatives of the public than as players in a political game played mostly on an elite field.

This literature is damning, in many ways, of journalists' latent democratic theory, but not all of the evidence supports this view. In a review of public opinion polls over decades, pollster Daniel

Yankelovich (1991) finds that the public has reached an informed, reasonable judgment on many issues. Public opinion toward the death penalty, for instance, became stable in the early 1980s and remained much the same through the rest of the decade. The same is true for abortion. Despite the best efforts of anti-abortion groups, solid majorities have been in favor for decades of a woman's right to choose. On other issues – from the environment to sex education in schools – public opinion shows a similar stability. Benjamin Page and Robert Shapiro (1992) have formalized Yankelovich's observations in a theory of the "rational public." Under certain conditions, Page and Shapiro argue, public preferences on political issues can be perfectly "reasonable," "responsible," and even "rational" (1992, p. 388). Among these conditions are the wide and consistent dissemination of information about the issues. In other words, they include a central role for journalism. Neither Yankelovich nor Page and Shapiro argue that the system always, or even often, works. But on certain big issues, which stay in the news for long periods of time, it appears that journalism does indeed inform the public well enough for it to develop reasonably consistent policy preferences.

On some occasions, this is to say, reality seems to confirm the theory reasonably well, at least well enough to warrant a bit of worrying about a future in which journalism no longer plays its accustomed role.

Worries

Worries about the future arise from the fact that the number of daily journalists, and of the newspapers that employ them, is shrinking. In 2006, daily newspapers employed roughly 55,000 journalists. By 2010 that number had fallen 25 percent, to 41,000 – or about the same number newspapers employed in 1975. According to the website Paper Cuts, in the same period hundreds of newspapers either folded or became online-only publications (March 3, 2011). Rick Edmonds (2010) estimates that, between 2006 and 2008, annual spending on newsroom expenses declined by about $1.6 billion. It is no exaggeration to say that this has been the most precipitous contraction of journalism in its history.

It has caused many people to worry that journalism can no longer play its proper role in public life. Defining that role with any specificity is difficult. Except for the First Amendment, journalism is not mentioned in the nation's founding documents, and even there it is coupled to the right of speaking available to anyone, an indication that the founders saw little distinction between the press and citizenship broadly understood. However, in the early twentieth century, journalism took on many new roles that were once performed by others (mostly by the political parties and Congress). These roles include at least the following: witnessing; verifying; explaining; and holding public officials accountable for their actions. The contraction of journalism has called into question whether journalism can continue to play these roles. Let me take each in turn.

Witnessing Journalists, as any journalist will tell you, represent the public. At a minimum, this means that journalists bear witness to public events and actions – everything from city council meetings to court proceedings – in place of citizens who cannot otherwise attend. As their numbers diminish, the worry is that journalists can no longer play this elementary role. Evidence is mounting that this worry is justified. As newsrooms have laid off reporters, newspapers cover fewer parts of city government. "There are strong signs," an FCC report concludes, "that [newsroom] cutbacks have weakened coverage of schools, health care issues, city government . . . and other important topics . . . even when beats have not been eliminated entirely, beat reporters have become responsible for covering more territory and 'feeding the beast'" (Waldman, 2011, p. 231). The same is true of statehouse coverage. In a census of statehouse reporters, the *American Journalism Review* (2009) found 352 full-time newspaper reporters at the nation's state capitols, a 32 percent decrease from a similar survey conducted six years before. The number of statehouse reporters in New Jersey dropped from thirty-five in 2003 to fifteen in 2009, and in California from forty in 2003 to twenty-nine in 2009. Fewer reporters also cover the federal government. A 2009 Pew study found that newspapers with Washington bureaus had declined by half in the past decade. This means, for example, that not a single daily reporter covers the Department of Agriculture (Enda, 2010). And it means that many congressional delegations go virtually uncovered by newspapers back home (Dorroh, 2009). The same story can be told for foreign affairs coverage. Since 2003, a year when the United States launched the first of two wars, eighteen newspapers have closed every one of their foreign news bureaus (Enda, 2011). In short, journalists no longer witness events that take place at many layers of government.

Verifying The decline in numbers of journalists means that public officials have new freedom to dominate the public discourse. In a study of news production in Baltimore, Pew researchers (Pew Research Center, 2010b) examined the news produced by all outlets over a seven-day period. They found that the "ecosystem" of news sources was expansive. Many different sorts of people and institutions produced news. But this diversity resulted in allowing government to dominate the news cycle. In fact, government agencies initiated over 60 percent of political news, and it was not unusual for news outlets to publish government press releases verbatim. Journalists initiated only 13 percent of news stories, and interest groups initiated the rest. This happened, the researchers surmise, because few news outlets have the resources to do independent reporting, and those that do – like the *Baltimore Sun* – have many fewer reporters. These reporters are asked to cover more agencies with fewer resources, and so have little time to verify the information they receive from those agencies. The same dynamics afflict every urban newspaper. If local government has more freedom to dominate the public discourse in Baltimore, it likely enjoys the same freedom in most every major American city.

Explaining   When Len Downie and Robert Kaiser (2002) conveyed the *News about the News*, they saw the *Raleigh News & Observer* (*N&O*) as a ray of hope. The *N&O* "stands out," they wrote, in its "ambition and execution" (p. 75). Writing seven years later, media economist James Hamilton (2009) reports that the *N&O* has been brought to its knees. Between 2004 and 2009, the newspaper lost nearly half its employees. While it may have the same ambitions, it simply does not have enough bodies to fulfill them. Ferrell Guillory (2009) notes one of the consequences. At one time, the *N&O* had four reporters covering health-related issues in North Carolina – everything from the pharmaceutical industry to researchers at Duke University. Now, the newspaper has only one reporter covering the same territory. Not only does this reporter simply miss many health-related events, she covers a wider expanse of issues in less time, and so cannot explain the issues she covers in any depth. "Public relations professionals," Guillory writes, "must provide background, context, and data to reporters who may not have much sense of what has happened" (2009, p. 361). Guillory's conclusions mirror those of a larger study of health journalism conducted by the Kaiser Foundation. Based upon a content analysis and survey of health editors, Kaiser's study found that health reporters have fewer training opportunities than in the past and are producing more "quick hit" and fewer explanatory or complex stories (Schwitzer, 2009, pp. 8–10). As the FCC's working group on the information needs of communities found, the same is true for subjects like technology, immigration, and the environment:

> The Society for Environmental Journalists had 430 newspaper reporters as members in 2004. Six years later, there were 256. "In a topic like environment, people spend a lot of years building up a knowledge base, and when you lose that, you have to rebuild it over a long time," says Beth Parke, executive director of the Society for Environmental Journalists. Tim Wheeler, who reports on the environment for the Baltimore Sun, says, "The work cycle here is changed . . . We're much more like wire service reporters than we were before. My job is to feed the beast." (Waldman, 2011, p. 54)

Accounting David Simon (2009), creator of the TV show *The Wire* and former crime reporter for the *Baltimore Sun*, recalls that, when he was a crime reporter for the newspaper, police department officials routinely refused to provide him information:

> Police commanders . . . felt it was their duty to demonstrate that crime never occurred in their precincts, desk sergeants . . . believed that they had a right to arrest and detain citizens without reporting it and . . . homicide detectives and patrolmen . . . argued convincingly that to provide the basic details of any incident might lead to the escape of some heinous felon. Everyone had very good reasons for why nearly every fact about a crime should go unreported.

It was Simon's job to ensure that this information came out and that officials were held to account for their conduct. So every day Simon engaged in a running battle with officials. That battle has now been waged, and journalists lost. As an example, Simon notes that the police department now refuses to release the names of police officers who use their weapons against Baltimore's citizens. Without this information, it is impossible for journalists to hold the department accountable for its actions.

It is difficult to say with any certainty that less accountability journalism has led to more political corruption. But researchers who study the matter find a correlation between the two. A study commissioned by the Inter-American Development Bank (Adserà et al., 2003) discovers that, across many nations, levels of newspaper readership are strongly correlated with levels of corrupt political practices. Using a different data set, Brunetti and Weder (2003) conclude that a "strong association" exists "between the level of press freedom and the level of corruption across countries" (p. 1820). In short, more journalistic scrutiny of public officials leads to lower levels of political corruption. So, for instance, as the *Los Angeles Times* decreased its coverage of suburban communities, it should come as no surprise that city officials of Bell, California, a small community just outside Los Angeles, were able to pay themselves exorbitant salaries – the city manager alone earned over $800,000. There was simply no one around to inform local citizens that this was happening.

Increased corruption is one consequence of the fact that fewer journalists are around to verify, explain, uncover, and disseminate information. Another is that citizens become less engaged in public life. The connection between news consumption and political/civic participation has been known for some time (e.g., Livingstone and Markham, 2008; Shah et al., 2007). Simply put, the more people consume news, the more likely they are to vote, to join a civic group, to volunteer, and to participate in a host of other political and civic activities. When there is less news to consume, we should expect less participation. That is precisely what Sam Schulhofer-Whol and Miguel Garrido (2009) find in a study involving the closure of the *Cincinnati Post*. The *Post* closed in 2007, leaving the *Cincinnati Enquirer* as the only daily newspaper in the region. In the next few years, fewer candidates ran for the city council, city commission, and school board. Incumbents were more likely to win re-election. Further, fewer people voted in elections or gave to political campaigns. Other research supports Schulhofer-Whol and Garrido's findings (Trounstine, n.d.). The *Post* was a small newspaper with a circulation of 27,000. The worry is that, when larger newspapers fold, more substantial declines in participation may follow.

Beyond specific worries about a rise in political corruption and a decline in political/civic participation, observers have expressed a series of vague concerns about public conversation in the absence of journalism. These worries arise from the fact that, as journalism shrinks, it is being replaced online by an avalanche of entertainment, opinion, and entertaining opinion, all of it personalized to the tastes of individual consumers. In a study of audience traffic for 162 news-based websites, Thomas Patterson (2007) found that "nontraditional" news sites like huffingtonpost.com were growing audiences much faster than traditional sites like those of daily newspapers. Moreover, the former tended to publish more entertainment and opinion news and less hard news. In fact, Patterson discovered that, in many cases, these sites had no capacity (i.e., reporters) to produce any hard news at all. Other research has duplicated Patterson's findings. The Pew Research Center's study of the Baltimore ecosystem of news (2010b) found that the daily newspaper, and to a lesser extent local television stations, produced the vast majority of new information. This information was then digested in an "echo chamber" by blogs, twitter feeds, and local niche sites. According to this research, the Internet is producing an abundance of information but very little news. "We are poised," Alex Jones warns, "to be a nation overfed but undernourished . . . swollen with media exposure, and headed toward an epidemic of social diabetes" (2009, p. 184).

The fear is that the reservoir of information created in a networked environment will be skewed in harmful ways. For one thing, it will be rife with innuendo, rumor, and false information. This claim is an empirical one (*more* false information) that we have no good way of testing. Does more unreliable information circulate through online public discourse than through newspapers of the past? It is difficult to say, and I know of no study on the question. Certainly, however, when the George W. Bush administration made misleading – some would say, false – arguments in support of going to war with Iraq, it was the mainstream and not online media that allowed these assertions to circulate virtually unchecked. It is also the case that newspapers routinely publish inaccurate information, and only some of these inaccuracies are ever corrected (e.g., Maier, 2005). Though in the past a larger corps of journalists existed to "get the facts straight," it is not clear that they were any more successful than the bloggers, citizen journalists, and niche sites that populate the Internet.

More evidence exists for three other biases in a networked public sphere. A first is that, compared to a mass-mediated public sphere, the networked public sphere will skew toward more partisan views. Small-group communication scholars have known for some time that people tend to adopt more extreme versions of previously held views when interacting with like-minded others (e.g., Isenberg, 1986). They have termed this process "group polarization." It means that, for example, if someone already believed that global climate science was suspicious, after interacting with like-minded others in a small group she may come to hold a more extreme version of this belief – say, that a conspiracy exists to convince the public of the danger posed by global climate change. Group polarization seems especially common online, where people tend to interact with like-minded others and to consume information that confirms their pre-existing views. In fact, legal scholar Cass Sunstein (2007) refers to the Internet as a "breeding ground of extremism" (p. 69), and on this basis calls for the reconstruction of "general interest intermediaries" – i.e., of journalism (p. 217).

An episode that occurred in Madison, Wisconsin, illustrates another way in which the online public sphere may be skewed. As described by Lewis Friedland and his colleagues (2007), the episode involved three school referenda to expand a local school in a poor, predominantly African-American, part of town. The authors observe that the referenda were strongly supported by the local political establishment, including local businesses, the teacher's union, the school board, and both local newspapers. This establishment dominated public debate of the issue, so much so that the referenda were widely predicted to pass. But they did not pass. Instead, they were defeated by an insurgent group of mostly upper-middle-class whites. Led by a dissident school board member, this group had been percolating below the surface for some time. But it had never gained traction before, largely because its views were never given much attention in mainstream political circles. With the advent of the Internet, however, the group discovered an alternative forum to share views and coordinate actions. Through a blog (schoolinformationsystem. org [SIS]), the group began to attract more adherents, which led to more publicity, which finally led to increased political power. In this way, a "well-organized minority" gained the ability to "speak to a broader public, and mobilize sufficient support to defeat referenda backed by both major media and an array of . . . important public actors" (Friedland et al., 2007, p. 56).

In theory, these benefits might accrue to any minority group wishing to make an impact on public debate. Clearly, however, minority groups that have a pre-existing base of resources (money, time, political expertise) and that enjoy a higher socio-economic status (SES), will be able to take advantage of this opportunity more than others. To the extent that SES correlates with race (as it does in the United States), members of these groups will also tend to be white. In the past, the value journalism placed on "afflicting the comfortable and comforting the afflicted" at least blunted the advantages of race and class in public debate. Journalism accomplished this by forcing political elites to frame issues in public terms. In Madison, for example, advocates for the new school framed their views in terms of a "public obligation" to address social inequality. As public debate moves online, this filter is lost, and minority groups are able to impose more self-interested frames. Given that white, upper-middle-class people are best positioned to take advantage of the opportunity afforded by the Internet, public debate will more likely be framed around their interests. In Madison, for instance, the SIS frame consisted of an opposition to property tax increases. Moving forward, the worry is that the Internet will exacerbate these sorts of inequalities and lead to an information environment skewed toward the interests of the wealthiest among us.

The Internet may skew the information environment in one final way – toward the interests of political elites. This claim can seem paradoxical. After all, hasn't the Internet freed individuals precisely from the manipulation of political elites? Yes and no. An argument can be made that the new medium actually strengthens the power of political elites over public discourse. It goes like this. In the past, primary and secondary social groups – family and friendship networks, religious groups, and so on – blunted the ability of political elites to shape public opinion. This insight is the basis of the Elihu Katz and Paul Lazarsfeld's (1955) "two-step" flow theory of communication, in which information is said to flow from media through a community's "opinion leaders" and on to individuals. To the extent that political elites had to negotiate with journalists, journalism also played a role in limiting their ability to shape public opinion.

But, as Lance Bennett and Jarol Mannheim (2006) note, American society has fragmented greatly since the 1950s. It has become less a mass society than a "lifestyle" society. This is a society in which people have fewer connections to others and are more intensely focused on personal pursuits (e.g, Giddens, 1991). New communication technologies have facilitated this transition by giving people greater control over their information environment. These same technologies have given marketers of all kinds – including political marketers – the ability to establish direct relationships with their consumers. Eli Pariser (2011) notes, for example, that the same Google search from different computers will yield different results because Google's algorithm automatically tailors results to the personal interests of users. What had been a "two-step" flow of political communication, Bennett and Manheim argue, is increasingly a "one-step" flow: from political elites directly to individual consumers. "Precisely because it is based on interest, preference and need data provided by the targeted individual himself or herself," they conclude, "[this communication] may be more effective than peer group exchanges in anticipating and responding to the personalized concerns of each audience member" (2006, p. 226). It may, in other words, enhance the ability of political elites to manage public opinion.

Behind all of these worries lurks an overarching fear, namely, that the loss of journalism amounts to a loss of community. It is tempting to dismiss this concern as merely an expression of journalists' illusion of grandeur. Journalism is simply not that important, and its loss cannot possibly lead to such a broad consequence. But an argument can be made that journalism is a linchpin for democratic community. Consider, for instance, Hegel's famous quote regarding early modern newspapers: "Reading the newspaper in early morning is a kind of realistic morning prayer. One orients one's attitude against the world and toward God [in one case], or toward that which the world is [in the other]. The former gives the same security as the latter, in that one knows where one stands."[16] Hegel's comment is set in the context of a rapidly secularizing society, one in which religion no longer seemed able to bind individuals to one another and to their communities as it had once done. How were these communal ties to be sustained in a modern world? In the eighteenth century and beyond, this question arises again and again (e.g., Delanty, 2003; Tönnies, 1957). Hegel provides one answer: journalism. On his view, the purpose of news is to offer public rituals out of which new communal attachments might form. This view of journalism's role in society is quite common. One finds traces of it in Alexis de Tocqueville's famous argument that "newspapers make associations and associations make newspapers" (1969, p. 518). It is implicit in John Dewey's image of the "Great Community" as arising when "free social inquiry is wedded to the art of full and moving communication" (1927, p. 184). It shows up in Benedict Anderson's history of nationalism, in his argument that newspaper reading constitutes a new "mass ceremony" that "visibly root[s]" community in the minds of modern citizens (1983, p. 43). It plays a central role in James Carey's "ritual" theory of journalism, when he argues that reading the news is akin to "attending a mass, a situation in which nothing new is learned but in which a particular view of the world is portrayed and confirmed" (1989, p. 20). It appears in a host of writings that see in journalism the raw material for collective fictions, rituals, and identities (e.g., Chaney, 1993; Katz and Dayan, 1992; Liebes and Curran, 1998). And it is central to journalists' self-conception. When Kovach and Rosenstiel (2001, p. 18) argue that "the concept of journalism" is intimately related to the "concept of community and later democracy," they express a view widely shared across the profession.

The particular concerns we have reviewed – the loss of journalism means more corruption, less civic participation, and a fragmented, skewed information environment – ultimately rest on this broader worry: that the loss of journalism will result in the loss of democratic community. No journalism = no democracy.

Responses

The worriers paint a bleak picture of the future. Corruption is rampant and citizens either do not know or do not care enough to become involved. Partisans dominate public debate. Wealthy and powerful groups use government to line their pockets, while they offer bread and circuses to the rest of us. This society is a bit like Gotham City without Batman.

In recent years, the bat signal has gone up over journalism, and many entrepreneurs have answered the call. The question that animates much of their work is whether public interest journalism can survive in the future. I say "much," but there is no way to know how much. To my knowledge, no census of innovation in the news exists. So many people are experimenting in so many places, it is doubtful that such a census could be taken. Certainly, however, it is fair to say that a great deal of activity has centered on journalism's central democratic functions: accountability, civic participation, and public conversation.

Consider efforts to reconstruct accountability journalism. Entrepreneurs around the country are working to make government more open and transparent and to make it easier for anyone to investigate government activities. Much of this work takes the form of new tools for making government databases more widely available and usable. For instance, the Sunlight Foundation, an organization created by Craig Newmark of craigslist fame, has created a host of online tools to make the work of Congress more transparent and accessible. As an example, one of its projects, Transparency Data, links a database of all federal and state contributions to congressional candidates to other databases of federal grants and earmarks. Similarly, Aaron Pilhofer, an editor of Interactive News at the *New York Times*, has teamed with Eric Umansky and Scott Klein of ProPublica to create DocumentCloud.org. DocumentCloud analyzes and sorts batches of documents by the dates, people, and places that are mentioned in them. A user can submit any number of public documents and quickly track relationships between people, make timelines of events, and map interactions across place. The Panda Project, a collaboration of several news organizations, recently won a Knight News Challenge grant to do something similar with local public databases. And Overview, an Associated Press project and also a Knight Challenge winner, is creating a set of open source tools for searching and visualizing information in these databases.

Other innovations put the power of crowds to the same purpose. For example, SeeClickFix, a for-profit company based in New Haven, Connecticut, has created a mobile application that allows users to document problems in their neighborhoods (everything from potholes to crime), send messages to government agencies, and interact with one another on Twitter and Facebook. Local media can use the tool to create widgets on their websites so that they too can document and discuss public problems. In a different vein, EveryBlock combines the power of computers (in the form of public databases on housing, crime, building permits, traffic violations, and so on) with the power of people (in the form of user-generated information) to create visual information maps of neighborhoods. A user can click on her neighborhood and map everything from all crimes committed in the last week to the most popular restaurants.

Still another set of tools makes it easier for people to participate together in news-oriented projects. The Public Laboratory for Open Technology and Science (PLOTS) – a project of MIT's Center for Civic Media – has created new ways for people to crowdsource investigations in environmental science. Its first project, called grassrootsmapping, allowed hundreds of individuals to participate in building an aerial map of the Gulf Coast oil spill via kites and balloons. Though its work focuses mostly on science, PLOTS' innovations have obvious implications for journalism, a fact recognized by the Knight Foundation, which awarded the group a 2011 News Challenge grant. A Canadian organization, OpenFile, has created a similar set of tools for doing specifically journalistic work. On its site, users may propose a story on any subject by opening a file. Once a file is opened, users may contribute content by submitting videos, photographs, or comments. At the same time, editors at OpenFile work with the community to flesh out the story and assign a reporter (chosen from thousands of freelance journalists) to write it up. A for-profit company, Ideascale, is actively marketing another set of crowdsourcing tools in the form of "ideascale communities." These virtual spaces make it possible for individuals to suggest ideas about how to solve a problem and allow the rest of the community to sort and rate those ideas. Storyful and Storify are different versions of this idea. Storyful's application allows users to build stories by scanning the web for related blog postings, videos, images, Facebook posts, and tweets. Storify works on the same premise. Its developers have created a search engine that allows users to build stories by aggregating tweets, blog posts, videos, Facebook posts, and other social media material. Together, these tools suggest that participation in the production of networked news may be a path to stimulating greater interest and participation in public life generally.

Other entrepreneurs are tackling the problem of civic conversation. Localocracy, a non-profit organization based in Massachusetts, has created a virtual "commons" for citizens in local communities to share views on issues of common concern. Its software organizes conversations by subject and, to ensure that users see all perspectives of an issue, presents views in "pro" and "con" columns side by side. In similar fashion, Uncaucus, a non-profit in Providence, Rhode Island, set up a website to help citizens participate more fully in the city's 2010 mayoral election. The site's managers posted a job description for the office, solicited applications from various members of the community, and then invited the community to conduct a virtual interview of applicants.

I could list more experiments, but I think the point is made. Worries about the past are fueling much innovation in the future of news. The editors of OpenFile are not just inventing a new form of news. As they say on the "About Us" page of their site, they are "connecting citizens to the reporters who cover their communities . . . [to] ensure that we all have a better understanding of the issues that affect where we live and work." Craig Newmark is not funding experiments in journalism because he is a news junkie. He is doing it because he believes, as he puts it on the "About Us" page of craig-connects.org, that "trustworthy media should be the immune system of democracy."

Of course, no particular experiment is guaranteed to succeed. In fact, many of those I have discussed will likely fail. This is true for any arena of innovation: many entrepreneurs try, most do not survive, and the few that do become templates for others. Since the work of finding solutions is still in its infancy – Wikipedia began in 2000, as did craigslist; Facebook was invented in 2004 and YouTube in 2005; none of the innovations I describe above existed before 2008 – we can expect a period of great churning as successes and failures sort themselves out. That said, there is every reason to believe that experimentation in networked forms of public interest news will continue apace. After all, we will not go back to a time when we have less technology, less information, or less capacity to connect to one another. Moving forward, we will only have more of these things. And much of the ensuing activity will be devoted to filling the democratic gaps left behind by journalism's unraveling.

It is important to understand that these efforts are not reinventing the past. Rather, they are solving old problems in new, networked forms. I have described the nature of networks elsewhere in this book. The innovations I describe in this chapter add more detail to this description. The logic of networks begins from the premise that the Internet allows organizations to distribute information quickly and coordinate with one another easily. For this reason, no organization needs to be very large to make an impact. In fact, to the extent that it makes organizations less flexible, in a networked environment size can be an impediment. None of the experiments discussed in this chapter involve more than a handful of people. Storify, for instance, employs three people and an intern. Three partners invented Documentcloud while retaining their day jobs, and two staffers see to the site's day-to-day work. Just nine people compose the team at SeeClickFix. As a network of networks, the Internet appears to reward smallness.

Precisely because they are small, networked organizations must rely on people outside the organization to complete some or most of their work. Obviously, a small organization has little capacity to pay others to complete its work. If it had this ability, the organization would simply hire more workers and become larger. So most of the people who help the organization will not be paid. In formal terms, they will be motivated by the pursuit of "intrinsic" rewards, like friendship, interest, and prestige. For example, the people who agreed to fly balloons and kites to track the Gulf of Mexico oil spill in 2010 for PLOTS did so because they were interested in the subject, or a friend asked them to participate, or they were passionate about science. People who contribute to Uncaucus, Storify, Localocracy and other networked news forums do so for similarly "intrinsic" reasons. To be successful, then, networked news organizations must devote a great deal of energy to creating and sustaining feelings of camaraderie, friendship, obligation, and responsibility among their members; put more simply, they must create a sense of community.

Another way to put this point is to say that, increasingly, crowds will perform the democratic functions once performed by journalists alone. Many worriers about the fate of journalism are happy to have the help. But few are as sanguine about one of its principal implications: letting crowds in means giving up control over news production. For nearly a century, journalists have done nearly the opposite. They have controlled which information they published, when, and in what form, and they have done so within bureaucratic structures strongly shaped by the dictates of editors. But people who inhabit communities are not professional journalists or employees; they are ordinary people and friends, and, as Jeff Howe (2009) observes, when they work together, "they can't be directed, they can only be guided" (p. 182).

This means that, if the crowd is uninterested in a story, it will not be done – no matter how much an editor may press or a journalist may feel that it is important or interesting. Conversely, if the crowd wants to move in a particular direction, much like a school of fish it will be difficult for a journalist to stop it. As an example, consider the website Digg. A site that allows users to share online content, Digg works via a user-rating system. Users are invited to post links to stories, videos, and photos they find on the web, and other users are then asked to vote on this content. Material that receives the most votes is placed higher on the page. On August 1, 2011, a day on which the national debt ceiling consumed the mainstream press, the top links on Digg included stories on HTML 5, censorship of online music, and a new Calvin Klein lingerie ad featuring a half-naked model. In networked journalism, journalists give up control to the crowd, and the crowd will go where the crowd wants to go.

This fact understandably gives many traditional journalists pause. But we must also recognize that, while much of the energy in networked journalism comes from the crowd, journalists still play a vital role. This role is apparent when we think about how networks change the work of news production. The 80/20 rule of networks suggests that not everyone will be willing to participate equally in the production of news. A few people will devote a great deal of time and energy to the work and many others only a very little. It has been estimated, for instance, that 10 percent of the people involved with Wikipedia, the online encyclopedia, perform 90 percent of its work. The same is true for Storyful, Storify, OpenFile, and any other networked news organization: a small percentage of the communities that form around these sites will produce much of their content. This is not necessarily a problem, but it does change several aspects of the work. Most obviously, if different people are willing to do different amounts of work, then the work will need to be "chunked" into different sizes – bigger sizes for the few passionate people and smaller sizes for the rest. So, for instance, OpenFile allows a passionate person to open files on new story ideas – a fairly large commitment. An open file, however, allows others who might have less passion for the project do smaller tasks. The same is true for Storyful. A person passionate about a subject may use Storyful to perform the time-consuming task of aggregating tweets, blog posts, videos, and photos. This willingness allows others to make smaller contributions – for example, by providing a link to a video or a blog post. Organizing work in this distributive fashion takes advantage of the incremental, additive nature of the Internet. Online, everything is always in a constant state of updating.

The question is this: Who will do the chunking? Crowds need people who can catalyze the community, organize its work in granular form, and put the pieces together when finished. They need, in other words, journalists. This point is sometimes lost on journalists. When they hear "crowdsourced journalism," they think it means "journalism without professionals." But this is not the case. OpenFile would not work without editors interacting with the community and journalists organizing their work into news stories. Conversations convened by Localocracy need moderators. One way to think of tools like Storify, Storyful, and Ideascale is that they enable professional journalists to sift through the work done by crowds (in the form of tweets, blog posts, photos, and videos), find the best material, and organize it into compelling narratives. Even the most ardent advocates of crowdsourcing recognize this fact. "We are all better served," Howe (2009) concludes, "when the crowd complements what journalists do, rather than trying to replicate it" (p. 220).

The use of crowds to help journalists do their jobs is so new that it is difficult to comprehend all that it implies. Certainly, however, it seems to change the role journalists play in news production. In traditional journalism, reporters imagined themselves as filters of information and producers of content (stories, videos, photos, and the like). More than one newspaper reporter with whom I have talked described themselves first and foremost as writers. Even the new "multimedia" journalist tends to understand her primary role as producing content. If the examples I have discussed are any indication, when working in networks journalists will still produce content. But they will also do a host of other things. They will convene communities and facilitate participation, moderate forums and code software, aggregate the work of others, and, at all times, interact, interact, interact.

As we saw in previous chapters, many if not most traditional journalists remain unable or unwilling to embrace these new practices. In many cases, they do not even see the new practices *as* journalism. However, their concerns have not stopped what now seems like an inexorable process of change. Whether journalists like it or not, the crowd has arrived.

To put the new role of journalism in context, it helps to take a step back for a moment. For one hundred years, journalists imagined their role as *informing* citizens. But that is not what networked journalists seem to be doing. In OpenFile's model, citizens do most of the reporting and produce most of the content. What do journalists do? Mostly, they catalyze, organize, and assist the crowds that form around stories. Individually and collectively, these crowds know as much about the topic as journalists. Journalists help by keeping the crowd engaged, aggregating its work, and packaging the result in narrative form. The same is true for Everyblock. In this model, Everyblock provides a platform for people passionate about neighborhoods to find one another. Journalists create a database that makes it easy for individuals to add and find information and to aggregate and represent the result. As with OpenFile, the journalist plays the role of convening and organizing crowds, amplifying their work, and making it useful for others.

These new activities suggest that journalism's new role is that of *engaging* citizens. Let's think through what this means. In the first instance, it means that a networked journalist tries to "attract the attention of" others. This is an ordinary meaning of the term, and it seems obvious that no networked journalist would survive long if she did not attract the attention of a community. However, the word "engage" has other meanings, and they are just as pertinent to the practice of networked journalism. Borrowing from the Oxford English Dictionary, four other meanings hold particular importance.

1 To "pledge," "bind oneself," or "promise." Examples of this usage include: "I have engaged rooms at a hotel" (as in promised to rent); "He is engaged" (as in betrothed); "I am engaged tomorrow" (as in promised to be somewhere). When used in this way, engagement conveys a sense of moral commitment.

2 "To be entangled with," "mix-up" with, or "interlock." This is a physical sense of the term. It comes out in Shakespeare's *Hamlet*, where he writes, "O limed soule, that struggling to be free, Art more ingaged." More commonly, we say that a cog has been "engaged" in a wheel, or that someone has been "engaged" in conversation. When used in this way, engagement raises the question of agreement.

3 "To enter into combat with." An example of this usage is: "The army engaged the enemy today . . ." This sense of the term carries with it an image of lines being drawn, of conflict, and therefore of an "us" in battle with "them."

4 "To hire or employ." An example is this usage is: "I engaged the services of this person." This usage refers to putting someone to work, or giving them something to do.

All of these senses of the term are mobilized in networked journalism. A journalist who engages citizens attracts their attention. She also pledges herself to others in a moral and ethical sense. It is only by doing so that she can create the conditions for community. This alone makes the practice of networked journalism very different from traditional journalism. By definition, a networked journalist is a passionate member of a community. She is committed, not neutral or impartial. Engagement also means "mixing it up" with citizens – conversing with them, arguing with them, establishing areas of agreement and disagreement. This can sometimes look like combat. Anyone with experience of the political blogosphere knows that online conversations can have the appearance of a battle. But this is the way that communities develop identities and establish boundaries. Finally, engagement means putting people to work – engaging their services. As we know, there will not be enough networked journalists to do all of the work once done by traditional journalists. Because this is so, networked journalists must put the communities of people that form around them to work.

The role of the networked journalist, then – to engage citizens – is different in striking ways from the role once played by a traditional journalist.

Networked Journalism and Democracy

Does this new role imply even more fundamental changes in journalism? Recall that the prevailing theory of journalism has reporters informing the public so that citizens may make judgments about the issues of the day, and the public may thereby infuse the democratic process. To borrow language from the last chapter, this is a constitutive rule of journalism; it is what journalism is for. Does networked journalism change this equation? Does it alter not only what journalists do, but also what journalism is for?

This is the crucial, but at this moment unanswerable, question, unanswerable in part because the changes in journalism have only just begun, but unanswerable too because the impact of networks on public life has yet to be settled.

There is some evidence that networks have not dramatically changed key aspects of public life. It is true, for instance, that networks lower the costs of public participation, but they do not change the underlying psychology of political participation or information consumption. Over a decade of research has shown that the Internet has done little to increase levels of public knowledge or political participation (e.g., Boulianne, 2009). Even today, most people prefer to ignore public affairs most of the time, and participation in most kinds of formal political activities (voting, petition-signing, organization-joining, and the like) is still strongly skewed toward the most educated and well-off members of the public (e.g., Brundidge and Rice, 2009). The Internet has expanded the number and variety of elites who may influence the political process, but it has not ushered in an age of participatory democracy that would require a change in how journalism imagines its role in the democratic process.

The structure of formal political institutions – from city hall to Congress – also remains much the same. Despite the dawn of the networked age, formal political institutions remain large and bureaucratic, in part for legislative and constitutional reasons, and in part because bureaucracies are simply a more efficient way to perform many state functions (e.g., Bimber, 2003, pp. 106–7). The Internet makes it theoretically possible for citizens to do more than express their opinions; the organization of formal political institutions makes this practically difficult. This suggests that the public will continue to play a relatively passive role in public affairs and, therefore, that journalism will continue to represent them in the corridors of power.

It is also the case that the onset of a networked society has not reduced the number of established political groups, most of which are large and bureaucratic, are populated by experts of various kinds, and have longstanding and deeply embedded roots in the political system. Quite naturally these groups are reluctant to give up their pride of place in the political system, and they have many resources to ensure that they do not (e.g., Pierson, 2000). Their relative ability to prevent incursions from others may blunt the impact of networks on public politics.

Finally, in many circumstances, political figures still need to capture the attention of mass audiences, and mass media are superior tools for this purpose. Take the case of national elections. Candidates for national office are interested less in stimulating public action than in shaping mass opinion. Political advertising distributed via mass media is most useful for this purpose. The same logic holds for occasions in which public officials wish to focus the mass public's attention on a particular problem. When the president wants the public to think about healthcare, mass media offer a more efficient and controllable venue for doing so than networks.

Networked journalism's new role, therefore, may require only a modest amendment to the field's underlying theory: journalists, *in collaboration with members of their communities*, produce news so that citizens can form judgments about the issues of the day, and the public may thereby infuse the democratic process. True, the political system is more fragmented, partisan, and populist than in the past. But in crucial ways it is still anchored to the progressive culture from which it arose. Bureaucratic organizations populated by technocrats still make most policy decisions, the public remains consigned to expressing opinions about these actions, and journalism mediates the relationship between the two. While new tools like DocumentCloud or Storify may change the practice of journalism and the role journalists play in news production, they do not seem to be altering its underlying purpose.

Other evidence indicates that a more fundamental transformation in public life may be underway. Michael Schudson (2010) makes the point that the Internet did not cause news to fragment online. "It is hard to imagine [this happening]," he writes, "without the civil rights movement, the women's movement, Students for a Democratic Society and the ideology of participatory democracy, the emergence of hundreds of new nonprofits and advocacy organizations in Washington, [and] aggregations of countercultural enthusiasts around the Whole Earth Catalog" (p. 103). These sorts of changes may anticipate basic changes in public life – and in journalism. It is becoming more fragmented, collaborative, and participatory because public life is fast becoming more fragmented, collaborative, and participatory.

Schudson identifies one kind of fragmentation: the enormous growth in "political observatories" in and around the formal institutions of government. These include Washington-based nonprofits and advocacy and interest groups that sponsor research and monitor governmental activity. And they include new rules and agencies designed to make government more open, transparent, and participatory. Among new rules are the requirement that the Environmental Protection Agency allow for a period of public comment before enacting new policies and the rule that political campaigns must disclose financial contributions. New agencies include the Inspector General's (IG) office that every cabinet-level federal agency now houses. Created as part of the Inspector General Act of 1978, IGs make reports to Congress on the internal workings of their agencies. Couple these with the new openness of government databases (e.g., Noveck, 2009) and, Schudson argues, you have the seeds of a new, more collaborative model for journalism. "Political observatories," he writes, "do not replace journalists . . . but the observatories are increasingly valuable partners for journalists . . . [they] offer promise for developing the kind of public information that makes democracy possible" (2010, p. 107).

Trends in local and regional government offer a different kind of evidence. A growing literature suggests that local government is fast becoming more open and participatory (e.g., Briand, 1999; Fung, 2004; Gastil and Levine, 2005; Putnam and Feldstein, 2003; Sirianni and Friedland, 2001). City managers and mayors are convening issues forums, study circles, citizen juries, citizens' conferences, and wisdom councils, to name just a few of the processes available for incorporating more public participation into government activities. There is no telling just how large this movement is, but the fact that 20,000 national issues forums alone are convened each year gives some sense of the scale.[17] As Matt Leighninger (2006) reports, this work has been spurred not by an idealistic pursuit of participatory democracy, but for the most pragmatic of reasons: the technocrats who inhabit government have concluded that they cannot solve their community's problems alone. Whether the problem is the decline of schools, the provision of healthcare, or race relations, they are so complicated that solutions require public participation.

Despite the many examples of participatory democracy that have piled up in the last fifteen years, a sea change in civic culture has yet to happen. Civic organizers have been stymied by problems in recruiting a broad base of citizens and sustaining initiatives over time. Perhaps, however, the granularity afforded by the Internet may help to overcome these problems. As Chadwick (2012) observes, in the past participation was all or nothing. A citizen either threw herself into the exercise or she did not. In contrast, online participation can be more flexible. "High-, medium- and low-threshold tools for democratic innovation," Chadwick writes, "may exist side-by-side in a panoply of online environments" (2012, p. 19). A citizen may be willing to do a great deal of work in one forum and very little in another. The Internet allows her to make this choice. As important, it makes it easier to aggregate the work of the group as a whole, and thus for initiatives to persist and build momentum over time – even when individual citizen participation is less consistent.

Thinking forward a decade or two, networked journalism might come to express a new sensibility of public life, one in which citizens play a more active role in public problem-solving.

How would this change journalism's purpose? It might move

it much closer to the vision announced by the public journalism movement of the 1980s and 1990s. Public journalism grew mostly in small and mid-sized daily newspapers, but also in a smattering of TV and radio stations. According to Lewis Friedland and Sandy Nichols (2002), by 2002 it had generated more than 600 journalistic experiments in the United States and abroad, a dozen or more books advocating its practice, and more than seventy academic studies investigating its results. This activity led Schudson to argue that public journalism represented the "most impressive critique of journalistic practice inside journalism in a generation" (1999, p. 118).

Tanni Haas (2007) is correct to note that, in all this activity, public journalism never developed a coherent public philosophy. But public journalists agreed on at least one principle: the purpose of journalism was to help citizens solve public problems. One prominent public journalist, Cole Campbell, listed this as his first belief: "Journalism is in the problem-solving business, not the truth business" (1999, p. xiv). Among public journalists, this sentiment was an article of faith. Nearly every summary of public journalism begins with the idea that journalism's overall mission is to re-create a vibrant, participatory democracy. As Jay Rosen put it, public journalism was intended to "help the community act upon, rather than just learn about, its problems" (1999b, p. 22). This problem-solving orientation stemmed from the movement's philosophical roots in the pragmatic tradition of John Dewey (Perry, 2003; Rosen, 1999a). It also was a natural consequence of public journalism's posture toward the public sphere. If journalists were responsible for stimulating public conversation, the next natural question was, "to what end?" The answer was to help citizens act on shared public problems. This is, to play off the title of Rosen's book, "what journalism is for."

At the time, most traditional journalists staunchly resisted this theory of journalism. In fact, by the early 2000s public journalism was, for all intents and purposes, dead (e.g., Haas, 2007; Nip, 2008). Perhaps, however, networked journalism will revive this tradition. Given that journalism takes its cue from the broader public culture, in some sense it is not up to journalists. Still, if networked journalism moved down this path, it would change not only journalism's role in public life but also its purpose. Journalists, the theory would go, *working in collaboration with members of their communities*, would produce news so that *citizens could act on the public problems they collectively face*. This would truly be a revolution in journalism.

A Revolution of a Kind

Worriers about the loss of traditional journalism may be right. It may be that networked journalism will not fill all of the gaps left behind by the loss of traditional journalism, and that we will all be the poorer for it. In the near-term future, the likelihood of this happening seems very high. Evidence is growing that the loss of journalism means less government accountability and a coarser public conversation. In the longer term, however, the worriers may be wrong. Journalists have only just begun to figure out how to leverage the power of crowds to serve the public interest. There is vibrancy and urgency in these innovations. Over time, it seems as likely as not that some of these experiments will show how crowds can perform at least some of journalism's democratic functions. One other alternative is possible. The worriers may be missing the real dynamic at work. Democracy itself may be changing, to become more distributed, fragmented, and participatory. In this eventuality, journalism may come to have entirely new democratic purposes that the worriers have not considered.

Whichever of these scenarios plays out, it seems clear that networked journalism's role in society will be different from that in the past. Networked journalists will seek to engage rather than inform people, and this will lead them to be involved in communities in ways that traditional journalism frowned upon, if not explicitly proscribed. This "revolution in the middle," as Bruce Bimber (2003, p. 229) refers to it, may or may not anticipate broader changes in journalism and society, but, as the term implies, it will nonetheless be a revolution of a kind.

Conclusion

In a strict sense, journalism is not dying; it is unraveling. In the future, there will still be journalists, and there will still be journalists working in commercially oriented news organizations. But the field is no longer cohesive and integrated, and journalists no longer control its boundaries.

Journalists who work for regional daily newspapers – which once constituted the backbone of journalism – feel the pain of this loss acutely. As I watched them over the years, they expressed indignation, frustration, anger, and confusion. They lashed out at their bosses and owners, the public, bloggers, government, and themselves, and they tried increasingly bold experiments to save their jobs and their profession. Nothing they did worked, and nothing they do is likely to work. A few of the premier news organizations will survive and even thrive. The rest will shrink, and some may cease to exist altogether.

Many of the journalists with whom I have talked recognize these trends. In every newsroom I visited, they pulled me aside before I left and peppered me with questions. Is it our fault? What could we have done differently? And, how long will this take?

It seems appropriate to end this book with the answers I gave them. The first two questions are related. Journalists could have done some things differently, and so are at least partly to blame for their circumstances. For instance, in the 1990s they could have made a better assessment of the new medium. I once talked to a journalist who worked in the 1990s for the *San Jose Mercury News*. This was the geographic heart of the digital revolution, and the *Mercury News* established a reputation in the field as one of the best sources of information on this revolution. Yet my journalist friend acknowledged to

me that the newspaper "missed the Internet." He described sitting
in a news meeting one day when someone circulated a press release
announcing the creation of a new company just up the road. It was
called "craigslist." The person who passed around the press release
thought the group might want to pay attention to this company. After
all, he noted, it seems to be doing the same thing as our classified
section. People in the room nodded their heads. A comment or two
followed, but then the group got back to the work of organizing the
next day's newspaper. My friend never heard the word "craigslist"
mentioned in the newsroom again. Journalists at the *Mercury News*
were so focused on covering the revolution that they missed its
implications for their own business. The same is true everywhere in
journalism.

Journalists might also have resisted less and innovated more. I call
this the "yes, but" syndrome. I have talked with dozens of journalists
about the future of their profession. As we chat, many return again
and again to "yes, but . . ." "Yes, I understand that we have to go
online, but let's not lose sight of our values." "Yes, I get it, but we
can't stop doing X, Y, or Z." "Yes, I see what you are saying, but . . ."
These "yes, buts . . ." carry energy in the wrong direction. Instead of
pushing toward the future, they lead journalists to fixate on the past.
In so doing, they stop conversations about the future of news in their
tracks. This isn't to say that more productive conversations would
save the field, but they may help journalists see the changes taking
place more clearly, and perhaps to respond more quickly.

Finally, journalists might have been better risk evaluators. Here,
I think of reporters at *The Herald*. Their investments in tradition
were certainly great, and worth protecting. By 2008, however, the
newspaper was considering some pretty drastic measures: reducing
the size of the newspaper, making do without an AP subscription,
getting rid of color, laying off a third of the newsroom. At this point,
it seemed that the risk of doing nothing became greater than the risk
of change. But most of the journalists in the newsroom did not see
that this balance had tipped. They remained convinced that the way
forward was to preserve the newspaper and to protect their investments in traditional practices and values. They simply made the
wrong calculation. Had more journalists been better assessors of risk,
they might have seen that dramatic and decisive change was now the
rational course to take.

All of this said, journalists are not entirely responsible for what has
happened to their profession. The Internet would have shrunk their
numbers regardless of what they did. In information industries, net-

works are simply hostile to large, bureaucratic organizations like the modern urban newspaper. Journalists also are not responsible for the decisions of upper management. It was not for them to take on new debt (or not), to make strategic investments in new technology (or not), or to demand increasingly higher profit margins. And journalists are not alone in seeing blogging, tweeting, aggregating, curating, and moderating, to name just a few new practices, as something other than journalism. In many quarters of society, especially among the experts and public officials with whom journalists routinely interact, this remains common sense. Whether and how journalism changes depends in part on whether and how the society around it, particularly political society, changes.

So, when journalists ask me these questions, I say, gently of course, that they could have done more, and so are partly to blame for what has happened in their field. I then follow this comment with the thought that other forces are at work as well, forces that are beyond their control.

On the issue of how long the transformation of news will take, I refer back to the last time journalism underwent a fundamental change. Beginning in the 1880s, the party-press system gave way to a modern, professional, commercially oriented system. This process took forty or fifty years to complete. It was only in the 1930s that modern journalism finally emerged. Networked journalism is only about ten to fifteen years old. In other words, it is at the same stage as modern journalism was in about 1900. At that time, many of the practices and values that would become modern news had been invented. They stood among other practices and values, some from the past, and some that were new but would not ultimately survive. It took another thirty years for journalists to cut through this thicket and to distinguish and organize the set of values and practices that would become modern journalism. This happened by trial and error. Entrepreneurs encountered problems and tried various solutions; some worked and some didn't. Other entrepreneurs copied what worked and dispensed with the rest. Over time, solutions to common problems were identified, codified, and institutionalized. The same is happening to networked journalism. Entrepreneurs are encountering problems posed by a networked environment. They are trying various solutions. Some will work and others will not. It will take time to identify which is which and for other entrepreneurs to copy successes. And it will take more time for these solutions to be codified and institutionalized.

For all the doom and gloom in newsrooms, this will be an exciting time in journalism's history. For interested observers like myself, we get to watch one of the great stories of our time, the dissolution of a social field and frantic efforts to stitch it back together. For citizens, this is a golden age of news, a time when people have never had greater access to more news and information. It is also an opportunity for citizens to become more involved in, and gain greater control over, the public sphere. And, for aspiring journalists, it is a rare moment when they get to invent their own jobs.

This last is a popular refrain among journalism educators. Yes, times are tough, we tell our students, but how often do you get to invent the future? I have written this book most of all for them, in the hope that it may serve as an explanation for what has happened, a guide for what is to come, and a spur to their creativity and ingenuity.

Notes

1 Except where noted below, the numbers presented in these last paragraphs come from the Newspaper Association of America (NAA: www. naa.org). The "state of the media" reports produced by the Project for Excellence in Journalism (www.journalism.org) are another excellent resource on economic trends in the industry. The reference to newspaper revenues falling to 1965 levels comes from Ryan Chittum, "Newspaper industry's ad revenue at 1965 levels," *Columbia Journalism Review*, August 19, 2009. Mutter's analysis of newspaper share prices can be found at: http://newsosaur.blogspot.com/2010/01/hefty-cost-cuts-fueled-surprise-news.html. Numbers on journalists who have taken a buyout or were laid off come from the "Paper Cuts" website: http:// newspaperlayoffs.com/. The reader can find a nice visual display of the newspaper industry's recent precipitous decline at: www.mint.com/blog/ trends/the-death-of-the-newspaper/?display=wide.

2 I should mention here that, when I say "Internet," I mean both the infrastructure of wires, computers, and routers that compose the "hardware" of the Internet and the content and applications that comprise the "world wide web."

3 These numbers can be found at: www.naa.org/Trends-and-Numbers/ Circulation/Newspaper-Circulation-Volume.aspx.

4 These age cohort numbers have continued to decline, which means that the average daily newspaper reader today is over fifty, while fewer than 20 percent of the "millennial generation" have picked up the habit. See Alan Mutter's analysis at: http://newsosaur.blogspot.com/2009/01/how-long-can-print-newspapers-last.html.

5 A chart representing Langeveld's data can be found at: www.niemanlab. org/images/Share-of-market-4908.PNG.

6 Apparently, this sensibility is common among executives at corporate newspapers. When I entered my first newsroom in 2005, I found a banner displayed on a wall in the middle of the newsroom. The banner

read, in part: "One of the strong insights of [our reader initiative] is that our definition of news doesn't always match readers."

7 Carroll's comments can be found at "Last call at the ASNE saloon," www.poynter.org/content/content_view.asp?id=100580; Harris' speech to ASNE can be found at: www.poynter.org/content/content_view. asp?id=4109&sid=14.

8 Kurt Lewin (1951) was the first to adapt field theories from science to psychological and sociological dynamics. But it was Pierre Bourdieu (1985) who popularized the concept in social theory and who has done the most to explore its uses for understanding social dynamics. The standard reference for field theory's application to journalism is Rodney Benson and Erik Neveu (2005). John Levi Martin's "What is field theory?" (2003) is a very good summary of field theory in sociology and includes a genealogy of its origins in the sciences.

9 Doing the math, this means that most people spend as little as 10 minutes per month on *The Herald's* news site. The 2010 *State of the Media* report, published by the Pew Project on Excellence in Journalism, confirms that about 10 minutes is the mainstream newspaper website industry average for a user's monthly time on site. See http://stateofthemedia.org/2010/special-reports-economic-attitudes/nielsen-analysis/. Scholars have only just begun to grapple with how data about online news habits are changing the structure of reporting. For more on this topic, see Anderson, 2010; Boczkowski, 2010; Usher, 2011.

10 Paton's "news summit" presentation can be found at: http://jxpaton. wordpress.com/2010/12/02/presentation-by-john-paton-at-inma-transfo rmation-of-news-summit-in-cambridge-mass/.

11 When I arranged to visit the *Gazette*, Peters insisted that I use his real name and that of the newspaper in any publication that came from this research. Steve Buttry, whom Peters hired as editor of the newspaper, also asked that I use his real name. I have honored their requests. However, as part of the agreement for access to the newsroom, I have kept the names of other employees anonymous.

12 My discussion of Buttry's experiment relies on personal interviews with him and Peters, as well as the following internal memos and presentations: Peters's presentation to the NAA, "Media X Change," March 10, 2009; Peters's "Corporate review" presentation to *Gazette* staff, May 11, 2009; Peters's GFOC employee meetings presentation, March 2009; Buttry's "A vision for the *Gazette*'s future," August 2008; Buttry's "Information Content Enterprise," September 2008; and Buttry's "Plan for launching C3 community engagement effort" (undated).

13 You might notice that ICE says little about traditional hard news. In none of Buttry's memos does there appear a superblog on city hall, the statehouse, the police department, and the like, that could generate revenue in the same way as one on weddings. When I pointed this out to him, Buttry told me that this is because hard news cannot pay for

itself – it never has and never will. "The audience for these stories is not there . . . People [just] aren't interested." It is not that this kind of news is unimportant. Rather, on Buttry's view, it would have to be subsidized by other parts of the company, just as it had been in the past.

14 Part of the regional newspaper's inability to attract a large enough audience will surely be the fact that consumers have direct access to the few, but much larger nationally and internationally oriented news organizations. In the not too distant past, the only way to get access to *New York Times* content was to subscribe to the local newspaper, which ran *Times* wire copy. Obviously, this is no longer true. Consumers mostly interested in national and international news no longer need to subscribe to the local newspaper. This means that the large news organizations now compete directly with regional newspapers for local consumers. I am indebted to Alan Deutschman for this point.

15 One study of these sites, for example, has found that most for-profit local news sites report revenues of $100,000 per year or less (McLellan, 2011).

16 Although often referenced, the exact provenance of this quote is difficult to track down. A reference in Anderson (1983, p. 35) traces back to Eisenstein's (1968, p. 42) essay. But, although Eisenstein makes the observation, she does not attribute it to Hegel. More recently, Buck-Morss (2000, p. 844) traces the reference to a German-language biography of Hegel by Rosenkranz (1977, p. 543), who apparently takes it from a note made by Hegel in his notebooks sometime in the years 1803 to 1805.

17 To gain more information about this movement, the interested reader may wish to visit the National Coalition for Dialogue and Deliberation, ncdd.org, the Deliberative Democracy Consortium (www.deliberative-democracy.net/), and participedia.net, a project created by Archon Fung of Harvard University and Mark Warren of the University of British Columbia.

References and Bibliography

Abramowitz, A. (2009) *The 2008 Elections*. New York: Longman.
Adserà, A., Boix, C., and Payne, M. (2003) "Are you being served? Political accountability and quality of government," *Journal of Law, Economics, & Organization* 19, pp. 445–90.
Alsop, J., and Alsop, S. (1958) *The Reporter's Trade*. New York: Reynal.
American Journalism Review (2009) "AJR's 2009 count of statehouse reporters" (April/May), available at: www.ajr.org/article.asp?id=4722.
Anderson, B. (1983) *Imagined Communities: Reflections on the Origin and Spread of Nationalism*. London: Verso.
Anderson, C. (2006) *The Long Tail: Why the Future of Business is Selling Less of More*. New York: Hyperion.
Anderson, C. (2009) *Free: The Future of a Radical Price*. New York: Hyperion.
Anderson, C. W. (2010) "Breaking journalism down: work, authority, and networking local news, 1997–2009," PhD thesis, Columbia University.
Archer, M. (1996) *Culture and Agency: The Place of Culture in Social Theory*. Cambridge: Cambridge University Press.
Bagby, M. A. (1991) "Transforming newspapers for readers," *Presstime* (April), pp. 18–25.
Baldasty, G. J. (1992) *The Commercialization of News in the Nineteenth Century*. Madison: University of Wisconsin Press.
Bantz, C. R. (1985) "News organizations: conflict as a crafted cultural norm," *Communication* 8, pp. 225–44.
Barabási, A.-L. (2002) *Linked: The New Science of Networks*. Cambridge: Perseus.
Bardoel, J., and Deuze, M. (2001) "Network journalism: converging competences of old and new media professionals," *Australian Journalism Review* 23, pp. 91–103.
Beniger, J. (1986) *The Control Revolution: Technological Change and the*

Origins of the Information Society. Cambridge, MA: Harvard University Press.

Benkler, Y. (2006) *The Wealth of Networks: How Social Production Transforms Markets and Freedom.* New Haven, CT: Yale University Press.

Bennett, W. L. (1983) *News: The Politics of Illusion.* New York: Longman.

Bennett, W. L., and Entman, R. M. (eds) (2001) *Mediated Politics: Communication in the Future of Democracy.* New York: Cambridge University Press.

Bennett, W. L., and Mannheim, J. B. (2006) "The one-step flow of communication," *Annals of the American Academy of Political Science* 608, pp. 213–32.

Benson, R. (2006) "News media as a 'journalistic field': what Bourdieu adds to new institutionalism, and vice versa," *Political Communication* 23, pp. 187–202.

Benson, R., and Neveu, E. (eds) (2005) *Bourdieu and the Journalistic Field.* Cambridge: Polity.

Benson, R., and Powers, M. (2010) *A Crisis of Imagination: International Models for Funding and Protecting Independent Journalism and Public Media (a Survey of 14 Leading Democracies).* Washington, DC: Free Press.

Benton, J. (2011) "Slip and slide: newspaper industry increases production of scary charts," available at: www.niemanlab.org/2011/03/slip-and-slide-newspaper-industry-increases-production-of-scary-charts/.

Bimber, B. (2003) *Information and American Democracy: Technology in the Evolution of Political Power.* Cambridge, MA: MIT Press.

Bimber, B., Flanagin, A. J., and Stohl, C. (2005) "Reconceptualizing collective action in the contemporary media environment," *Communication Theory* 15, pp. 365–88.

Bird, E. (1992) *For Enquiring Minds: A Cultural Study of Supermarket Tabloids.* Knoxville: University of Tennessee Press.

Boczkowski, P. (2004) *Digitizing the News: Innovation in Online Newspapers.* Cambridge, MA: MIT Press.

Boczkowski, P. (2010) *News at Work: Imitation in an Age of Information Abundance.* Chicago: University of Chicago Press.

Bogart, L. (1991) *Preserving the Press: How Daily Newspapers Mobilized to Keep their Readers.* New York: Columbia University Press.

Botein, S. (1975) 'Meer Mechanics' and the open press: the business and political strategies of colonial American printers," *Perspectives in American History* 9, pp. 251–67.

Boulianne, S. (2009) "Does Internet use affect engagement? A meta-analysis of research," *Political Communication* 26, pp. 193–211.

Bourdieu, P. (1971) "Intellectual field and creative project," in M. K. D. Young (ed.) *Knowledge and Control: New Directions for the Sociology of Education.* London: Collier Macmillan, pp. 161–88.

Bourdieu, P. (1985) "The genesis of concepts of habitus and of field," *Sociocriticism* 2, pp. 11–24.

Bourdieu, P. (2005) "The political field, the social science field, and the field of journalism," in R. Benson and E. Neveu (eds) *Bourdieu and the Journalistic Field*. Cambridge: Polity, pp. 29–47.

Bourdieu, P., Wacquant, L., and Farage, S. (1994) "Rethinking the state: genesis and structure of the bureaucratic field," *Sociological Theory* 12, pp. 1–18.

Boyer, D., and Hannerz, U. (2006) "Introduction: worlds of journalism," *Ethnography* 7, pp. 5–17.

Breed, W. (1955) "Social control in the newsroom: a functional analysis," *Social Forces* 33, pp. 326–35.

Briand, M. (1999) *Practical Politics: Five Principles for a Community that Works*. Urbana: University of Illinois Press.

Brundidge, J., and Rice, R. E. (2009) "Political engagement online: do the information rich get richer and the like-minded more similar?" in A. Chadwick and P. N. Howard (eds) *Routledge Handbook of Internet Politics*. New York: Routledge, pp. 145–56.

Brunetti A., and Weder, B. (2003) "A free press is bad news for corruption," *Journal of Public Economics* 87, pp. 1801–24.

Buchanan, M. (2002) *Nexus: Small Worlds and the Groundbreaking Science of Networks*. New York: W. W. Norton.

Buck-Morss, S. (2000) "Hegel and Haiti," *Critical Inquiry* 26, pp. 821–65.

Caggiano, J. (2011) "Online media guide – Washington State," *Washington News Council*, available at: http://wanewscouncil.org/omgwashington/.

Campbell, C. (1999) "Foreword: journalism as a democratic art," in T. Glasser (ed.) *The Idea of Public Journalism*. New York: Guilford Press, pp. xiii–xxx.

Carey, J. W. (1987) "The press and public discourse," *Center Magazine* 20, pp. 4–32.

Carey, J. W. (1989) *Communication as Culture: Essays on Media and Society*. Winchester, MA: Unwin Hyman.

Carr, D. (2007) "All the world's a story," *New York Times* (March 19), available at: www.nytimes.com/2007/03/19/business/media/19carr.html?scp=1&sq=&st=nyt.

Castells, M. (2010) *The Rise of the Networked Society*. 2nd edn, Malden, MA: Wiley-Blackwell.

Chadwick, A. (2012) "Recent shifts in the relationship between the Internet and democratic engagement in Britain and the United States: granularity, informational exuberance, and political learning," in E. Anduiza, M. J. Jensen, and L. Jorba (eds) *Digital Media and Political Engagement Worldwide: A Comparative Study*. Cambridge: Cambridge University Press.

Chaney, D. (1993) *Fictions of Collective Life: Public Drama in Late Modern Culture*. London: Routledge.

Charity, A. (1995) *Doing Public Journalism*. New York: Guilford Press.

Christensen, C. (1997) *The Innovator's Dilemma: When New*

Technologies Cause Great Firms to Fail. Cambridge, MA: Harvard Business School.

Chung, D. (2007) "Profits and perils: online news producers' perceptions of interactivity and uses of interactive features," *Convergence: The International Journal of Research into New Media Technologies* 13, pp. 43–61.

Columbia Journalism Review (1991) "Doing the Boca: an interim report from a reinvented newspaper" (May/June), p. 15.

Compaine, B. M., and Gomery, D. (2000) *Who Owns the Media? Competition and Concentration in the Mass Media Industry.* 3rd edn, Mahwah, NJ: Lawrence Erlbaum.

Cook, T. E. (1989) *Making Laws and Making News: Media Strategies in the U.S. House of Representatives.* Washington, DC: Brookings Institution.

Cook, T. E. (1998) *Governing with the News: The News Media as a Political Institution.* Chicago: University of Chicago Press.

Cottle, S. (2009) "New(s) times: towards a 'second wave' of news ethnography," in A. Hansen (ed.) *Mass Communication Research Methods.* London: Sage, pp. 366–86.

Cranberg, G., Bezanson, R., and Soloski, J. (2001) *Taking Stock: Journalism and the Publicly Traded Newspaper Company.* Ames: Iowa State University Press.

D'Andrade, R. G. (1984) "Cultural meaning systems," in R. Shweder and R. LeVine (eds) *Culture Theory: Essays on Mind, Self, and Emotion.* Cambridge: Cambridge University Press, pp. 88–119.

Delanty, G. (2003) *Community.* London: Routledge.

Delli Carpini, M. X., and Keeter, S. (1996) *What Americans Know about Politics and Why it Matters.* New Haven, CT: Yale University Press.

Dewey, J. (1927) *The Public and its Problems.* New York: Henry Holt.

Doctor, K. (2010) "The newsonomics of the fading 80/20 rule," available at: www.niemanlab.org/2010/08/the-newsonomics-of-the-fading-8020-rule/?utm_source=feedburner&utm_medium=feed&utm_campaign=Feed 3A+NiemanJournalismLab+28Nieman+Journalism+Lab29.

Doctor, K. (2011) "The newsonomics of oblivion," available at: www.niemanlab.org/2011/03/the-newsonomics-of-oblivion/.

Domingo, D. (2008) "Interactivity in the daily routines of online newsrooms: dealing with an uncomfortable myth," *Journal of Computer-Mediated Communication* 13, pp. 670–704.

Domingo, D., Quandt, T., Heinonen, A., Paulussen, S., Singer, J. B., and Vujnovic, M. (2008) "Participatory journalism practices in the media and beyond," *Journalism Practice* 2, pp. 326–42, available at: http://jclass.umd.edu/classes/jour698m/domingo.pdf.

Dorroh, J. (2009) "Statehouse exodus," *American Journalism Review* (April/May), available at: www.ajr.org/article.asp?id=4721.

Downie L., Jr., and Schudson, M. (2009) "The reconstruction of American journalism," *Columbia Journalism Review* (October 19), available at: www.cjr.org/reconstruction/the_reconstruction_of_american.php?page=all.

Downie, L., Jr., and Kaiser, R. G. (2002) *The News about the News: American Journalism in Peril.* New York: A. A. Knopf.

Durkin, J., Glaisyer, T., and Hadge, K. (2010) "An information community case study: Seattle, a digital community in transition," New America Foundation (June), available at: http://mediapolicy.newamerica.net/.../ An_Information_Community_Case_Study_Seattle_Version1point1.pdf.

The Economist (2010) "Emperors and beggars: can technology help make online content pay?" (April 29), available at: www.economist.com/ node/16010291.

Edelman, M. J. (1988) *Constructing the Political Spectacle.* Chicago: University of Chicago Press.

Edmonds, R. (2010) "Newspapers: news investment," in Pew Research Centre Project for Excellence in Journalism, *The State of the News Media 2010,* available at: http://stateofthemedia.org/2010/newspapers-summary-essay/news-investment/.

Eisenstein, E. (1968) "Some conjectures about the impact of printing on Western society and thought: a preliminary report," *Journal of Modern History* 40, pp. 1–56.

Eliasoph, N. (1988) "Routines and the making of oppositional news," *Critical Studies in Mass Communication* 5, pp. 313–34.

Emirbayer, M. (1997) "Manifesto for a relational sociology," *American Journal of Sociology* 103, pp. 281–317.

Emirbayer, M., and Mische, A. (1998) "What is agency?" *American Journal of Sociology* 103, pp. 962–1023.

Enda, J. (2010) "Capital flight," *American Journalism Review* (June/July), available at: www.ajr.org/article.asp?id=4877.

Enda, J. (2011) "Retreating from the world," *American Journalism Review* (December/January), available at: www.ajr.org/article.asp?id=4985.

Entman, R. (1989) *Democracy without Citizens: Media and the Decay of American Politics.* New York: Oxford University Press.

Epstein, E. J. (1973) *News from Nowhere: Television and the News.* New York: Random House.

Fallows, J. (1996) *Breaking the News: How the Media Undermine American Democracy.* New York: Pantheon.

Fancher, M. R. (2011) "Seattle: a new media case study," in Pew Research Center Project for Excellence in Journalism, *The State of the News Media 2011,* available at: http://stateofthemedia.org/2011/mobile-survey/seattle-a-new-media-case-study/.

Ferguson, N. (2002) *Nexus: Small Worlds and the Groundbreaking Science of Networks.* New York: W. W. Norton.

Fishman, M. (1980) *Manufacturing the News.* Austin: University of Texas Press.

Folkenflik, D. (2009) "In rush to reinvent, media rivals become classmates," *National Public Radio* (August 10), available at: www.npr.org/templates/ story/story.php?storyId=111724595.

Fourcher, M. (2010) "AOL"s Patch revenue model makes no sense," *Business Insider.com* (May 21), available at: www.businessinsider.com/ aols-patch-revenue-model-makes-no-sense-2010-5.

Friedland, L., and Nichols, S. (2002) *Measuring Civic Journalism's Progress: A Report across a Decade of Activity.* Washington DC: Pew Center for Civic Journalism, available at: www.pewcenter.org/doingcj/research/ measuringcj.pdf.

Friedland, L. A., Long, C. C., Shin, Y. J., and Kim, N. (2007) "The local public sphere as a networked space," in R. Butsch (ed.) *Media and Public Spheres.* Basingstoke: Palgrave Macmillan, pp. 43–57.

Fung, A. (2004) *Empowered Participation: Reinventing Urban Democracy.* Princeton, NJ: Princeton University Press.

Galbi, D. A. (2001) "Some economics of personal activity and implications for the digital economy," available at: www.galbithink.org/activity. htm#_ftnref25.

Gans, H. (1979) *Deciding What's News: A Study of CBS Evening News, NBC Nightly News, Newsweek, and Time.* New York: Pantheon Books.

Gastil, J., and Levine, P. (eds) (2005) *The Deliberative Democracy Handbook: Strategies for Effective Civic Engagement in the Twenty-First Century.* San Francisco: Jossey-Bass.

Geertz, C. (1973) "Religion as a cultural system," in Geertz, *The Interpretation of Cultures: Selected Essays.* New York: Basic Books, pp. 87–125.

Giddens, A. (1979) *Central Problems in Social Theory: Action, Structure, and Contradiction in Social Analysis.* Berkeley: University of California Press.

Giddens, A. (1991) *Modernity and Self-Identity: Self and Society in the Late Modern Age.* Stanford, CA: Stanford University Press.

Gissler, S. (1997) "What happens when Gannett takes over," *Columbia Journalism Review* (November/December), p. 42.

Glasser, T. (ed.) (1999) *The Idea of Public Journalism.* New York: Guilford Press.

Gluckstadt, M. (2009) "Can anyone tap the $100 billion potential of hyperlocal news?" *Fast Company* (September 1), available at: www.fastcompany.com/magazine/138/get-me-rewrite-hyperlocals-lost.html.

Gordon, R. and Johnson, Z. (2011) *Linking Audiences to News: A Network Analysis of Chicago Websites,* Chicago Community Trust, available at: www.cct.org/sites/cct.org/files/CNM_LinkingAudiences_0611.pdf.

Guillory, F. (2009) "Weaker media, weaker health news reporting," *North Carolina Medical Journal* 360, available at: www.ncmedicaljournal.com/ wp-content/uploads/NCMJ/Jul-Aug-09/Guillory.pdf.

Haas, T. (2007) *The Pursuit of Public Journalism: Theory, Practice and Criticism.* London: Routledge.

Hallin, D. (1994) "The passing of the 'high modernism' of American journalism," in Hallin *"We Keep America on Top of the World": Television Journalism and the Public Sphere.* New York: Routledge, pp. 170–80.

Hallin, D., and Mancini, P. (2004) *Comparing Media Systems: Three Models of Media and Politics*. Cambridge: Cambridge University Press.

Hamilton, J. T. (2004) *All the News that's Fit to Sell: How the Market Transforms Information into News*. Princeton, NJ: Princeton University Press.

Hamilton, J. T. (2009) "Subsidizing the watchdog: what would it cost to support investigative journalism at a large metropolitan daily newspaper?" Duke Conference on Non-Profit Media, May 4–5, available at: http://sanford.duke.edu/nonprofitmedia/documents/dwchamiltonfinal.pdf.

Harp, D. (2007) *Desperately Seeking Women Readers: U.S. Newspapers and the Construction of a Female Readership*. Lanham, MD: Lexington Books.

Hermida, A., and Thurman, N. (2008) "A clash of cultures," *Journalism Practice* 2, pp. 343–56.

Hiar, C. (2010) "Writers explain what it's like toiling on the content farm," MediaShift (July 21), available at: www.pbs.org/mediashift/2010/07/writers-explain-what-its-like-toiling-on-the-content-farm202.html.

Hindman, M. (2011) "Less of the same: the lack of local news on the Internet," unpublished manuscript, School of Media and Public Affairs, George Washington University.

Hoftstadter, R. (1963) *The Progressive Movement, 1900–1915*. Englewoods Cliffs, NJ: Prentice-Hall.

Howe, J. (2007) "Did Assignment Zero fail? A look back, and lessons learned," *Wired Magazine* (July 16), available at: www.wired.com/techbiz/media/news/2007/07/assignment_zero_final.

Howe, J. (2009) *Crowdsourcing: Why the Power of the Crowd is Driving the Future of Business*. New York: Random House.

Hughes, H. M. (1940) *News and the Human Interest Story*. Chicago: University of Chicago Press.

Humphrey, C. S. (1996) *The Press of the Young Republic, 1783–1833*. Westport, CT: Greenwood Press.

Irwin, W. ([1911] 1969) *The American Newspaper*. Ames: Iowa State University Press.

Isenberg, D. J. (1986) "Group polarization: a critical review and meta-analysis," *Journal of Personality and Social Psychology* 50, pp. 1141–51.

Iyengar, S. (1991) *Is Anyone Responsible?: How Television Frames Political Issues*. Chicago: University of Chicago Press.

Jacobs, R. (1996) "Producing the news, producing the crisis: narrativity, television and news work," *Media, Culture & Society* 18, pp. 373–97.

Joas, H. (1993) *Pragmatism and Social Theory*. Chicago: University of Chicago Press.

Johnstone, J. W. C. (1976) "Organizational constraints on newswork," *Journalism Quarterly* 53, pp. 5–13.

Jones, A. (1989) "Issue for editors' meeting: news vs. profits," *New York Times* (April 12), p. 24.

Jones, A. (2009) *Losing the News: The Future of the News that Feeds Democracy*. New York: Oxford University Press.

Kaiser Family Foundation. (2010) "Generation M2: media in the lives of 8- to 18-year-olds," available at: www.kff.org/entmedia/8010.cfm.

Kaniss, P. (1991) *Making Local News*. Chicago: University of Chicago Press.

Kaplan, R. (2002) *Politics and the American Press: The Rise of Objectivity, 1865–1920*. Cambridge: Cambridge University Press.

Katz, E., and Dayan, D. (1992) *Media Events: The Live Broadcasting of History*. Cambridge, MA: Harvard University Press.

Katz, E., and Lazarsfeld, P. (1955) *Personal Influence: The Part Played by People in the Flow of Mass Communications*. Glencoe, IL: Free Press.

Kodrich, K. (1998) "How reporters react to Knight-Ridder's 25/43 project," *Newspaper Research Journal* 19, pp. 77–94.

Kovach, B., and Rosenstiel, T. (2001) *The Elements of Journalism: What Newspeople Should Know and the Public Should Expect*. New York: Crown.

Kwitny, J. (1990) "The high cost of high profits," *Washington Journalism Review* (June), pp. 19–29.

Lanham, R. A. (2006) *The Economics of Attention: Style and Substance in the Age of Information*. Chicago: University of Chicago Press.

Leighninger, M. (2006) *The Next Form of Democracy: How Expert Rule is Giving Way to Shared Governance – and Why Politics Will Never Be the Same*. Nashville: Vanderbilt University Press.

Lewin, K. (1951) *Field Theory in Social Science*, ed. D. Cartwright. New York: Harper & Brothers.

Liebes, T., and Curran, J. (eds) (1998) *Media, Ritual, and Identity*. New York: Routledge.

Lippmann, W. (1920) *Liberty and the News*. New York: Harcourt, Brace, & Howe.

Lippmann, W. (1922) *Public Opinion*. New York: Macmillan.

Lippmann, W. (1925) *The Phantom Public*. New York: Harcourt, Brace.

Lipset S., and Schneider, W. (1987) *The Confidence Gap*. 2nd edn, Baltimore: Johns Hopkins University Press.

Livingstone, S., and Markham, T. (2008) "The contribution of media consumption to civic participation," *British Journal of Sociology* 59, pp. 351–71.

Lowrey, W. (2011) "Institutionalism, news organizations and innovation," *Journalism Studies* 11, pp. 64–79.

Maier, S. R. (2005) "Accuracy matters: a cross-market assessment of newspaper error and credibility," *Journalism and Mass Communication Quarterly* 82, pp. 533–51.

Martin, J. L. (2003) "What is field theory?" *American Journal of Sociology* 109, pp. 1–149.

McCombs, M. (2004) *Setting the Agenda: The Mass Media and Public Opinion*. Cambridge: Polity.

McGerr, M. (1986) *The Decline of Popular Politics: The American North, 1865–1928*. New York: Oxford University Press.

McLellan, M. (2011) "Emerging economics of community news," Pew Research Center Project for Excellence in Journalism, *The State of the*

News Media 2011, available at: http://stateofthemedia.org/2011/mobile-survey/economics-of-community-news/.

Meaney, T. (2010) "Why demand media is just like KFC," available at: http://blog.arc90.com/2010/04/19/why-demand-media-is-just-like-kfc/.

Meyer, P. (2004) *The Vanishing Newspaper: Saving Journalism in the Information Age*. Columbia: University of Missouri Press.

Mindich, D. T. Z. (1998) *Just the Facts: How "Objectivity" Came to Define American Journalism*. New York: New York University Press.

Mindich, D. T. Z. (2004) *Tuned Out: Why Americans under 40 Don't Follow the News*. New York: Oxford University Press.

Morgan, F., and Perez, A. (2010) "An information community case study: the research triangle, North Carolina," New America Foundation, available at: http://mediapolicy.newamerica.net/publications/policy/the_research_triangle_north_carolina.

Mortenson, E. (2011) "As Portland media shrink, Metro joins a national trend by hiring a reporter to cover itself," *The Oregonian* (January 17), available at: www.oregonlive.com/environment/index.ssf/2011/01/as_portland_media_shrink_metro.html.

Morton, J. (2006) "Buying and selling newspapers," in J. A. Bridges, B. R. Litman, and L. W. Bridges (eds) *Newspaper Competition in the Millennium*. New York: Nova Science, pp. 49–60.

Mutter, A. D. (2010) "Newspaper ad sales head to 25-year low," *Reflections of a Newsosaur* (September 7), available at: http://newsosaur.blogspot.com/2010/09/newspaper-ad-sales-head-to-25-year-low.html.

Mutter, A. D. (2011) "Hyperlocals like TBD: more hype than hope," *Reflections of a Newsosaur* (February 24), available at: http://newsosaur.blogspot.com/2011/02/hyperlocals-like-tbd-more-hype-than.html.

Neuman, W. R. (1986) *The Paradox of Mass Politics: Knowledge and Opinion in the American Electorate*. Cambridge, MA: Harvard University Press.

Niles, R. (2010) "Why I am skeptical of Patch.com," *Online Journalism Review* (August 27), available at: www.ojr.org/ojr/people/robert/201008/1880/.

Nip, J. (2008) "The last days of civic journalism: the case of the *Savannah Morning News*," *Journalism Practice* 2, pp. 179–86.

Noveck, B. S. (2009) *Wikigovernment: How Technology Can Make Government Better, Democracy Stronger, and Citizens More Powerful*. Washington, DC: Brookings Institution.

Nye, J. (1997) "The decline of confidence in government," in J. Nye, P. D. Zelikow, and D. C. King (eds) *Why People Don't Trust Government*. Cambridge, MA: Harvard University Press, pp. 1–18.

The Oregonian (2009) "The demise of the *Seattle Post-Intelligencer*" (March 17).

O'Sullivan, J., and Heinonen, A. (2008) "Old values, new media: journalism role perceptions in a changing world," *Journalism Practice* 2, pp. 357–71.

Ostrow, A. (2010) "Social networking dominates our time spent online" (August 12), available at: http://mashable.com/2010/08/02/stats-time-spent-online/.

Overholser, G. (1998) "State of the American newspaper, editor inc.," *American Journalism Review* (December), available at: www.ajr.org/article.asp?id=3290.

Page, B. I., and Shapiro, R. Y. (1992) *The Rational Public: Fifty Years of Trends in Americans' Policy Preferences.* Chicago: University of Chicago Press.

Palser, B. (2010) "The hazards of hyperlocal," *American Journalism Review* (September), available at: www.ajr.org/article.asp?id=4902.

Pariser, E. (2011) *The Filter Bubble: What the Internet is Hiding from You.* New York: Penguin.

Pasley, J. (2001) *"The Tyranny of Printers": Newspaper Politics in the Early American Republic.* Charlottesville: University Press of Virginia.

Paterno, S. (1996) "Whither Knight-Ridder?" *American Journalism Review* (January/February), available at: www.ajr.org/article_printable.asp?id=3595.

Patterson, T. (2000) *Doing Well and Doing Good: How Soft News and Critical Journalism are Shrinking the News Audience and Weakening Democracy – and What News Outlets Can Do about It.* Faculty Research Working Paper RWP01-001, John F. Kennedy School of Government. Cambridge, MA.

Patterson, T. (2003) *The Vanishing Voter: Public Involvement in an Age of Uncertainty.* New York: Vintage Books.

Patterson, T. (2007) *Creative Destruction: An Exploratory Look at News on the Internet.* Cambridge, MA: Joan Shorenstein Center on the Press, Politics and Public Policy, available at: www.hks.harvard.edu/presspol/research/carnegie-knight/creative_destruction_2007.pdf.

Pedelty, M. (1995) *War Stories: The Culture of Foreign Correspondents.* New York: Routledge.

Perry, D. K. (2003) *The Roots of Civic Journalism: Darwin, Dewey, and Mead.* Lanham, MD: University Press of America.

Pew Research Center's Project for Excellence in Journalism (2009a) "The new Washington press corps: as mainstream media decline, niche and foreign outlets grow," available at: www.journalism.org/analysis_report/new_washington_press_corps.

Pew Research Center's Project for Excellence in Journalism (2009b) *State of the Media 2009,* available at: http://stateofthemedia.org/2009/.

Pew Research Center's Project for Excellence in Journalism (2010a) *State of the Media 2010,* available at: http://stateofthemedia.org/2010/.

Pew Research Center's Project for Excellence in Journalism (2010b) "How news happens: a study of the news ecosystem of one American city," available at: www.journalism.org/analysis_report/how_news_happens.

Picard, R. (2002) *Evolution of Revenue Streams and the Business Model of Newspapers: The U.S. Industry between the Years 1950–2000,* School of

Economics and Business Administration, Series C Discussion Paper, Tufts University.

Picard, R. (2008) "Shifts in newspaper advertising expenditures and their implications for the future of newspapers," *Journalism Studies* 9, pp. 704–16.

Pierson, P. (2000) "Increasing returns, path dependence, and the study of politics," *American Political Science Review*, 94, pp. 251–67.

Presstime (1991) "Gannett's News 2000 project builds on community ties" (July), p. 50.

Preston, P. (2008) "The curse of introversion," *Journalism Practice* 2, pp. 318–25.

Putnam, R., and Feldstein, L. (2003) *Better Together: Restoring the American Community*. New York: Simon & Schuster.

Quandt, T. (2008) "(No) news on the world wide web? A comparative content analysis of online news in Europe and the United States," *Journalism Studies* 9, pp. 717–38.

Rainey, J. (2010) "On the media: trying to Patch into the hyper-local news market," *Los Angeles Times* (April 24), available at: http://articles.latimes.com/2010/apr/24/entertainment/la-et-onthemedia-20100424.

Rauch, J. (2010) "How Tea Party organizes without leaders," *National Journal Magazine* (September 11), available at: http://conventions.nationaljournal.com/njmagazine/cs_20100911_8855.php.

Redman, E. (2010) "US: time spent on top news websites falls," available at: www.editorsweblog.org/multimedia/2010/02/us_time_spent_on_top_news_websites_falls.php.

Reston, J. (1991) *Deadline: A Memoir*. New York: Random House.

Roberts, G., and Kunkel, T. (2002) *Breach of Faith: A Crisis of Coverage in the Age of Corporate Newspapering*. Fayetteville: University of Arkansas Press.

Robinson, S. (2011) "Convergence crises: news work and news space in the digitally transforming newsroom," *Journal of Communication* 61, pp. 1122–41.

Rosen, J. (1999a) *What Are Journalists For?* New Haven, CT: Yale University Press.

Rosen, J. (1999b) "The action of the idea: public journalism in built form," in T. Glasser (ed.) *The Idea of Public Journalism*. New York: Guilford Press, pp. 21–48.

Rosen, J. (2009) "Sources of subsidy in the production of news: a list," available at: http://jayrosen.tumblr.com/post/243813457/sources-of-subsidy-in-the-production-of-news-a-list.

Rosenkranz, K. (1977) *Georg Wilhelm Friedrich Hegels Leben*. Darmstadt: Wissenschaftliche Buchgesellschaft.

Rosse, J. (1975) *Economic Limits of Press Responsibility*. Studies in Industry Economics, no. 56, Stanford University, Department of Economics.

Roth, D. (2009) "The answer factory: demand media and the fast, disposable, and profitable as hell media model," *Wired Magazine* (October 19), available at: www.wired.com/magazine/2009/10/ff_demandmedia.

Schiller, D. (1981) *Objectivity and the News: The Public and the Rise of Commercial Journalism*. Philadelphia: Temple University Press.

Schlesinger, P. (1978) *Putting Reality Together: BBC News*. Beverly Hills, CA: Sage.

Schnettler, S. (2009) "A structured overview of 50 years of small-world research," *Social Networks* 31, pp. 165–78.

Schudson, M. (1978) *Discovering the News: A Social History of American Newspapers*. New York: Basic Books.

Schudson, M. (1995a) "Question authority: a history of the news interview," in Schudson, *The Power of News*. Cambridge, MA: Harvard University Press, pp. 72–93.

Schudson, M. (1995b) "What is a reporter?," in Schudson, *The Power of News*. Cambridge, MA: Harvard University Press, pp. 94–112.

Schudson, M. (1998) *The Good Citizen: A History of American Civic Life*. New York: Martin Kessler Books.

Schudson, M. (1999) "What public journalism knows about journalism but doesn't know about the public," in T. Glasser (ed.) *The Idea of Public Journalism*. New York: Guilford Press, pp. 118–34.

Schudson, M. (2001) "The objectivity norm in American journalism," *Journalism* 2, pp. 149–70.

Schudson, M. (2010) "Political observatories, databases & news in the emerging ecology of public information," *Daedalus* 139, pp. 100–9.

Schulfhofer-Whol, S., and Garrido, M. (2009) *Do Newspapers Matter? Short-Run and Long-Run Evidence from the Closure of the Cincinnati Post*, NBER working paper no. 14817, available at: www.nber.org/papers/w14817.pdf.

Schwitzer, G. (2009) *The State of Health Journalism in the U.S.* Menlo Park, CA: Kaiser Family Foundation, available at: www.kff.org/entmedia/upload/7858.pdf.

Searle, J. (1969) *Speech Acts: An Essay in the Philosophy of Language*. Cambridge Cambridge University Press.

Sewell, W. (1992) "A theory of structure: duality, agency, and transformation," *American Journal of Sociology* 98, pp. 1–29.

Shah, D. V., McLeod, D. M., Freidland, L., and Nelson, M. R. (2007) "The politics of consumption/the consumption of politics," *Annals of the American Academy of Political and Social Science* 611, pp. 6–15.

Sharples, T. (2009) "After the *P-I*'s demise, will Seattle news live?" *Time Magazine* (March 17), available at: www.time.com/time/nation/article/0,8599,1885819,00.html.

Shaw, D. (1976) "Newspapers challenged as never before," *Los Angeles Times* (November 26), p. A1.

Shirky, C. (2008) *Here Comes Everybody: The Power of Organizing without Organizations*. New York: Penguin.

Shirky, C. (2009) "Newspapers and thinking the unthinkable," available at: www.shirky.com/weblog/2009/03/newspapers-and-thinking-the-unthinkable/.

Sigal, L. (1973) *Reporters and Officials: The Organization and Politics of Newsmaking*. Lexington, MA: D. C. Heath.

Sigelman, L. (1973) "Reporting the news: an organizational analysis," *American Journal of Sociology* 79, pp. 132–51.

Simon, D. (2009) "In Baltimore, no one left to press the police," *Washington Post* (March 1), available at: www.washingtonpost.com/wp-dyn/content/article/2009/02/27/AR2009022703591.html.

Singer, J. (2004) "More than ink-stained wretches: the resocialization of print journalists in converged newsrooms," *Journalism and Mass Communication Quarterly* 81, pp. 838–56.

Sirianni, C., and Friedland, L. (2001) *Civic Innovation in America: Community Empowerment, Public Policy, and the Movement for Civic Renewal*. Berkeley: University of California Press.

Sloan, W. D., and Williams, J. H. (1994) *The History of American Journalism: The Early American Press, 1690–1783*. Westport, CT: Greenwood Press.

Smith, A. (1980) *Goodbye Gutenberg: The Newspaper Revolution of the 1980s*. New York: Oxford University Press.

Smith, C. (1977) *The Press, Politics, and Patronage*. Athens: University of Georgia Press.

Smolkin, R. (2006) "Adapt or die," *American Journalism Review* (June/July), available at: www.ajr.org/article.asp?id=4111.

Sparrow, B. (1999) *Uncertain Guardians: The News Media as a Political Institution*. Baltimore: Johns Hopkins University Press.

Squires, J. (1993) *Read All About It! The Corporate Takeover of America's Newspapers*. New York: Times Books.

Stelter, B. (2009) "When Chevron hires ex-reporter to investigate pollution, Chevron looks good," *New York Times* (May 10), available at: www.nytimes.com/2009/05/11/business/media/11cbs.html.

Stepp, C. S. (1991) "When readers design the news," *Washington Journalism Review* (April), pp. 20–4.

Stepp, C. S. (2002) "Then and now," in G. Roberts and T. Kunkel (eds) *Breach of Faith: A Crisis of Coverage in the Age of Corporate Newspapering*. Fayetteville: University of Arkansas Press, pp. 89–116.

Sunstein, C. (2007) *Republic.com 2.0*. Princeton, NJ: Princeton University Press.

Swidler, A. (2006) "What anchors cultural practices?," in T. R. Schatzki, K. Knorr-Cetina, and E. von Savigny (eds) *The Practice Turn in Contemporary Theory*. London: Routledge, pp. 83–102.

Tapscott, D., and Williams, A. D. (2006) *Wikinomics: How Mass Collaboration Changes Everything*. New York: Portfolio.

Temple, J. (2011) "Week 49: Hawaii governor holds fake press conference," *Honolulu Civil Beat* (April 9), available at: www.civilbeat.com/articles/2011/04/09/10214-week-49-hawaii-governor-holds-fake-press-conference/.

Tocqueville, A. de ([1831–40] 1969) *Democracy in America*, ed. J. P. Mayer, trans. G. Lawrence. Garden City, NY: Doubleday.

Tönnies, F. (1957) *Community and Society*, trans. C. P. Loomis. East Lansing: Michigan State University Press.

Toossi, M. (2002) "A century of change: the US labor force, 1950-2050," *Monthly Labor Review* (May), pp. 15–28, available at: *www.bls.gov/opub/mlr/2002/05/art2full.pdf*.

Trillin C. (2003) "Newshound: the triumphs, travels, and movable feasts of R.W. Apple, Jr.," *New Yorker* (September 29), available at: www.newyorker.com/archive/2003/09/29/030929fa_fact1.

Trounstine, J. (n.d.) "Incumbency and responsiveness in local elections," available at: *faculty.ucmerced.edu/jtrounstine/low_info_draft4.pdf*.

Tuchman, G. (1972) "Objectivity as strategic ritual: an examination of newsmen's notions of objectivity," *American Journal of Sociology* 77, pp. 660–79.

Tuchman, G. (1978) *Making News: A Study in the Construction of Reality.* New York: Free Press.

Underwood, D. (1993) "The very model of the reader-driven newsroom?," *Columbia Journalism Review* (November/December), pp. 42–4.

Usher, N. (2011) "Making business news in the digital age," PhD thesis, University of Southern California.

van der Wurff, R. (2005) "Impacts of the Internet on newspapers in Europe," *Gazette: The International Journal for Communication Studies* 67, pp. 107–20.

Waldman, S. (2011) *The Information Needs of Communities: The Changing Media Landscape in a Broadband Age.* Washington, DC: Federal Communications Commission, available at: www.fcc.gov/infoneeds report.

Weaver, D., and Wilhoit, G. C. (1986) *The American Journalist: A Portrait of U.S. News People and their Work.* 2nd edn, Indianapolis: Indiana University Press.

Weaver, D., and Wilhoit, G. C. (1996) *The American Journalist in the 1990s: U.S. News People at the End of an Era.* Mahwah, NJ: Lawrence Erlbaum Associates.

Wenger, E. (1998) *Communities of Practice: Learning, Meaning, and Identity.* New York: Cambridge University Press.

White, D. M. (1964) "The 'gatekeeper': a case study in the selection of news," in L. A. Dexter and D. M. White (eds) *People, Society and Mass Communications.* New York: Free Press, pp. 160–72.

Wiley, N. (1994) *The Semiotic Self.* Chicago: University of Chicago Press.

Williams, R. (1976) *Keywords: A Vocabulary of Culture and Society.* New York: Oxford University Press.

Yankelovich, D. (1991) *Coming to Public Judgment: Making Democracy Work in a Complex World*. Syracuse, NY: Syracuse University Press.

Zaller, J. (1992) *The Nature and Origins of Mass Opinion*. New York: Cambridge University Press.

Zuckerman, E. (2009) "Clay Shirky and accountability journalism," available at: www.ethanzuckerman.com/blog/2009/09/22/clay-shirky-and-accountability-journalism/.

Index